Resurrecting the Brother of Jesus

Resurrecting the Brother of Jesus

The James Ossuary Controversy and the Quest for Religious Relics

Edited by
RYAN BYRNE &
BERNADETTE MCNARY-ZAK

The University of North Carolina Press
Chapel Hill

Designed by Kimberly Bryant
Set in Whitman by Keystone Typesetting, Inc.
Manufactured in the United States of America

The paper in this book meets the guidelines for permanence and durability of the Committee on Production Guidelines for Book Longevity of the Council on Library Resources.

The University of North Carolina Press has been a member of the Green Press Initiative since 2003.

Library of Congress Cataloging-in-Publication Data
Resurrecting the brother of Jesus : the James Ossuary controversy and the quest for religious relics / edited by Ryan Byrne and Bernadette McNary-Zak.
p. cm.
Includes bibliographical references and index.
ISBN 978-0-8078-3298-1 (cloth : alk. paper)
1. James Ossuary. 2. James, Brother of the Lord, Saint.
3. Protestant churches—Doctrines. I. Byrne, Ryan.
II. McNary-Zak Bernadette.
BS2454.J3R47 2009
225.9′3—dc22 2009002896

cloth 13 12 11 10 09 5 4 3 2 1

Contents

Illustrations

Acknowledgments

This book is one of the products of a collaborative teaching and learning effort in the Department of Religious Studies at Rhodes College in the spring of 2004. Seeking a way to work interdepartmentally and to provide an upper-level research opportunity for our students, four of this volume's authors created a seminar course on the James Ossuary phenomenon. The course allowed us to work closely with four undergraduate students, Robert Edgecombe, Lindsey Hammond, Marion Heckethorn, and Mary Claire Giffin, who were eager to explore and understand various aspects of the public response to this object. In many ways, their work was the foundation for the essays in this volume, and therefore we are especially grateful to them.

Our work was funded by an Andrew W. Mellon Foundation Grant for Faculty Career Enhancement (Local Initiative). We are grateful to those who helped make this funding possible and for the institutional support that we received from our colleagues at Rhodes College, especially Professors Robert Llewellyn, Robert Strandburg, and Ellen Armour and the members of the Department of Religious Studies. Special thanks go to Professors Georgia Frank, Byron McCane, Leigh Schmidt, and Jonathan Reed, who graciously accepted our invitation to speak at the college on topics pertaining to the James Ossuary phenomenon and spent time in conversation with our students. Our study of the James Ossuary phenomenon was further enhanced by conversations with Professor Jonathan Z. Smith at the Midwest Regional Meeting of the American Academy of Religion in Chicago in April 2004, during which our students presented some of their finds and participated in a panel discussion in a special session on religion and education. We are especially grateful to Professor Smith and to those in the American Academy of Religion and the Society of Biblical Literature for their interest in, and support of, our work.

This study would not have been possible without those in the city of Toronto who were willing to meet with Professor Thomas S. Bremer and

Robert Edgecombe to share their thoughts on the ossuary and its display. We are particularly grateful to the Royal Ontario Museum, whose staff provided invaluable assistance. Special thanks go to Ed Keall, Francisco Alvarez, Suzan Sabir, and the security guards at the James Ossuary display. We would also like to extend our gratitude to Terry Donaldson of the University of Toronto, Professor John Kloppenborg, Professor John Marshall, Professor Peter Richardson, Professor Leif Vaage, June Alloway, Tom and Kay Hayes, Frank Petersen, and Rev. Dr. Fritz T. Kristbergs.

Finally, we are grateful to the anonymous readers of an earlier version of this manuscript and to Elaine Maisner and the staff of the University of North Carolina Press, including Tema Larter and Jay Mazzocchi, for their work in bringing this volume to publication.

RYAN BYRNE & BERNADETTE MCNARY-ZAK

Introduction

World Exclusive! Evidence of Jesus Written in Stone

Thus ran the cover of the popular newsstand magazine *Biblical Archaeology Review* (BAR) in the autumn of 2002.[1] In a private antiquities collection, Sorbonne professor Andre Lemaire had discovered an Aramaic inscription on an ancient Jewish ossuary—a burial box for skeletal remains—that read, "Jacob [James] son of Joseph, brother of Jesus." The find was heralded as the final resting place of James, the brother of Jesus of Nazareth.[2] The *New York Times*, the *Guardian*, the *Washington Post*, *Le Monde*, and other newspapers around the world acclaimed the ossuary as perhaps the greatest archaeological find of all time. The *Lehrer News Hour*, *60 Minutes*, the Discovery Channel, the *Tonight Show*, and the *New Yorker* all offered perspectives on the potential significance of the discovery. On November 7, 2002, the *Daily Show*'s Jon Stewart offered the barb: "Heaven's Crate: scientists have found the burial box of Jesus' brother James, who was sort of the Emilio Estevez of the Holy Land." The abstruse pop culture reference was apt, in part because James had never enjoyed a prominent role in Protestantism, while Catholicism could not grant him a blood relationship with Jesus, the son of a perpetual virgin. In other words, the religious public needed a kind of introduction to James. It fell to scholars, specifically biblicists and epigraphers, to repackage James as a central Christian figure and cause for religious excitement. It fell to the media to sensationalize the find and polemicize its potential theological meaning. These choices of deliberate interpretation offer us an instructive look at the commercialization of biblical antiquity, the academy's dialogue with

The James Ossuary in its hallowed context in the Royal Ontario Museum (With permission of the Royal Ontario Museum © ROM; photo credit: Brian Boyle)

religion, and religious people's responses to the interpretation framed for them. The interests of scholars and faith communities converged with the discovery of the James Ossuary, an ordinary limestone box that the media transformed into a relic overnight and a forgery only a few months later.

Nearly 100,000 visitors flocked to see the ossuary in the short time it resided on display in Toronto's Royal Ontario Museum (ROM) in late 2002. At first glance, the phenomenon resembled a pilgrimage of sorts. And why not? The box bore the name "James," who may have been the brother of Jesus identified in the New Testament. Print and Internet media had sensationalized the ancient Jewish burial box as an archaeological connection to Jesus, a complication for Catholic doctrine, and a relic of enduring religious significance. In keeping with the curators' wishes to accommodate displays of reverence from the visiting public, the museum exhibit was designed to feel like a sanctuary, with deep red-purple walls visible through a dimly lit room punctuated by a shaft of raking light illuminating the box. The opening lines of the exhibit informed visitors that the James Ossuary was a "tangible relic" that "puts us in contact with an age when there were still people alive who knew Jesus of Nazareth."[3] Indeed, the initial staging and reception of the ossuary focused as much, or possibly more, on its appeal to the interests of religion and religious people as to its historical or archaeological importance. In the summer of 2003, however, a blue-ribbon panel of experts declared the artifact's inscription a modern forgery, and the Israeli police arrested its owner in a sting foreshadowing a sensational trial that began in late 2005.[4]

Featuring an extensive witness list of international experts in ancient inscriptions and geochemistry, the Israeli prosecution's case initiated a long and detailed examination of the most obscure of topics, yet one perhaps freighted with deeply resonant consequences for people who follow material developments in matters of faith. As the ossuary trial confronted the ambiguity surrounding the discovery and vetting of this object, the phenomenon it created still requires explanation. Why did the James Ossuary elicit such a passionate response from believers, scholars, and the media? Why do some still interpret its inscription along denominational lines, thereby emphasizing the evidentiary relevance to traditional claims about Jesus Christ?

JEWISH BURIAL AND OSSUARIES IN ROMAN PALESTINE

Burial is both an emotional and intellectual channel of release; its customs absorb pain, fury, horror, reminiscence, and celebration. It is an archaeological commonplace that burial patterns reveal a strong correlation between economic status and the quality of inhumation.[5] For ancient Mediterranean religions that emphasized the connection between the quality of burial and the quality of the afterlife, class might have unimaginable repercussions beyond death for the have-nots. From the early to mid-first millennium BCE (the Iron Age), Israelite and Judean elites interred their dead in commissioned family tombs hewn into dense bedrock or adapted from preexisting caves. Finer tombs featured hewn benches on which the dead could be laid until the corpse's initial decomposition, when the remains could be easily removed and merged with the bones of other deceased family members. Thus literally "gathered with their fathers," these bones of multiple corpses often commingled in special bedrock hollows that served as multigenerational repositories. This genealogical conflation of mortal remains may have arisen organically from long-standing traditions of symbolic ancestor veneration and an ethos of corporate identity, but the factor of cost was pertinent; it was expensive to hew individual bench tombs out of bedrock, and so the commingling of family remains may have signified a necessary, if rationalized, result of spatial and monetary constraints. Many such tombs characterize the vicinity of Jerusalem, and the bone repositories sometimes produce remarkable grave goods, like the Ketef Hinnom amulets bearing an inscription with the earliest biblical quotation.[6] By the Hellenistic period (third to first centuries BCE), Greek influence had found purchase in elite Jewish tombs with monumental proportion and decoration. Mausolea occasioned more than the proper disposal of the dead. While the earlier Iron Age bedrock tombs indeed serviced the prestige interests of elite families, there was an incidental modesty to their subterranean character. The Hellenistic memorials, on the other hand, introduced salient beacons of status above ground—some of which dominate the northern approach to Jerusalem in a style reminiscent of the extramural epitaphs bidding one welcome to a traditional Greek *polis*. Death became a domain where the Hellenization of Judaism could find an enduring material expression. Death may have exposed a cross-cultural discourse in its extreme form if the sporadic Jewish practice of providing the corpse with coins derived from or mirrored the Greek practice of subsidizing the soul's fee to the underworld ferryman for crossing the river Styx.[7] Appearing within the monumental Hellenistic Jewish tombs, as well as within those bedrock-cut tombs without extravagant facades, were now individual burial chambers called *loculi* (Hebrew *kokhim*) carved into the walls. These *loculi* frequently take the form of rectangular niches extending perpendicularly from the tomb wall like tunnels reaching deeper into the dense, dark rock. While the bench niches continue, the Roman period would see the *loculus* style proliferate among the Jewish population of Judea and surrounding areas in the southwestern foothills, the Jordan Valley, and the Galilee.

Consistent with earlier periods, Roman-period Judaism distinguished between primary and secondary burial. After the mortuary rites of shrouding and anointing, family members slid the decedent into an individual *loculus*, sometimes within a thin lead or wooden coffin but often without any container for the body. A year of desiccation afforded enough natural decomposition to remove remains piecemeal and deposit the bones into an ossuary, or bone box. After the bones were collected in the ossuary, the box might be grouped with others out of the way or even reshelved into another *loculus*. Sometimes several ossuaries are discovered crammed into a *loculus*, and sometimes each has its own niche. In other cases, it is difficult to avoid tripping over the clutter of boxes scattered throughout the tomb floor. Square footage matters in death as in life. Jewish burial seems to have introduced this secondary-burial practice called *ossilegium* in the last quarter of the first century BCE. Ossuary interment enjoyed its apex during the bulk of the first century CE, after which it declined into sporadic practice through the third century CE. The precision with which archaeologists date burials and specific mortuary practices depends upon the recovery of artifacts *in situ*, that is, in their original spatial context. Only largely undisturbed contexts like the family tombs from Jericho from the Roman period permit archaeologists to reconstruct the ritual procedures that in turn afford an examination of the religious dimensions of mortuary behavior.[8] Too often, however, looters penetrate the tombs before archaeologists can undertake a controlled excavation. Most of the intact ceramic vessels that populate the legal antiquities shops in Israel are grave goods from pillaged tombs. Many ossuaries make their way into private collections through the black market, but not before looters have discarded the bones.[9] Such disturbance of mortal remains may deny scholars the primary context necessary to evaluate the particulars of the burial, but it lucidly testifies to the modern disregard for those remains. The black market is an instructive prism wedged between what Jonathan Z. Smith calls first-order religion (that which is practiced) and second-order religion (that which is ascribed to or denied the practitioner). Where the question of a looted ossuary's *intrinsic* religiosity is concerned, we glean much more about the present attitudes of traffickers, collectors, and gawkers than the past attitudes of those within the boxes and without.

The ossuaries were predominantly carved from soft limestone readily available in the Jerusalem quarries that also supplied the stone for the manufacture of ritually sanctioned purity vessels. Ossuaries could be plain limestone boxes with flat or gabled lids, or they could feature elaborately carved decoration with rosettes, floral patterns, geometric designs, architectural iconography, and occasionally painted images. They might be inscribed in one or more languages or simply left anonymous. The diversity of quality and detail reflects in part the financial consideration of the purchase. Could the family afford the elaborate rosette additions? The majority of the population was illiterate and many extant inscriptions represent elite commissions. Could the family afford to pay the scribe to incise an epitaph? Some have argued that poorly executed inscriptions on ossuaries might reflect the penmanship of semiliterate family members. In any case, there is as much variation in the epigraphic handwriting in the wider ossuary corpus as there is diversity of craftsmanship and flourish in the boxes themselves. As with any material purchase, the choice of ossuary may reflect cost as much as taste.

This returns us to the consideration of means. General archaeological surveys of burial patterns run the risk of misrepresenting a prominent practice as illustrative of common practice, but extant remains are often misleading precisely because of their survivability. It is expensive to be memorialized in such a fashion as to be remembered (or discoverable) millennia hence. The rock-cut Jewish family tombs popular from the Iron Age to the Roman period do not in fact represent common practice; they reflect luxury purchases of the elite. There are no surviving markers for most of the dead; no elaborate tombs; no lead coffins procured for customized cavities carved into bedrock; and no ossuaries.

"JAMES SON OF JOSEPH, BROTHER OF JESUS"

On October 21, 2002, before a throng of journalists assembled at the Marriott Hotel in Washington, D.C., Hershel Shanks, the publisher of the BAR and founder-impresario of the Biblical Archaeology Society (BAS),[10] held an elaborate press conference to announce the exclusive public presentation of an ossuary that once contained the remains of Jesus' blood brother, James. An assembled cadre of world-renowned experts sat on the dais ready to interpret the knotty linguistic and historical details of the amazing object. This limestone box, purchased from the black market, bore a first-century CE Aramaic inscription, which read, "Jacob son of Joseph, brother of Jesus." This "Jacob" was purportedly none other than James, brother of Jesus, biological son of Mary and Joseph, and founder of the Christian church in Jerusalem.[11] For Shanks, this discovery signified nothing less than the first direct archaeological connection to the historical Jesus and a cause for people interested in the historicity of the biblical narratives to rejoice.

The interpretation of the box's significance prompted several serious questions, each of which Shanks had anticipated. Was the box authentic? Scientists at the Geological Survey of Israel had examined the surface of the ossuary on the microscopic level and determined that natural, prolonged exposure to the elements had deposited a *patina*, or natural environmental encrustation, on top of the limestone surface over the duration of centuries.[12] The limestone itself was also consistent with the natural deposits of the Jerusalem quarries that produced certifiable ossuaries in the Roman period. Was the inscription authentic? The patina also coated the surface of the letters incised into the limestone. Therefore the inscription had been executed well before the long-term environmental deposition that covered the grooves of its characters. Andre Lemaire, an elite paleographer at the Sorbonne, had deciphered the inscription and authenticated its first-century date on the basis of the handwriting. Joseph Fitzmeyer of the Catholic University of America had authenticated the Aramaic on the basis of its spelling and grammar. How could Shanks be certain that this Jacob was *the* Jacob to whom the New Testament refers? While all three names on the ossuary (*Yaʿaqob*, *Yosef*, and *Yeshua*) were indeed very common for the period, it is statistically unlikely that this specific set of paternal and fraternal relationships coincidentally referred to anyone but *the* James. Were there physical remains within the ossuary? The box originally included a few bone fragments, but the owner had repackaged them in a Tupperware container, which he stored in his refrigerator. And who was the owner of the ossuary? That individual preferred to remain anonymous for the time being. He claimed to have purchased the ossuary several years earlier from a dealer in Jerusalem. The burial box had no known provenance and therefore no controlled archaeological context. As with all ossuaries that made their way into private hands through the antiquities market, looters had no doubt disturbed a family tomb, stolen the ossuary, and desecrated the human remains by dumping most of the bones. The penultimate repository of Jacob, whoever he was, was a criminal discovery, not an archaeological one.

At the Marriott press conference, Shanks added a dimension of immediacy to the discovery with the announcement that the ossuary would soon visit the ROM in Toronto as a special exhibit to coincide with the annual meetings of the Society of Biblical Literature, the American Academy of Religion, and the BAS's Bible and Archaeology Fest, a series of popular lectures for a paying audience. It is unclear from the ROM's internal memoranda whether the museum had already agreed to exhibit the ossuary by the time the press conference was held; Shanks's negotiating tactics and personal request for a finder's fee had apparently complicated his unsolicited offer to ROM chief curator Ed Keall to display the box. By the following afternoon, however, internal ROM e-mails began to acknowledge that the museum would indeed consent to the exhibition. It is also unclear, therefore, whether Shanks's public statements pressured the ROM to capitulate to the exhibition and forgo a qualifying examination prior to a contractual acceptance.[13]

The day after Shanks's press conference at the Marriott, the promotional dividends of his efforts emerged, as newswires worldwide trumpeted the discovery of the burial box as nothing less than a direct historical link to Jesus Christ. A host of prominent scholars opined on the ossuary, hailing it as significant not only for its historical importance but also for its pertinence to the traditions of people of faith. The ROM's design team readily agreed; the museum offered visitors a framework for interpretation just before they entered the exhibit room to view the ossuary:

> The ossuary is a tangible relic. Whatever its associations in terms of personages, it puts us in contact with an age when there were still people alive who knew Jesus of Nazareth. Written accounts of Jesus may reflect eyewitness reports of his life, but most of the texts were composed decades after the Crucifixion, in Greek, and almost all of the hard copies that still exist were made centuries later.[14]

Visitors were left to wonder whether and how the object was to be situated in the context of competing Christian denominational frameworks of interpretation.

The exhibit itself was hardly the sole venue in which the ossuary saga would play out. By early November, a few weeks prior to the exhibit's opening, the Israel Antiquities Authority had established that Oded Golan, a prolific Israeli collector, was the owner of the ossuary. Since Israeli law nationalizes all antiquities acquired after 1978, there was an initial investigation to determine whether Golan had obtained the ossuary illegally. Then in January 2003, yet another unprovenanced blockbuster artifact appeared from the black market. This time it was a stone tablet with Hebrew text purportedly commissioned in the ninth century BCE by King Jehoash (or Yehoash) of Judah to commemorate repairs to the Temple of Solomon as described in 1 Kings 12. Eminent scholars immediately rejected the inscription as a forgery.[15] The script's paleography—the execution of the incised letters—was impossible for the period, and the language seemed to contain certain curious modern Hebrew idioms. There was another serious problem: the tablet had arrived for its media debut with authentication from the very same geologists who had determined the James Ossuary's inscription to be ancient. A pall of scholarly suspicion immediately fell upon the previously convincing geological merits of the James Ossuary's authenticity, even as the Discovery Channel aired a ballyhooed documentary on the ossuary over Easter weekend. In the summer of 2003, a team of experts convened by the Israel Antiquities Authority issued a report finding both the Jehoash Inscription and the James Ossuary to be modern forgeries.[16] Israeli police raided the house of Oded Golan, reportedly discovering a plethora of incriminating evidence.[17] In a widely circulated photograph on the Internet, the media revealed the spot where Golan, one of Israel's savviest and most affluent private collectors, had been displaying his priceless artifact: on the seat of a toilet. The James Ossuary had migrated from pedestal to "throne." In December 2004 Golan was indicted on charges of forgery and antiquities trafficking. Four years later, after more than seventy witnesses have taken the stand in criminal case 482/04, the *State of Israel v. Oded Golan*, the trial, headlines, and agitation to religious sensibilities continue.[18]

FOR SCHOLARS OF RELIGION

Golan stands accused not only of illegal collecting, but also of masterminding a forgery ring responsible for contaminating the market, peer-reviewed publications, and museums with objects intended to prey on the religiosity of consumers, collectors, readers, and scholars.[19] The zeal of the Israeli prosecution speaks to the rancor of public reaction to the alleged crimes. Perhaps it was the exploitation of *piety*, the eagerness to embrace the divine significance of the box, that generated this outrage and its unending publicity. The role of the academy, which circumvented its own rules of peer review to lionize the box, comes into play here as well. Did scholars also try to manipulate public perception? How was an object without a corroborated history, context, or provenance transformed into an object of reverence? The emotional eruption caused by the allegation of forgery reveals how religiously important many believed the box to be. Were its forgers "exploiting the deep emotional need of Jews and Christians to reinforce their faith" as some argued?[20] The humanistic dividends of the ossuary caper may ultimately lie in the convergence of diverse voices and interests from the journalistic, academic, clerical, congregational, and secular communities. The burial box elicited a host of religious behaviors, disputes, and alliances. Who holds the authority to serve as the interpreter of religious significance for people of faith? In the case of the ossuary, epigraphers and biblicists assumed this position, while clergy and scholars of religion (in contrast to scholars of the Bible) sat on the sidelines.[21] The box was promoted first and foremost as a vessel of religious, nay, theological, importance, yet it was housed in a museum, not in a place of worship. As John Dominic Crossan and Jonathan L. Reed write, "The intellectual problem we have with the James box and its 'discovery' is that the archaeological process has been circumvented while a presentation to the public has reduced it to an arbiter of faith over unbelief."[22]

The James Ossuary tests the observable boundaries of concepts like "pilgrimage" and "relic" because it occasioned certain behaviors among visitors and promoters that simultaneously resembled and resisted a religious description. The phenomenon of mass visitation looked like pilgrimage. The rhetoric of tangibility linking the pious to the historical Jesus sounded like relic veneration. It was the scholars and curators promoting the ossuary, however, who assumed a religiosity inherent in the object's resonance and public reception. Many people indeed visited the ossuary out of religious curiosity but declined to place a religious value on it. The box did not seem to validate faith or undermine it, however much partisans attempted to conscript or dismiss its purported religious essence. ROM employees offered differing recollections about demonstrable acts of piety by museum visitors. The BAR marketed the ossuary as something approaching a relic. Perhaps the ossuary also tests the conceptual boundaries of religion itself. It is difficult to ignore Jonathan Z. Smith's famous controversial dictum that religion is nothing more than an act of academic classification: "Religion is solely the creation of the scholar's study. It is created for the scholar's analytic purposes by his imaginative acts of comparison and generalization. Religion has no independent existence apart from the academy. For this reason, the student of religion, and most particularly the historian of religion, must be relentlessly self-conscious. Indeed, this self-consciousness constitutes his primary expertise, his foremost object of study."[23] Smith's position has not gone unchallenged, and we do not adopt his definition here, but the phenomenological circumstances of the ossuary's story allow us to examine the Smithian characterization of *religiosity* as an ascribed quality rather than an inherent reality.

The essays in this volume will examine whether the ossuary bears an innate religious character or acquires it vis-à-vis assumptions about its funerary origins and putative connection to earliest Christianity. They revisit familiar questions in a new context. What makes an object religious? Why is it relevant that an object might have some connection to the ancient world or to Jesus Christ? How do we account for the distinctiveness in the meaning of the ossuary in the particular context of modernity?[24] Our reconstruction of the reception history of the ossuary requires examination of the deep human need for sensory experience of objects and the processes whereby people construct religious categories. The ossuary's etiology had to be considered in the context of an already contested and incomplete narrative about the family of Jesus. Museum officials, scholars, and the media offered a host of rubrics for interpreting the religious significance of the ossuary that centered on its role as further evidence for the incarnation of Jesus Christ. Thus, we consider the relationship between object and narrative, relic and story, and the opportunity to visualize, empathize, and imagine such tangibility afforded as a tool for enabling a particular interpretation as legitimate and true. We explore important questions about the protocols of scholarship where religious interpretation, historical presentation, and ethical accountability are concerned. We ask whether discourses of kinship, sexuality, and modernity in fact underpin the continuing media coverage of an otherwise uninteresting limestone box. The ossuary's saga offers an intriguing account of scholars of religion as well as of religion itself. It is a cautionary tale about self-consciousness and consciousness about others, both the living and the dead. It is a very good story.

OVERVIEW OF THIS BOOK

The essays in this volume critically evaluate the popular, theological, and scholarly receptions of the James Ossuary as it emerged from its chrysalis in the antiquities black market to become a Protestant relic in the media's custody. The essayists are not only interested in how responses to the ossuary phenomenon inform the presumption of religious meaning incarnate in an object; they also consider how those responses illuminate the landscape of religious studies as an academic discipline and the role of academicians as public interpreters of discoveries with religious significance.

In the first essay, "Archaeological Context and Controversy: The Bones of James Unpacked," biblical archaeologist Byron McCane guides readers through the thorny question of authenticity. He situates the ossuary both within Jewish burial practices of the Roman period and the modern dynamics of the antiquities market. He argues that the absence of an archaeological context for the James Ossuary complicates the means to connect it to Jesus of Nazareth in a responsible manner. Perhaps most pointedly, McCane juxtaposes the evangelical celebration of the ossuary's discovery with the willful disregard for the role of looters, who unceremoniously discarded the bones of the decedent (whoever he or she was). For McCane, this rationalization of exploitation and desecration amounts to archaeological pornography and highlights the theological commercialization of Holy Land material culture.

After its initial introduction in the BAR, the ossuary traveled to Toronto for its public unveiling at the ROM. A media circus ensued when the box, insured for seven figures, was damaged en route thanks to faulty packing. ROM curators had just a few weeks to plan a special exhibit that would accommodate, in the words of internal memoranda, space for "acts of reverence." Soon afterward, controversy erupted concerning the ossuary's authenticity and the museum's confusing roles as custodian of a sacred relic, collaborator with the black market, and shaper of public interpretation with carefully crafted docent literature for visitors. In the second essay, "The Brother of Jesus in Toronto," historian of religion Thomas Bremer discusses the ROM's construction of museum space for the display of a religiously charged object, the official interpretation of the ossuary in the exhibit, and the public response to the ossuary by museum visitors, including religious people. He also addresses the museum's official stance on the crisis of authenticity and the feedback from visitors. As part of his research, Bremer interviewed dozens of museum personnel and exhibit visitors from academic and religious communities. His unique "inside look" benefits from hundreds of internal ROM documents and e-mails, generously provided to this project's contributors by the museum's chief curator, Ed Keall. Bremer concludes that the ossuary's polemical story arc represents a discourse on modernity in its bizarre confluence of piety, skepticism, science, and hokum.

Theological debate among Christian believers created by competing interpretations of the inscription on the James Ossuary provides a way to examine embodied religious practice in contemporary Christianity. In the third essay, "Finding True Religion in the James Ossuary: The Conundrum of Relics in Faith Narratives," Bernadette McNary-Zak, a scholar of early Christianity, explores how this debate intersects with the notion of "relic," both as an academic category and an emblem of religious experience. Her research outlines several different interpretive narratives and asks how people evaluated these narratives in order to make meaning of the James Ossuary. She concludes that, while ROM visitors used preexisting patterns and language to make sense of their experiences, the box's uncertain origin and its inscription's equivocation ensure that a shroud of ambiguity will veil its appropriation into any Christian worldview.

Reports about the James Ossuary in TV documentaries, tabloids, and news outlets provide an interesting database to study the role of scholars in the production and dissemination of information in the age of mass media. Archaeologist and scholar of Christian origins Milton Moreland examines the roles and responsibilities that scholars assume as interpreters of religious arcana for public consumers in essay four, "Christian Artifacts in Documentary Film: The Case of the James Ossuary." Moreland considers how books on religion are published, marketed, and reviewed in an effort to understand how the ossuary conformed to, and defied, conventional patterns of scholarly dialogue with the public. He concludes that the theological interpretation of the object could only have unfolded as it did within the contours of modernity. Had the ossuary surfaced two centuries ago, both the artifact and *materiality* might have found a very different place in the Protestant tradition.

Essay five, "Anatomy of a Cargo Cult: Virginity, Relic Envy, and Hallowed Boxes," by Semitist and archaeologist Ryan Byrne, explores the larger media circus that pitted the Aramaic inscription against the Catholic doctrine of Mary's perpetual virginity, thereby involving the James Ossuary in a centuries-long dispute about Mary's postpartum sex life. In fact, it is in the series of Western historical discourses on *virginity* that we must locate the cultural buttons that the familial reference to James pushed. In the light of Julia Kristeva's work on the *Stabat Mater* tradition, Byrne examines denominational subtexts of the ossuary's academic treatments and a Protestant curiosity that he terms "relic envy." The James Ossuary epitomizes the scale of fraud that unsound ethical protocols may permit when museum professionals and biblicists associate with dealers and collectors. Professional archaeological societies have developed decisive ethical responses to the dilemma, but biblicists have thus far hesitated to bite the hand that feeds them unprovenanced inscriptions (sometimes forged, always suspect), which ostensibly validate biblical authority. Byrne discusses the impulse of academicians to adopt the mantle of religious professionals in order to interpret objects of historical significance for faith communities. It is clear that potential evangelical consumerism played a large role in the BAS's strategy to market the James Ossuary and the book *The Brother of Jesus*. He concludes that the introduction and public vetting of the object violated every scholarly protocol of *editio princeps* and peer review in a strange evasion of what Thomas Aquinas called the "sin of curiosity." As Martha Kaplan asserts that Western scholarship constructed the myth of Polynesian cargo cults, so too did scholars impose religious trappings on a box of prosaic character. The ossuary fracas revealed as much about the seduction of the academy as it did about religious behavior outside its towers.

In the sixth essay, "Overcoming the James Ossuary and the Legacy of Biblical Archaeology," Jonathan Reed, a best-selling author of popular and scholarly books about the archaeology of early Christianity, offers a privileged, critical perspective on the James Ossuary phenomenon. Reed was approached by HarperSanFrancisco to pen the popular book companion to the James Ossuary's museum tour. Believing the artifact to be a fraud, he declined the offer and enjoyed unique insights into the publishing world's competition to market the ossuary to evangelical readers by promoting the ossuary as a tangible link to Jesus. He and John Dominic Crossan went on to include discussion of the James Ossuary in their revised edition of *Excavating Jesus: Beneath the Stones, Behind the Texts* in order to explain how the James Ossuary is "almost a poster warning about the distinctive effects of paralegal artifact collecting, about the potential criminal sanctions for selling and buying on the illegal antiquities market, and about the moral difference between scientific archaeology and cultural looting."[25] From this exclusive vantage point, Reed reflects on his personal experiences as widely consulted documentary expert, popular author, and professional spectator of the ossuary's public odyssey.

The sustained fascination and willing suspension of critical faculties with regard to the discovery and vetting of ancient objects like the ossuary is the focus of the epilogue. A comparative look at the more recent phenomenon surrounding the public presentation of the Talpiot Tomb, identified as the family tomb of Jesus and allegedly the possible origin of the James Ossuary, provides an opportunity to witness similar political, scholarly, and marketing forces at work and to revisit factors central to the contemporary characterization of religiosity.

NOTES

1. André Lemaire, "Burial Box of James, the Brother of Jesus: Earliest Archaeological Evidence of Jesus Found in Jerusalem," *Biblical Archaeology Review* 28, no. 6 (2002): 24–33, 70.

2. Whereas looters had previously dumped the bones, perhaps "penultimate resting place" might have proved a more suitable description.

3. "James Ossuary Exhibit: Final text, except for conservation item, Version: 08 November 2002," Royal Ontario Museum document provided by Suzan Sabir.

4. For a popular overview of the personalities and events leading from the ossuary's public introduction to its scholarly condemnation, see Neil Asher Silberman and Yuval Goren, "Faking Biblical History," *Archaeology* 56, no. 5 (2003): 20–29; and David Samuels, "Written in Stone," *New Yorker*, April 12, 2004, 48–59. Regarding the trial, see Nina Burleigh, *Unholy Business: A True Tale of Faith, Greed, and Forgery in the Holy Land* (New York: Harper-Collins, 2008).

5. For a representative survey and bibliography of burial practices in ancient Israel from the Iron Age to the Roman period, see Elizabeth Bloch-Smith, *Judahite Burial Practices and Beliefs about the Dead* (Sheffield, England: Sheffield Academic Press, 1992); Rachel Hachlili, *Jewish Funerary Customs, Practices, and Rites in the Second Temple Period* (Leiden and Boston: Brill, 2005); and Byron R. McCane, *Roll Back the Stone: Death and Burial in the World of Jesus* (Harrisburg, Pa.: Trinity Press International, 2003). Relevant specialized studies include Eric M. Meyers, *Jewish Ossuaries: Reburial and Rebirth* (Bibliotheca et Orientalia 24; Rome: Biblical Institute, 1971); Levi Y. Rahmani, *A Catalogue of Jewish Ossuaries in the Collections of the State of Israel* (Jerusalem: Israel Antiquities Authority, 1994); Levi Y. Rahmani, *A Catalogue of Roman and Byzantine Lead Coffins from Israel* (Jerusalem: Israel Antiquities Authority, 1999); Rachel Hachlili and Ann E. Killebrew, *Jericho: The Jewish Cemetery of the Second Temple Period* (Jerusalem: Israel Antiquities Authority, 1999); Andrea Berlin, "Power and Its Afterlife: Tombs in Hellenistic Palestine," *Near Eastern Archaeology* 65 (2002): 138–48; Jodi Magness, "Ossuaries and the Burials of Jesus and James," *Journal of Biblical Literature* 124 (2005): 121–54; Yifat Peleg, "Gender and Ossuaries: Ideology and Meaning," *Bulletin of the American Schools of Oriental Research* 325 (2002): 65–73; and Eyal Regev, "Family Burial, Family Structure, and the Urbanization of Herodian Jerusalem," *Palestine Exploration Quarterly* 136 (2004): 109–31.

6. For the Ketef Hinnom texts paralleling the blessing in Num. 6:24–26, see Gabriel Barkay, "The Priestly Benediction on the Silver Plaques from Ketef Hinnom in Jerusalem," *Tel Aviv* 19 (1992): 139–92.

7. The significance and meaning of this practice in Jewish burial are hotly disputed. See Rachael Hachlili and Ann Killebrew, "Was the Coin-on-Eye Custom

a Jewish Burial Practice in the Second Temple Period?," *Biblical Archaeologist* 46 (1983): 147–53; and William Meacham, "On the Archaeological Evidence for a Coin-on-Eye Jewish Burial Custom in the First Century A.D.," *Biblical Archaeologist* 49: 56–59.

8. See Hachlili and Killebrew, *Jericho*.

9. Black market ossuaries typically come into private hands without reliable provenance, but they also compromise the integrity of public museum corpora. Around 20 percent of the ossuaries in Israel's state collection are unprovenanced; compare Rahmani, *A Catalogue of Jewish Ossuaries in the Collections of the State of Israel*.

10. BAS is the magazine's umbrella nonprofit organization.

11. English-speaking Christianity had long ago anglicized "Jacob" (Greek *Iacobus*, from the original Semitic *Yaʿaqob*), whom the New Testament calls the "brother of Jesus," as "James." In fact, English translations of early Christian literature would accord only this Jacob the distinction; no other Jacob became anglicized as James in the Christian tradition. Thus the decision to brand the burial box the "James Ossuary" conceded the identification of the box's former occupant.

12. The report on the SEM-EDS analyses of the ossuary, as conducted by Amnon Rosenfeld and Shimon Ilani of the Geological Survey of Israel, was published in *Biblical Archaeology Review* 28, no. 6 (2002): 29.

13. Financial figures obtained from an interview with the ROM's curator, Ed Keall, in Toronto on March 4, 2004. Keall also generously provided access to e-mail correspondence regarding details of the ROM staff's internal discussions of the exhibition's merits and obstacles, as well as the apparent time frame of the museum's decision to exhibit the ossuary later than Shanks had announced.

14. "James Ossuary Exhibit: Final text, except for conservation item, Version: 08 November 2002."

15. For studies representing the mainstream consensus about the Jehoash Inscription's inauthenticity, see Frank Moore Cross, "Notes on the Forged Plaque Recording Repairs to the Temple," *Israel Exploration Journal* 53 (2003): 119–22; Israel Ephʿal, "The 'Jehoash Inscription': A Forgery," *Israel Exploration Journal* 53 (2003): 124–28; and Yuval Goren, Avner Ayalon, Miryam Bar-Matthews, and Betina Schilman, "Authenticity Examination of the Jehoash Inscription," *Tel Aviv* 31 (2004): 3–16. For a minority perspective offering evidence for the text's possible antiquity, see Chaim Cohen, "Biblical Hebrew Philology in the Light of Research on the New Yeho'ash Royal Building Inscription," in *New Seals and Inscriptions, Hebrew, Idumean and Cuneiform*, ed. Meir Lubetski (Sheffield, England: Sheffield Phoenix Press, 2007), 222–84. For a defense of the original geological authentication, see Shimon Ilani, Amnon Rosenfeld, and Michael Dvorachek, "Archaeometry of a Stone Tablet with Hebrew Inscription Referring to Repair of the House," *Geological Survey of Israel Current Research* 13 (2003): 109–16.

16. Uzi Dahari, ed., *Final Report of the Examining Committees for the Yehoash Inscription and James Ossuary* (Jerusalem: Israel Antiquities Authority, 2003). The conspectus of the report is republished in Hershel Shanks and Ben Witherington III, *The Brother of Jesus: The Dramatic Story and Meaning of the First Archaeological Link to Jesus and His Family*, rev. ed. (San Francisco: HarperOne, 2004), 227–37. See also Avner Ayalon, Miryam Bar-Matthews, and Yuval Goren, "Authenticity Examination of the Inscription on the Ossuary Attributed to James, Brother of Jesus," *Journal of Archaeological Science* 31 (2004): 1185–89.

17. Samuels, "Written in Stone"; Michael Posner, "Israel Police Arrest Owner of Controversial Ossuary," *Globe and Mail* (Toronto), July 23, 2003; Zev Singer, "Ossuary Dealer Accused of Forgery, He Seemed Honest: ROM," *National Post* (Toronto), July 23, 2003.

18. "Israel Antique 'Forgers' Charged," BBC News, December 29, 2004; Matthew Kalman, "Trial Sheds Light on Shadowy Antiquities World," *Boston Globe*, May 16, 2006; Nadav Shragai, "The Art of Authentic Forgery," *Haaretz*, April 14, 2008.

19. Oded Golan claims to have purchased the limestone box for a few hundred dollars on an unknown date in the 1970s from an antiquities dealer whose identity also remains unknown. In an interview with *Time* magazine, Golan was "familiar" with the inscription but "unaware" that the names were "special" (November 4, 2002).

20. CNN.com, "Museums Warned on Bible-Era Relics," December 29, 2004.

21. Jeffrey Weiss, "Searching for Proof on 'Holy Ground': Many Archaeologists Are Reluctantly Drawn into Debates about Claims of Faith," *Edmonton Journal*, August 2, 2003.

22. John Dominic Crossan and Jonathan L. Reed, *Excavating Jesus: Beneath the Stones, Behind the Texts*, revised and updated edition (San Francisco: HarperSanFrancisco, 2002), 32.

23. Jonathan Z. Smith, *Imagining Religion: From Babylon to Jonestown* (Chicago: University of Chicago Press, 1982), xi.

24. If the response to the James Ossuary is unique in comparison to the response elicited by other ossuaries, then we are required to ask, what features make it unique? "Uniqueness is an ordinary presupposition of definition and classification," Smith writes, "it is not some odd point of pride" (Smith, *Imagining Religion*, 6).

25. Crossan and Reed, *Excavating Jesus*, xvi.

BYRON R. MCCANE

Archaeological Context and Controversy

The Bones of James Unpacked

The October 2002 issue of the popular magazine *Biblical Archaeology Review* featured a cover story on the James Ossuary, in which epigrapher André Lemaire asserted: "It seems very probable that this is the ossuary of the James in the New Testament. If so, this would also mean that we have here the first epigraphic mention—from about 63 CE—of Jesus of Nazareth."[1] This highly extraordinary claim was immediately met with skeptical responses from many archaeologists, who considered the so-called James Ossuary interesting and potentially significant but expressed concern that it had come to light from the antiquities market and a private collection rather than through a controlled archaeological excavation. Since its context and provenance were unknown, these archaeologists warned, the authenticity of the ossuary and its inscription could never be conclusively established. In subsequent news reports during early November 2002, further questions came to light regarding the circumstances under which the artifact had been brought to public attention. The time, place, and method of its acquisition all became matters of uncertainty and suspicion, prompting one leading archaeologist to remark, "To say the least, I have a very bad feeling about the matter."[2]

Despite these concerns, however, the general excitement about the James Ossuary and its inscription seemed to prevail. An exhibition was scheduled for the Royal Ontario Museum in Toronto, Canada, at the time of the annual meetings of the Society of Biblical Literature (SBL) and the American Schools of Oriental Research (ASOR) in Toronto during mid-

November 2002. Arrangements for the exhibition were made by the Royal Ontario Museum in conjunction with Hershel Shanks, editor of *Biblical Archaeology Review*, but without input from the Israel Antiquities Authority (IAA), the governing body for all archaeological activity in the nation of Israel. At the exhibition and the annual meetings, in other words, an artifact with no known archaeological context or provenance was presented to the SBL and to ASOR by persons with no scholarly credentials or academic affiliations. These persons, who stood to profit substantially by displaying the artifact at the SBL, were not cooperating with governmental authorities of the nation in which the artifact had originated. These facts of the situation were enough to give pause. Dazzled, however, by the possibility of an archaeological connection to Jesus of Nazareth, and titillated by the glare of mass media attention, the guild of biblical scholars largely ignored the warnings of experienced archaeologists. The result was an event that, it is now clear, was certainly not biblical scholarship's finest hour.

There is much to be learned, however, from the events that surrounded the appearance, promotion, and exposure of the James Ossuary, for the public phenomenon of this artifact encompassed a broad range of historical, financial, scientific, religious, and cultural factors. To that end, the remarks that follow will seek to establish an archaeological foundation for the larger task of understanding and evaluating the public excitement about the James Ossuary. Since the ossuary was an archaeological artifact, the starting point for thoughtful reflection on it must be archaeology, and more specifically, the archaeological fact that the inscription "Yaʿacob bar Yosef ahui diYeshua" is a modern forgery. Whatever else it might turn out to have been, the James Ossuary was surely not "the earliest known documentation of Jesus outside the Bible."

A Jewish ossuary from the Early Roman period is a chest or box, usually made of stone but occasionally of clay or wood, used for secondary burial —that is, the reburial of human bones after the flesh of a corpse has decayed. Early Roman Jewish ossuaries were usually made by hollowing out blocks of the soft limestone that is so common in the geology of Syro-Palestine. In keeping with their function as containers for human bones, ossuaries are typically proportional in size to the large and long bones of the body (skull and femur, for example). Thus the average size for an adult's ossuary is approximately 60 by 35 by 30 centimeters, with smaller measurements for the ossuaries of children. Ossuaries have removable lids, most of which are flat, although some are domed or gabled. The majority of ossuaries are plain and undecorated, but many are ornamented with decorations typical of artistic motifs in Early Roman Jewish art.[3] Geometric designs, for example, appear frequently, the most common of which is a rosette chip-carved into the side of the ossuary using a chisel and compass.[4] Representations of Jewish religious themes also sometimes appear, including palm branches, *menoroth*, and Torah shrines. Inscriptions, when present, are usually scrawled with charcoal or scratched with a nail or sharp object, and they may be found virtually anywhere on the ossuary, including on the sides, ends, or lid or even along the inside edge. These inscriptions typically identify the person whose bones are contained in the ossuary and most often include only the name of the deceased, sometimes adding a nickname, father's name, or place of origin. Occasionally, a distinguishing fact about the deceased may also be added.

Ossuaries are found in Jewish tombs from Early Roman Palestine, primarily in tombs within the vicinity of Jerusalem.[5] The typical tomb is a nearly square underground chamber (approximately 3.5 meters on a side), cut from bedrock, with a shallow rectangular pit in the floor creating a low shelf (about knee-high) around the walls. Several *loculi* (Hebrew, *kokhim*)—deep narrow niches for the primary burial of a single body—are usually carved into the walls. Ossuaries may be found in several locations around such a tomb, including on the shelf, in the niches, and on the floor. Other typical finds in these burial caves include human bones on the shelf and in the niches, perfume bottles (piriform unguentaria), juglets, cooking pots, and lamps. Coins, by contrast, are rare.

The James Ossuary has all the essential characteristics of a typical Jewish ossuary from the Early Roman period. It was formed, for example, from a block of limestone. Testing by the Geological Survey of the Ministry of National Infrastructures of Israel, in fact, identified the likely source of the stone as the area around Mt. Scopus in Jerusalem. With dimensions of 50.5 by 25 by 30.5 centimeters, the ossuary is slightly smaller than is typical for ossuaries used in the reburial of bones of full-grown adults. Like most Jewish ossuaries from this period, it is roughly and unevenly hewn. One of the short sides, for example, is not quite perpendicular to the base, giving the ossuary a slightly trapezoidal shape. Chisel marks and scratches are evident across all its surfaces. The lid is nearly flat, very slightly convex, and the bottom is flat, with no feet. It shows signs of the beginnings of an attempt at decoration. Each face (including the lid) is framed by two thinly incised straight lines running along the outside edge 1.2 centimeters from the edge, and on one long side (the side opposite the inscription) are the preliminary marks used by carvers for creating two chip-carved rosettes. All of these features are entirely typical of Jewish ossuaries from the Early Roman period in Jerusalem.

An inscription, incised with a nail or other sharp object, runs across the middle of the right half of one of the long sides. Made up of twenty Aramaic letters, the inscription is 19.5 centimeters long and 0.9 centimeters high. The script is slightly smaller than is typical for most ossuary inscriptions, and it is very neatly rendered, with no spaces between the words. The reading is clearly legible, with no letters uncertain: "Yaʿacob bar Yosef ahui diYeshua," or "James son of Joseph, brother of Jesus." The form and content of this inscription are, like the other features of this ossuary, typical of the Early Roman period in Jerusalem. The script includes some of the common variations in the ancient spellings of names like "James," "Joseph," and "Jesus." "Yaʿacob," for example, which was sometimes written without the letter *waw*, is written with the *waw*. "Yosef," which could be written with the letter *he* ("Yehosef"), is written without the *he*. "Yeshua" is a common variation in the spelling of a name that could also be rendered "Yehoshua" or "Yeshu." The script includes both cursive and formal lettering, with cursive forms of *aleph*, *daleth*, and *yod* in the words "ahui diYeshua." Early in the archaeological analysis of the ossuary, several epigraphers commented that the presence of these cursive forms was a sign that the closing phrase "ahui diYeshua" must have been added to the inscription later by a second hand. The cursive shapes in question are typical of Jewish funerary inscriptions from the first century CE, but the presence of both cursive and formal lettering in the same inscription, although unusual, is not by itself sufficient to establish the presence of two hands, especially in an ossuary inscription. Variations in spelling and forms of letters in these inscriptions are frequent, because these inscriptions were usually written at the time of secondary burial by members of the immediate family. In such circumstances, for example, in the cramped and dark confines of a Jewish family tomb, variations occurred naturally. Finally, the content of the inscription is also typical of Jewish ossuary inscriptions. It identifies the deceased in the way that Jews of this region and period customarily identified themselves: "X son of Y." On the whole, then, this ossuary could hardly be a more typical Early Roman Jewish artifact. If not for the constellation of names in the inscription, its authenticity would not be in doubt; indeed it would probably be regarded as a generally unremarkable specimen.

The constellation of names in the inscription is, however, anything but unremarkable. "James son of Joseph, brother of Jesus" configures a set of relationships that coincides exactly with the present state of our knowledge about one of the important figures in primitive Christianity. Appearing in such early Christian documents as the books of Matthew, Mark, Acts, 1 Corinthians, and Galatians, and outside the New Testament in the Gospel according to the Hebrews (quoted by Jerome in *de Vir. Ill.* 2), James is remembered as both the brother of Jesus and as an influential leader in the earliest Christian community in Jerusalem. Josephus mentions that "James, the brother of Jesus" was convicted and condemned by the Sanhedrin around the year 62 CE (*Ant.* 20.200). The cordial coincidence of these historical data with the names in the inscription was the spark that set off the assertion that an otherwise ordinary ossuary was "very probably" the burial container of the brother of Jesus.

From the beginning, however, there were significant problems with this assertion. The first had to do with statistics. The known frequencies of the names "Yaʿacob," "Yosef," and "Yeshua" in Jewish funerary inscriptions from Early Roman Palestine allow an approximate estimate of the likelihood that a Jewish male in Jerusalem during the first century CE might have been named Yaʿacob and had a father Yosef and a brother Yeshua. These three names are among the most common for Jewish males in this region and period. After examining inscriptions from across Early Roman Palestine, for example, Rachel Hachlili calculated that the rate of occurrence for the name "Yosef" was 14 percent; "Yeshua" was 9 percent and "Yaʿacob" 2 percent of the total of Jewish male names.[6] Levi Rahmani's study of ossuary inscriptions produced similar frequencies.[7] Estimating (conservatively) that the average Jewish male had two brothers, the particular constellation of names and relationships in this inscription was likely to occur in about 0.05 percent of the male population. In other words, in Early Roman Palestine, one Jewish male out of every 2,000 was named Yaʿacob with a father Yosef and a brother Yeshua. If our current population estimates for first-century Jerusalem are generally correct, then "in Jerusalem during the two generations before 70 CE, there were probably only about 20 people who could be called 'James/Jacob son of Joseph brother of Jesus.'"[8] At first glance, such calculations might seem to establish the likelihood of a connection between the historical Jesus and the James Ossuary. Rational reflection, however, shows that this statistical analysis actually supports the opposite conclusion. It is in fact very *un*likely that the inscription refers to James, the brother of Jesus of Nazareth. As a matter of statistical probability, there would have been approximately twenty men in first-century Jerusalem who could have been identified as "James son of Joseph, brother of Jesus," and the James Ossuary thus could have belonged to any one of those twenty men. Only one of the twenty, however, would have been James, the brother of Jesus of Nazareth. Thus the statistical calculations actually establish that there was only one chance in twenty that the ossuary was connected to Jesus of Nazareth. One out of twenty equals 5 percent, an extremely low level of probability that certainly does not make it "very probable that this is the ossuary of the James in the New Testament." People who are inclined to think that 20–1 odds are "very probable" are neither good poker players nor good scholars. On the basis of statistical arguments, in other words, it was never reasonable to imagine that this ossuary represented a material connection with Jesus of Nazareth. The probability was always strongly against it. At best, the inscription was an interesting coincidental combination of common Jewish male names, like another well-known ossuary that is inscribed, "Jesus, son of Joseph."

A responsible argument on behalf of this ossuary and its inscription could not therefore rest on statistical probabilities. Perhaps that was the reason that the most ardent proponents of the authenticity of the ossuary tended to emphasize the fact that the inscription included the phrase, "ahui diYeshua," or "brother of Jesus." This phrase appears in the inscription, they argued, because there must have been something special about being the brother of Yeshua. And what, it was suggested, could have been more special than to be the brother of Jesus of Nazareth? At first glance, this proposal, like the statistical argument, appears to be compelling. It is, after all, very rare for a brother's name to appear alongside the name of the deceased in an ossuary inscription. In addition, some ossuary inscriptions do include information about the deceased that family members regarded as socially or religiously significant. The inclusion of a brother's name therefore might be due to the fact that, in the eyes of the family, that brother had some particular social or religious standing. Yet this argument, too, is not probative. For the mention of a brother's name in an ossuary inscription did not necessarily carry any special social or religious significance. There could be other, more mundane reasons for including a brother's name. In the corpus of ossuary inscriptions surveyed by Rahmani, for example, there is an inscription that has exactly the same form as that on the James Ossuary: "X, son of Y, brother of Z." This inscription, scrawled on the side of an ossuary found in a tomb on Mount Scopus, reads "Shimi bar ʿsiah ahui Hanin," or "Shimi son of Asiah, brother of Hanin."[9] In this inscription, there is no apparent social or religious significance to the inclusion of the brother's name, and no reason for an archaeologist to construct one. Rahmani comments drily: "In certain cases, relatives found it important to indicate a sibling relationship in addition to a patronymic."[10] Among the possible reasons for including the name of a brother is a very practical one. Jewish ossuaries are typically found in Early Roman Jewish burial caves, and such caves typically hold the remains of multiple generations of extended family members. In addition, male names are often repeated across generations. Finally, the purpose of ossuary inscriptions was to identify the deceased. Thus a brother's name may have been added to an ossuary inscription for no more serious purpose than to differentiate between a grandson and a grandfather or between second cousins. Indeed, in one well-known tomb, two ossuaries were found side by side in the same *loculus* niche, and each of them was inscribed with the name "Jesus." In order to tell these two members of the family apart, one inscription added a surname and the other added a nickname. In the case of the James Ossuary, since the original archaeological context is unknown, an ordinary explanation of this sort can never be ruled out.

At this point, we come upon the third and most serious problem with the argument for the authenticity of the James Ossuary: the archaeological context of this artifact has been irretrievably lost. In the absence of such a context, carefully observed and recorded by excavators, it is not possible to make extraordinary claims about this ossuary. It came to light through suspicious circumstances. The location, date, and manner of its discovery were all unknown. As a result, interpreters were forced to rely upon guesswork, calculation, and imagination rather than upon archaeological data. There were no field notebooks, excavation reports, or analyses of the finds—only statistical probabilities, laboratory examinations, and articles in the media. Consider for a moment how different the situation would be today, if the people who first discovered the tomb in which this ossuary was found had, as the laws of the state of Israel require, contacted the IAA. In that case the ossuary would have been recovered through a controlled excavation. Questions about its provenance and significance would be answered with great confidence. Excavators would have drawn a plan of the tomb, recording not only the find spot for this ossuary but also for those of all the other ossuaries that would have been found with it. Some (or all) of those other ossuaries would also have been inscribed, and the names in all the inscriptions could have been interpreted in the light of each other. Human skeletal remains contained in the ossuary—and we must never forget that this artifact was the last resting place of a human being—would have been carefully preserved for analysis by physical anthropologists, who would have established the age and gender of the person whose bones were collected within. The cause of death might even have been evident. Reports on the pottery and lamps found in the tomb would have added further detail and richness to the archaeological context. Under such conditions, excavators have (at times) been able to establish that a particular tomb was related to this or that prominent historical figure from antiquity. But in such cases, everything depends upon information gleaned from the context, for the context of an artifact often provides far more information than the artifact itself. In the case of this ossuary, that information is gone forever. When looters picked it up from the shelf or niche in which it lay, dumped the bones onto the floor of the tomb, and sold it to an antiquities dealer, they permanently obliterated all of what we might have known about its history.

Before looking further into the forgery of the inscription, it is important at this point to pause long enough to point out another often-overlooked fact about the James Ossuary: even if its inscription had been shown to be genuine, the sensational claims of its proponents would still have been unjustified. Even if the words "James son of Joseph, brother of Jesus" had been an authentic ancient inscription, and even if they had referred to Jesus of Nazareth, they would not have told us anything we did not already know about James, Joseph, Jesus, ossuaries, ossuary inscriptions, Jewish burial practices in Early Roman Jerusalem, or even primitive Christianity there. This inscription did not contain any new information. We already knew that Jesus of Nazareth existed, that he had a father named Joseph and a brother named James, and that this James had died in Jerusalem during the early sixties of the first century CE. Most practicing biblical scholars, historians, and archaeologists never doubted any of those facts. In addition, we already knew that the earliest Christians in Jerusalem had practiced the typical Jewish burial customs of that time and place, including secondary burial in ossuaries.[11] The James Ossuary and its inscription thus unfortunately never held much significance for scholarship. From the moment it first appeared, this artifact was a typical Jewish ossuary. Such discoveries are indeed exciting to archaeologists, but they do not belong in the headlines of the *New York Times*. The public reporting of this ossuary was, in other words, entirely sensationalistic.

And now we know that the inscription is a fake. The ossuary itself is from an unknown context in Early Roman Jerusalem, but its inscription is from a well-known context in postmodern Tel Aviv. Examination by the IAA has exposed the truth. Chemical analysis of the ossuary's patina (the buildup of chemical and organic material on the surface of an archaeological artifact over the centuries during which it lies in the dirt), for example, proves that the inscription is recent. Hershel Shanks originally asserted—incorrectly—that the inscription did not cut through the natural patina on the ossuary and thus had to be ancient rather than modern. The IAA, however, demonstrated that the inscription actually does cut through the patina, proving that while the ossuary is ancient, the inscription is certainly not. Further, the inscription and the area immediately around it were found to have been coated with an *artificial* patina produced by a mixture of chalk and water. The percentages of calcium carbonate in this mixture "suggested that its crystallization took place in heated water,"[12] at a temperature of approximately 122 degrees Fahrenheit—too high for the environment of a typical Jewish burial cave from Early Roman Palestine. Only the surface area immediately in and around the inscription was found to have been covered with this fake patina. Finally, the renderings of the names in the inscription have now been shown to correspond closely to squeezes (rubbings) of inscriptions already published by Levi Rahmani in his *Catalogue of Jewish Ossuaries in the Collections of the State of Israel*. The name "Yaʿacob," for example, is taken from inscription number 396 in the catalog; "bar Yosef" is a copy of number 573; and "brother of" is taken from number 570. We now know, in other words, not only that the inscription is fake (since it cuts through the natural patina and was coated with an artificial one), but also how the forgery was created. Oded Golan found inscriptions in Rahmani's *Catalogue* that contained the names he needed to create the illusion of a connection with Jesus of Nazareth. He scanned the published squeezes of these inscriptions, resized the scanned images, and used them as a template with which he carved the inscription. He then covered his work with a coating of chalk and hot water. Worse yet, from the evidence collected in his home, we know that this was not the first time that Golan had created a forged inscription for profit.

The use of scanned images from multiple inscriptions accounts for the feature of the James Ossuary inscription that had been most puzzling to epigraphers. The script of each individual name looks genuine, since it includes typical forms and common variations in the ancient spellings of "James," "Joseph," and "Jesus." As we have already noted, many epigraphers were puzzled by the fact that the inscription includes both cursive and formal lettering, with cursive forms of *aleph*, *daleth*, and *yod* only in the words "ahui diYeshua." Some epigraphers had argued that the words "ahui diYeshua" must have been added by a later hand. Now we know the actual source of these variations in the script: Rahmani's *Catalogue*. Inscriptions number 396 and 573 in the catalog feature formal spelling of *aleph* and *yod*, while number 570 has cursive spellings of those same letters.

There is no longer any doubt that the inscription on the James Ossuary is not an archaeological artifact related to Jesus of Nazareth. The ossuary itself is authentic, robbed from a Jewish burial cave somewhere in or near Jerusalem. The inscription, however, is a pastiche of squeezes of published ossuary inscriptions, created through the clever use of digital scanning technology. In addition, we now know that the arguments for the authenticity of the ossuary and its inscription were not convincing. Scholarly archaeological interpretation, conducted on the basis of long-established disciplines in the field, would never have arrived at the extraordinary claim that this inscription referred to Jesus of Nazareth.

A final observation that is not strictly about archaeology may advance the conversation that follows in this book about the public phenomenon of the James Ossuary. It has to do with the most basic reasons for our work in the field of archaeology and religion. Those of us who are archaeologists and/or professors of religion teach a subject that belongs to the area of the college curriculum called the "humanities." In the subjects of the humanities—which include philosophy, history, religion, literature, and art—we study "human-ness," seeking to understand and illumine the most significant contours of what it means to be human. In particular, we esteem those aspects of our shared condition that distinctively mark us as human beings. Few of those shared human qualities are as deeply compelling as our mortality. The temporal horizon of our biological existence inscribes itself powerfully upon our lives. In this regard, the most troubling aspect of the phenomenon of the James Ossuary was the utter disregard that was shown toward its human—and humane—significance. Whatever else it may have been, this ossuary was the last resting place of a human being who lived, loved, laughed, worked, hoped, prayed, dreamed, wept, sang, wondered, feared, and (eventually) died. To forge an inscription upon such an artifact, and then to display that artifact sensationalistically—playing upon people's needs and anxieties for the purpose of financial profit—is an activity that can fairly be described as pornographic. For this reason, it is critically important for us to get to the bottom of what went on here. The archaeological judgment that the inscription is a fake is only the beginning. The James Ossuary must now be put in the context where it belongs: namely, as an event that, if studied carefully, can display more fully the varying contours of light and shadow that make up our all-too-human condition.

NOTES

1. André Lemaire, "Burial Box of James, the Brother of Jesus: Earliest Archaeological Evidence of Jesus Found in Jerusalem," *Biblical Archaeology Review* 28, no. 6 (2002): 33.

2. Eric M. Meyers, quoted in "Experts Question Authenticity of Bone Box for 'Brother of Jesus,'" *New York Times*, December 3, 2002.

3. Pau Figueras, *Decorated Jewish Ossuaries* (Leiden and Boston: Brill Academic Publishers, 1983). Also see Levi Y. Rahmani, *A Catalogue of Jewish Ossuaries in the Collections of the State of Israel* (Jerusalem: Israel Antiquities Authority, 1994), 28–52.

4. Levi Y. Rahmani, "Chip-Carving in Palestine," *Israel Exploration Journal* 38 (1988): 59–75.

5. Ossuaries do not appear in Galilee, for example, until the early second century CE, as at Huqoq; compare B. Ravani, "Rock Cut Tombs at Huqoq," *ʿAtiqot* 3 (1961): 128–43.

6. Rachel Hachlili, "Names and Nicknames of Jews in Second-Temple Times," *Eretz Israel* 17 (1984): 188–211.

7. Rahmani, *A Catalogue of Jewish Ossuaries in the Collections of the State of Israel*, 13.

8. Lemaire, “Burial Box of James, the Brother of Jesus,” 33.

9. Rahmani, *A Catalogue of Jewish Ossuaries in the Collections of the State of Israel*, no. 570.

10. Ibid., 15.

11. Byron R. McCane, *Roll Back the Stone: Death and Burial in the World of Jesus* (Harrisburg, Pa.: Trinity Press International, 2003).

12. Neil Asher Silberman and Yuval Goren, “Faking Biblical History,” *Archaeology* 56, no. 5 (2003): 28.

THOMAS S. BREMER

The Brother of Jesus in Toronto

At the Royal Ontario Museum (ROM) in Toronto, Ontario, officials regularly receive "all sorts of strange inquiries," according to Ed Keall, former head of the museum's Department of Near Eastern and Asian Civilizations. Thus, Keall initially regarded the call he received in October 2002 from Hershel Shanks, editor and publisher of the *Biblical Archaeology Review* (BAR) as just another "crank call."[1] But as he listened to the caller's proposal, Keall's curiosity grew. Shanks offered to arrange for the ROM to be the first institution to display the James Ossuary, a newly discovered artifact of great archaeological and religious significance. Although ossuaries are rather common (the ROM already had several in its collection), this particular burial box, according to Shanks, bore an inscription of monumental importance: "James son of Joseph, brother of Jesus," written in the Aramaic of first-century Palestine. Experts who had examined the ossuary had concluded that this small stone box had held the bones of the biblical character James, the purported brother of Jesus of Nazareth.

Keall's initial skepticism gradually gave way to intrigue. He still had questions, but Shanks pressed for a quick answer. He insisted that the ROM display the ossuary in time for the annual meetings of religious scholars that would be convening in Toronto in November, only six weeks away.[2] This seemed like an unreasonable request; the museum usually needed six months to a year to prepare this sort of exhibit. But Keall, as he recalls the conversation, "was talking with a very high-pressure person." Shanks threatened to take his offer elsewhere.[3] Bowing to the pressure, Keall agreed to at least present the offer to the museum's top administrators.

When Keall told William Thorsell, the chief executive officer of the

ROM, and other museum administrators of Shanks's offer, they were immediately "enthusiastic to pursue it."[4] But caution tempered their enthusiasm somewhat. A newly discovered object of unknown provenance, held by an anonymous collector and not subjected to the usual scrutiny of experts in the field, left the ROM vulnerable to rushing into a regrettable situation. On the other hand, museum officials welcomed the opportunity to display what Shanks would call "the most astonishing find in the history of archaeology—an inscription that many scholars believe is the first attestation of Jesus of Nazareth in the archaeological record."[5] With museum attendance down for the year, the possibility of a high-profile object like the James Ossuary appealed to them. Thorsell instructed Keall to go ahead and explore the possibility of bringing the James Ossuary to the ROM.[6]

The exhibition of an object at a major institution like the ROM does more than merely enhance the museum's gate receipts. In this case, the display of the James Ossuary in Toronto contributed to its transformation from an unknown stone box in the collection of an Israeli antiquities dealer to an object of cultural importance at the center of heated debates regarding its scholarly merits and theological implications for various Christians. At the museum, this ancient box became a very modern object, appealing to modern sensibilities and entangled in the discourses of modernity.[7] Moreover, the public interest generated by the museum exhibition would benefit those with a financial stake in the ossuary, people like its owner, Oded Golan of Israel, as well as Shanks, whose Biblical Archaeology Society profited from the 2003 book on the ossuary that he cowrote with Ben Witherington. Indeed, the ROM's agreement to show the James Ossuary confirmed its worth as a highly valued commodity.

DISPLAYING THE OSSUARY

Agreeing to display the James Ossuary was a risky proposition for officials at the ROM. The prestige, even the legitimacy, of a museum as a cultural institution rests on the authority of its expertise, and, as Steven Lavine and Ivan Karp point out, museums can lose their audiences if that authority is called into question.[8] A key issue in maintaining the authority of a museum is the authenticity of the objects it exhibits and the validity of claims about those objects. Museums rely on expert curators with specialized knowledge and professional experience to establish authenticity and develop appropriate exhibits for the public display of items in its collection. But the ROM had no such experts when it came to the James Ossuary. Keall's training and experience had little to do with ossuaries of first-century Palestine, although as an archaeologist of Islamic materials, he had some familiarity with the issues at stake in displaying the James Ossuary.[9] Without experts on their staff to reliably confirm for certain the ossuary's authenticity, officials were inclined to proceed slowly. They insisted on examining the box for themselves before agreeing to exhibit it. Cautiously, ROM officials arranged for a loan of the ossuary without committing to actually displaying it publicly.

Urgency displaced their caution, however, when Shanks announced the discovery of the James Ossuary to the world with a press conference on October 21, 2002. In his announcement to the media, he revealed that "plans are under way to exhibit the box at the Royal Ontario Museum in Toronto, Canada, during the annual meeting of Bible scholars in November," according to the report on CNN's website.[10] ROM officials were caught off guard by this sudden announcement. The next morning, Meg Beckel, the museum's chief operating officer, clarified to museum staff that the James Ossuary would be lent to the ROM initially "for inspection only," and only after closely examining the box and its accompanying documentation would the museum's officers consider displaying it. But by that same afternoon, as the museum's public-relations department staff prepared a press release, Beckel revealed in a subsequent communication that the museum planned to actually display the ossuary during the scholarly conferences in November. It appears as if Shanks may have forced their hand by announcing to the world that the James Ossuary would be on display in Toronto. Museum officials quickly abandoned their course of caution that called for a close examination and reasonable authentication of the object.[11] The world was clamoring to see this important discovery.

With a clear commitment to display the James Ossuary, the museum's staff began working on a design for the exhibit. The design team, under the direction of project manager Suzan Sabir, considered several possible formats for displaying the stone burial box. Their first inclination was to show it alongside the ossuaries from their own collection. Then they thought about building a cave or a replica of an ancient tomb, creating a context for the ossuaries. But they were under severe time constraints, and such an elaborate display would have taken months to design and build. Finally, they decided to concentrate on quotations about James. The curator, Keall, produced a series of texts drawn from ancient sources, and the graphic designer covered the walls of the exhibition room with the quotes in exceptionally large lettering. The object itself would take center stage in a freestanding display case, with the museum's other ossuaries left in their normal place in another room not far from the James exhibit. Images of the other ossuaries encouraged visitors to view them after leaving the James exhibit, and signage showed the way to the other room.[12]

The emphasis on text, in Keall's estimation, was a fortuitous decision that added to the success of the exhibit. "The whole thing was words," he notes, "and I think it was very powerful that way. Because in a sense the power of the ossuary itself are the words. So in that magnification of writing, for me it was a very, very successful design presentation, largely accidental because of the circumstances of what we were up against."[13] Indeed, the box is of relatively little interest in itself. The words of the inscription make the ossuary a sensational object that arouses public interest. These words, in their original Aramaic form with transliterations in Roman letters (one running right to left, like the original, and a second written in conventional left to right form), plus translations in both French and English, dominated the walls of the exhibition room.[14]

In addition, the designers included a great deal of supplemental text. "The exhibition was actually extremely text heavy," notes Sabir, "and we literally covered all four walls of the gallery with text, so that when people came in it wasn't just a matter of the object."[15] In the hallway before viewing the ossuary, visitors had their initial introduction to the importance of the object:

> The ossuary is a tangible relic. Whatever its association in terms of personages, it puts us in contact with an age when there were still people alive who knew Jesus of Nazareth. Written accounts of Jesus may reflect eyewitness reports of his life, but most of the texts were composed decades after the Crucifixion, in Greek, and almost all of the hard copies that still exist were made centuries later.

A second introductory text offered information about James:

> James was the first permanent head of the Christian Church in Jerusalem. Clement, the man who replaced Peter as bishop of Rome, wrote to him as "James, bishop of bishops, who rules Jerusalem, the holy church of the Hebrews." He was visited in 58 CE in Jerusalem by

> Paul, who referred to him as "the Lord's brother." He was sometimes referred to as James the Just. He was martyred in Jerusalem in 62 CE after refusing to deny to the High Priest and the Pharisees that Jesus was the Messiah.

This text included a clarifying footnote: "Note on dating: In preference to using BC (Before Christ) and AD (*Anno Domini*, Year of the Lord), we adopt the current practice of using CE (Common Era) and BCE (Before Common Era)."

Following the introduction, the exhibit included three ancient quotations, all under the caption "References in textual scripture to the family relationship of James to Jesus, and his role in the early Christian Church in Jerusalem." Two are from the Christian Bible (Luke 2:17, "Reference to Jesus as the first born of Mary"; and Galatians 1:18–19, "Reference to James brother of Jesus"), and the other is from the *Ecclesiastical History* of Eusebius ("Reference to James as spokesperson and revered leader of the Christian community in Jerusalem"). Elsewhere in the exhibit were quotations from Jerome, the Gospel of Thomas, and Flavius Josephus. Also displayed was a reproduction of the official letter of the Geological Survey of Israel stating the results of their analysis confirming the authenticity of the James Ossuary and its inscription; it concluded, "No evidence that might detract from the authenticity of the patina and the inscription was found." Other information included an explanation regarding the age of the ossuary; an acknowledgement of varying interpretations of James's relationship to Jesus according to different Christian traditions (James as full brother of Jesus, dominant among Protestants; James as half brother of Jesus and son of Joseph by a previous marriage, dominant among Orthodox Christians; and James as cousin of Jesus and son of Clopas and the Mary who stood near the cross, dominant among Roman Catholics), which included diagrams of various family trees taken from the article first announcing the James Ossuary (November/December 2002 issue of the BAR); and explanations of Aramaic writing and the use of ossuaries in Jerusalem up until 135 CE. Altogether, the exhibit featured far more textual materials than usually provided for a single object.

Museum officials were very much aware of the religious potential of the James Ossuary. Expecting devotional behaviors from devout visitors, the design team discussed whether they should provide a place for them to kneel in solitude before the object. At stake in the decision was whether to regard the ossuary as primarily religious or historical in nature. As Sabir asks, "Do we make this into a religious piece that we treat as an icon, or are we treating it as 'here's an artifact with a very interesting history that you may or may not wish to believe, but which has religious impact'?"[16] In the end, they decided on the latter. They justified their decision, however, with concern about crowd control. Accommodating religious devotions would slow down the flow of visitors, creating a logjam that the museum was not prepared for.

VIEWING THE OSSUARY

As preparations to display the James Ossuary at the ROM took shape, the museum's Communications Department planned for the arrival of the bone box. A media event was scheduled for the official uncrating of the object on the afternoon of October 31, 2002. But as the media gathered at the museum, the event was suddenly cancelled. Museum officials were shocked when the courier delivered the ossuary in a cardboard box, so they had decided to sneak a look at the box prior to its public unveiling. As Francisco Alvarez, the museum's director of communications, exclaims, "No object has ever arrived in a cardboard box to the museum, probably in fifty years. . . . It was a cardboard box. It looked like the corners had been smashed in a little bit. . . . It had written on it in Hebrew 'Fragile,' but not in English. And it had traveled from Tel Aviv to New York, to Hamilton, to Toronto. Why? We don't know. We didn't arrange it. This was all arranged by the owner, packing and transport. We were just told it was going to arrive at 11:00. . . . It was Halloween Day."[17] What they found inside confirmed their worst fears. The ossuary was set inside the box with only bubble wrap wound around it for protection. "As soon as we opened the box and saw that there was this bubble wrap," Alvarez recalls, "we could see a crack right at the top. We couldn't actually open it because we knew that it was just going to fall, like pieces were just going to fall out. It was in five pieces."[18] With such shoddy packaging, it seemed that the James Ossuary, valued according to museum documents at $2 million (U.S.), "was almost guaranteed to break," according to the reaction of Dan Rahimi, the ROM's director of collections management.[19]

The cancellation of the official uncrating in front of the media unleashed a tempest of rumors. But museum officials could do little to quell the media's consternation; their immediate priority was to communicate with the owner of the ossuary and develop a conservation plan for it. As Alvarez notes, "We were in a particularly strange position because we don't own the object, and we couldn't decide to do anything until we had permission from the owner. He had to approve exactly what steps were being taken, how they were being communicated, and what pictures we were releasing to the media."[20] The delays, however, only added to the press's curiosity and heightened the suspense about the James Ossuary and its arrival in Toronto. When museum officials finally announced that the famous bone box had suffered damage en route to the museum, the story warranted banner headlines in Toronto and elsewhere. In fact, the news media gave at least as much attention to the breakage as they had to Shanks's original announcement introducing the James Ossuary to the world.

Meanwhile, the ROM's conservation experts, led by Ewa Dziadowiec, quickly devised a plan for fixing the damaged bone box, but they could not begin work on it until the insurance adjuster arrived a few days later to inspect the object and approve the conservation plan. By the time everyone had agreed to the repairs, the opening of the exhibition was looming, and the conservators worked frantically to prepare the ossuary for display. In the rush to get it ready, however, museum officials had no time to conduct a close inspection of the box to determine its authenticity. Only the conservators viewed the ossuary up close, and they were more concerned with repairing it than determining its age. Nevertheless, several of the conservators who worked on the ossuary harbored doubts about the authenticity of its inscription. They conveyed their concerns to the curator, but their opinions were apparently disregarded. In fact, a member of the conservation team took exception to a museum press release the following summer that said, in part, that "the studies that were carried out on the inscription and broken fragments of the Ossuary, however, satisfied *the ROM's curators and conservators* that it was an authentic artifact with an authentic inscription" (emphasis added). The unnamed conservator stated in an internal communication that several of the conservators told museum officials at the time that they were not convinced of the inscription's authenticity as a genuine first-century work. The press release that was subsequently posted on the museum's website was changed to read: "The studies that were carried out on the inscription and broken fragments of the Ossuary, however, satisfied *the ROM's investigative team* that it was an authentic artifact with an authentic inscription that might make it the Ossuary of James, the brother of Jesus" (emphasis added).[21]

As the ROM's conservation team worked to repair the James Ossuary, the damage it had incurred in transit to the museum only added to the appeal of the object. Not only did it generate a tremendous amount of publicity, but the breakage also made the stone box a more interesting artifact. The cracks in the object, both old and new, accentuated the antiquity and the consequent fragility of the ossuary. In fact, the designers of the exhibit drew attention to the damage, explaining in text on the walls of the exhibit room how museum conservators treated the box and noting the difference between the new cracks and the old ones that were a part of the natural aging of the stone.[22]

Despite the pressures of an unusually short time to prepare—and the added pressures of repairing the damaged object under the heightened scrutiny of constant attention in the press—the staff at the ROM put together a remarkable exhibit that opened on time on November 15, 2002. Responses to the exhibition were mostly favorable. As Peter Richardson, professor emeritus in the Department for the Study of Religion at the University of Toronto, recalls: "I thought they had done a good job. I was happy with it. I didn't think they embarrassed Toronto or the ROM in the way they did it."[23] Others, like Professor John Kloppenborg of the Centre for the Study of Religion at the University of Toronto, were disappointed that the museum's other ossuaries or additional funerary items were not included; he would have preferred a richer contextual display. Nevertheless, Kloppenborg thought that the exhibit was very good. He appreciated how the textual material helped to situate what people were looking at.[24]

Another scholar, John Marshall, who also teaches in the Department for the Study of Religion at the University of Toronto, noticed a strong parallel between the museum exhibit and the initial article about the James Ossuary in the *BAR*, published by Shanks.[25] He recalls: "When I read the *Biblical Archaeology Review* article, I realized how thoroughly indebted to that article the museum exhibit was. The museum exhibit was substantially a retyping and an enlargement of that article."[26] Nevertheless, the abundance of information on the exhibition walls provided museum visitors with a satisfying experience. As Marshall observes, "It was one of those exhibitions that you go to it and since there's only one item, you feel that you ought to be getting more, but how do you spend more time on a box with an inscription that you can't read?" But the text on the walls supplemented visitors' experience of the ossuary. Marshall recalls that most visitors "would read and they would look at it, and they would read, and leave."[27]

At least a few museum visitors did more than merely read the text on the walls and look at the ossuary. Some Christian visitors brought their religious devotion to the museum. Determining exactly how many of the approximately 95,000 people who saw the James Ossuary in Toronto came for specifically religious reasons is a difficult task. Museum officials confirm that a number of churches arranged organized group trips to the museum, and numerous individuals likely visited out of a devotional impulse.[28] Certainly, museum officials anticipated the likelihood of religious practices at the exhibit when they considered whether to make space for visitors to kneel in front of the display case. But their decision to not facilitate such practices may have put a damper on the willingness of adherents to display religious behaviors in the museum setting; it seems that the occurrence of such behaviors was far less common and somewhat more subdued than might be expected.[29]

Although their presence at the museum was less obvious than some predicted, Christian adherents did visit the James Ossuary at the ROM, and for some, at least, there was a feeling that they were viewing an object of monumental importance for their faith. Glen Taylor, on the faculty of the University of Toronto, felt "a sense that this was something out of the ordinary and potentially inspiring." In talking to other visitors at the museum, he recalls, "There was a sense that we Christians might be standing beside a piece of history tied to the life of our LORD."[30] Another visitor, identified only as "Sisi," attended a panel discussion at the ROM that included Oded Golan, owner of the James Ossuary, and various scholars. They were debating whether or not the ossuary was genuine. Sisi writes: "I remember that while the box was becoming authenticated, Jesus was becoming more real and tears began to roll down my eyes in the middle of the lecture. I don't need a box to tell me that Jesus walked on this planet, but sometimes these little events bring the reality of Christ a breath away; which brings about the question: what will you do with the man called Jesus? That is what makes people uncomfortable. Quite often it is not the box they want to reject but Christ Himself."[31] Even among Christians who were uncertain about the claim that the ossuary had once held the bones of Jesus' brother, the exhibit played an important evangelistic role. One visitor who remained "dubious as to its authenticity" remarks: "The one good thing about the artifact was that it did bring a number of people to the ROM to read a Christian message. If that assisted someone in their faith journey, fine, but as to actual history, that is another matter."[32]

Sisi's assertion that she does not "need a box to tell me that Jesus walked on this planet" reveals a more common theme among Christians interested in the James Ossuary. As exciting as its discovery may be, the burial container of the brother of Jesus has very little theological significance for most Christians. The author of a local church newsletter asked, "Does this ossuary add to our knowledge of the life of Jesus? No. Do you need to worry whether it is genuine or not: In terms of faith, not really. The ossuary of James, with its inscription (if genuine), does not affect in any way the central teachings of the Christian faith."[33] Likewise, James A. Beverly, professor of theology and ethics at Tyndale Seminary in Toronto, insisted that "the ossuary is more of a curiosity than a faith-building discovery."[34] Whether authentic or not, many Christians felt that the James Ossuary had little consequence for personal faith, although it did have a profound effect on some faithful Christians who visited the ROM. For example, Isa Hauser, a theology student at the University of Toronto, recalls viewing the ossuary: "I thought, 'Wow! This most probably held the bones of the brother of our Lord Jesus Christ!!' It made Jesus as a human being somehow more real."[35]

For religious visitors to the ROM, another issue proved more contentious than the theological implications of the box that may have held the bones of Jesus' brother. The museum's explanation of the widely accepted convention of CE and BCE nomenclature for dating purposes angered a significant number of Christian visitors and even caught the attention of the conservative Christian press. Alvarez recounts that "many visitors had never seen that before and took great exception to the fact that we were unilaterally excising the name of the Lord from generally accepted practice. We got literally dozens and dozens and dozens of e-mail[s] and letters on that issue alone."[36]

Yet, regardless of whatever religious interest that the Christian faithful had in the museum display, the vast majority of visitors viewed the James Ossuary, in the words of James Beverly, "more of a curiosity than a faith-building discovery." For faithful, practicing Christians, the ossuary adds little to their appreciation of the tradition. Terry Donaldson, the Lord and Lady Coggan Professor of New Testament Studies at Wycliffe College,

University of Toronto, notes that the ossuary may be "of intrinsic interest, but it doesn't add anything to our understanding of the first-century context of the ministry of Jesus." Donaldson continues by emphasizing that despite the claims of Shanks and others in the BAR, this was not a momentous discovery for practicing Christians; in terms of what it adds to our understanding of Christianity, the James Ossuary is not comparable to something like the Dead Sea Scrolls, "which just continue to generate new insights and open new windows and raise new questions."[37]

Because of this, even devout Christians tended to regard the ossuary less as an object of religious devotion and more of "an object of interest, of intellectual and sort of cultural interest."[38] The public came to the ROM not to honor James or pray to him, but as consumers of an object created in part by the cultural work of museum practices. In this sense, regardless of its authenticity as a first-century box that once held the bones of the brother of Jesus, the James Ossuary certainly is a genuine artifact of modernity, produced by that most modern of institutions, the museum, and designed precisely for the modern sensibilities of a twenty-first-century museum-going public. As a modern object, it participates in discourses regarding Christianity in the modern world.

AUTHENTICATING JAMES

Modernity arises in a discourse on difference. The term "modern" invokes both a temporal difference (the modern present as qualitatively different from the premodern past) and differences in social identity (the modern self as qualitatively different from the premodern other). In this regard, Bruno Latour describes what he calls the "double asymmetry" of the modern: "It designates a break in the regular passage of time, and it designates a combat in which there are victors and vanquished."[39] The temporal difference, as Gustavo Benavides wryly suggests, remains perpetual, involving a self-conscious distinction between oneself as *moderni* and others as *antiqui* that goes back in the European context at least to the eighth century.[40] Thus, regarding one's identity as "modern" consists of a claim of knowing oneself through a knowledge of the past. Most often this insinuates a claim of superiority over the premodern past, with the modern self representing distinctive progress in moral, intellectual (especially in its reliance on rational authority), social, political, technological, and economic domains.[41]

Western modernity, in Benavides's characterization, consists of an interaction between the exercise of reflexivity (a self-conscious reflection on the differences that constitute the self) and the ability to exercise power over others and over nature.[42] The resulting self-understanding as "modern" organizes itself on the social level around particular points of reference. One of the more prevalent of these that Benavides draws attention to involves market relations. He refers to the work of Jacques Bidet in recognizing "a 'matrix of modernity' constituted by a market in which individuals engage in contractual relations, the contract being the pivot around which everything gyrates."[43] In the consequent marketplace matrix that constitutes a key element in the discursive performance of a self-conscious modernity, the acquisition and aestheticization of the material objects of nonmodern peoples and cultures carries significant rhetorical force. One way that modern westerners perform their self-understanding as the agents of modernity is through practices of acquiring, collecting, interpreting, and displaying the things of the nonmodern other, usually regarded as primitive and therefore inferior to the modern self.

Thus, in this manner museums serve the rhetorical aims of modernity in the Western world. In fact, the historical rise of museums parallels the history of the modern West. Beginning with the emergence of powerful merchants in Renaissance Italy in the fifteenth century who built palaces to display the fruits of their wealth, continuing through the great nationalistic museums built upon the colonial exploits of European empires, and extending to the plethora of museums that today offer a varied choice of cultural experiences for a knowledge-hungry public, museums follow closely the course of the Western modern world.[44]

Sociologically, museums reinforce the values of modern society. In nineteenth-century Britain, for instance, museums "were seen as playing their part in the development of the reliable and orderly citizens which the Victorian establishment desired to see."[45] They accomplished this with impressive collections of material objects that gave evidence of, and thus legitimized, the prevailing worldview of the normative social order. Susan Pearce notes that museums have "the ability to display, to demonstrate, to show the nature of the world and of man within it by arranging the collected material in particular patterns which reflect, confirm and project the contemporary world view. With this go the modes of curatorial care, study and interpretation which, in themselves, make up elements in the constituting modern discourses."[46] Indeed, museum practices do more than merely inform the public about the items in their collections; they participate in the constitutive discourses of modernity itself.

Participation in these discourses involves both the authoritative production of knowledges and the public dissemination of these knowledges.[47] Museums utilize their collections to produce knowledges that support dominant narratives of the society, making museum practices a key component in what Pearce terms "the social code (or system, or rules, or habitus) of enlightened modernity, grounded in the belief in overarching narratives which tell of the reality of scientific reason, the value of past historical experience, and the conviction that there exist realities to know about, that people are capable of knowing about them, and that they are able to use this knowledge to create better social systems."[48] In short, museums occupy a prominent place in the social landscape of modernity because they produce socially useful knowledge. A crucial aspect of this knowledge are the narratives that give definition and meaning to the existing social order. Museums affirm the society's self-understanding of its history and the propriety of its dominant institutions.[48]

The appearance of the James Ossuary at the Royal Ontario Museum contributed to a particular narrative of Western society by taking up a long-standing issue in the modern West: the uneasy relationship between modernity and Christianity. Certainly, the modern West's debt to Christianity remains undeniable. Yet the rise of modern science and the concomitant investment in the authority of rational inquiry has, despite its own roots in Christian Scholasticism—or perhaps *because* of those roots—largely displaced the authority of the Church as the dominant institution in Western society. Nevertheless, rational westerners are reluctant to discard religion altogether. In fact, much of modern intellectual history in the West seeks to incorporate Christian assumptions into the discourses of modernity.

In this context, a museum exhibit featuring the stone box that once held the remains of a significant character in the Christian story appends a modern authority to the religious narrative—the rational authority of expert scrutiny and interpretation provided by the museum's curatorial practices. At the same time, it bolsters the legitimacy of Christianity in general in the modern order by providing material evidence of its historical claims. In short, Christian claims acquire a verifiable material reality with the appearance of the burial container of Jesus' brother in the Toronto museum.

Museums exercise their authority primarily through the process of selection, interpretation, and presentation of material objects. But materiality in general carries little inherent value in modern Western thought. Western philosophy allots a subordinate or secondary role to material culture "in which objects are seen as merely the outcome or the product—or even the detritus—of primary thinking, feeling and acting which is carried out elsewhere."[50] It is therefore up to the museum to give its objects meaning through curatorial practices. The process begins with selection, the choices regarding objects deemed worthy of the narratives and values that museums support.[51] Transforming the selected items into museum pieces requires interpretation, relying on the curatorial expertise of recognized authorities. Finally, museums display their objects to the public in exhibits that give meaning to larger social and cultural narratives. Consequently, the viewers' experiences of museum exhibits reinforce the normative values of society.

The James Ossuary contributes to a narrative regarding the origins of Western society. The bone box of Jesus' brother lends credence to biblical accounts of those origins as historical reality; at least the ROM's exhibit made it seem so by employing what Hooper-Greenhill calls "an ethos of obviousness."[52] Thus, a bone box inscribed with "James son of Joseph, brother of Jesus" is something more than a first-century funerary item. The curatorial strategies employed in the interpretation and display of the ossuary highlighted the obviousness of the connection to the Christian tradition. At the same time, visitors had little access to other possible narratives about the stone box. Instead, the obvious reference to personages of the Christian story emphasized a particular narrative: the historical account of the Christian church.

The exhibition at the ROM affirmed this particular historical narrative by presenting the James Ossuary as an object of religious significance. The exhibit began by claiming that "the ossuary is a tangible relic," thus situating the ossuary in a religious framework from the outset. Characterizing it as a relic framed the museum visitors' experiences of the object in terms of religious pilgrimage; like Christian pilgrims, they came to the museum to be in the presence of relics.[53]

Reinforcing the religious context of the ossuary were the documentary references to James and the explanations of his relationship to the main character in the Christian narrative, Jesus of Nazareth. By posting quotes from sources (both biblical and extrabiblical) used to verify the Christian story, the museum exhibit situated the object in the narrative context of Christianity. Even the diagram of family trees that explained the different interpretations by various Christians of how they interpret the sibling relationship between James and Jesus (as full brother, half brother, or cousin) told visitors that this item must have great significance for Christians.

The ROM also made the James Ossuary into a religious object in the performative aspects of the exhibit. Museums employ what Barbara Kirshenblatt-Gimblett calls "the agency of display." As she notes, "Exhibitions are fundamentally theatrical, for they are how museums perform the knowledge they create."[54] This performance arises out of carefully constructed display space that serves as "an interface that mediates and thereby transforms what is displayed into heritage." Heritage, Kirshenblatt-Gimblett explains, is not something old but actually rather new, "a mode of cultural production in the present that has recourse to the past."[55] Indeed, items like the James Ossuary have their significance in the world of modernity, not in the ancient world of James, Joseph, and Jesus.

The exhibition at the ROM employed its theatrical agency in dramatic fashion that evoked religious awe. As visitors entered the hallway outside the exhibit space, a scrim curtain blocked their view of the ossuary. On the curtain projected in light was the title of the exhibition, creating a sense of anticipation. Visitors entered the room by turning first to their left and then around the scrim curtain to their right. The ossuary was not visible until the viewer stood right in front of it.[56] It rested in an altar-like case at the center of the room, surrounded by deep red walls covered floor-to-ceiling with text, most prominently the transliterations and transcriptions of the letters inscribed on the stone box. Special lighting raked across the ossuary itself, highlighting the inscription.[57] There was little doubt that this was a very special object, a "tangible relic" set in what seemed like a temple space.

This performance of the James Ossuary as a religiously significant object followed closely the interpretive story being pushed by Hershel Shanks. In fact, in their acceptance of Shanks's proposal and the subsequent reliance on his interpretation of the ossuary as published in the pages of the BAR, officials at the ROM abdicated their own curatorial authority. Instead, they allowed those with a financial interest in promoting the ossuary to determine the interpretive framework for their display.

On the other hand, the ethos of obviousness makes the Christian context the most plausible, perhaps the only, interpretive framework for understanding the James Ossuary. After all, the obvious context for this box is the early Christian church and specific characters named in the canonical texts of the tradition.[58] An exhibit that ignored this context would seem somewhat disingenuous or entirely misinformed. Yet, other curatorial possibilities were available. For instance, rather than situating their interpretation of the ossuary firmly within the Christian narrative, Ed Keall and his staff could have told the ossuary story from an archaeological perspective. By asking what makes this object interesting to archaeologists (rather than what makes it interesting to Christians), the museum's performance could have discussed what it might tell us about funerary practices in first-century Palestine, the sociological implications of the inscription, the kinds of scientific questions it might raise, and the caveat of inferring too much from an unprovenanced object of questionable origins. A discussion of the ossuary's possible implications for Christians and an understanding of their tradition would certainly be an appropriate dimension of such an exhibit, but it would be peripheral to the more pertinent issues of the object's archaeological relevance.

Both interpretive possibilities regard the James Ossuary as an object of modernity by furthering modern narratives and positing normative values of modern society. The story behind a predominately Christian interpretation tells an origin story of Western society grounded firmly in Christianity. The ossuary bolsters claims that the modern West has its beginnings in the longer Christian narrative by providing material evidence of that story. From a Christian perspective, the West's beginnings in the Christian tale are self-evident knowledge. Archaeological evidence, although justifying this understanding, remains superfluous to the revealed truth of the human condition. In contrast, an interpretation focused on the archaeology of the ossuary demonstrates a different set of values. It shows that knowledge is a product of the human effort at rational truth. The normative values posited by this sort of interpretation have to do with skepticism and rational discernment rather than faithful acceptance of an ancient tale. It presents questions about what such an object can tell us about the world we live in and what conclusions we must remain suspicious of. It remains less certain about conclusive answers.

Yet a more scientific, archaeologically focused interpretation of the James Ossuary presents a significant drawback: it lacks a strong appeal to the public imagination. Consequently, the alternative take on the burial box would have little appeal to its owner, to Shanks (who had money to gain in placing the box in the Christian story), or to news organizations clamoring to break the next big story. Moreover, it would not make sense for the museum. Indeed, a bone box with an archaeologically interesting inscription would not sell nearly as many tickets as would the first material link to Jesus.

THE REAL JAMES

The pressure to sell tickets led the ROM staff to pay less attention than perhaps they should have to what turned out to be a crucial issue: whether or not the James Ossuary, or at least its inscription, was authentic. The urgency of the circumstances under which the ROM agreed to show the ossuary did not allow them to investigate thoroughly the possibility that they were dealing with a forgery. Instead, they relied only on the opinion of noted epigrapher André Lemaire of the Sorbonne and a scientific study by two geologists at the Geological Survey of Israel (completed in only one day) that concluded: "No sign of the use of a modern tool or instrument was found. No evidence that might detract from the authenticity of the patina and the inscription was found."[59] This minimal body of evidence was enough to convince museum officials to put the box on display.

Forgery is a constant concern of museums. Because so much is at stake (in terms of financial considerations as well as reputations) in the authentication of museum objects, museums are, in the words of Susan Pearce, "particularly vulnerable to authentication's dark angel, the practice of faking." Pearce goes on to describe faking as "a subversive activity intended to make illegitimate money out of human gullibility, to discredit scholars and undermine the world of expertise, and to falsify the record of the past, sometimes in the interests of specific individuals or groups." But the work of forgers plays an important role in the museum world. "Fakers need fakees or, to put it another way, successful fakes work because the perception of them by collectors, scholars and museums is set by the structure of expectations which underpins the activities of both parties. Fakes, with the originals which they mimic, are the right- and left-hand sides of the same system."[60] In other words, forgers know all too well the expectations of experts, and they exploit the desires that those expectations generate. Thus, the same desires that give value to authentic originals also make collectors and experts susceptible to well-executed fakes.

There were skeptics regarding the authenticity of the James Ossuary from the outset, but their views were not heard by ROM officials.[61] In fact, Keall insisted that up until the time they shipped the ossuary back to Israel, the consensus seemed to be that it was a valid, genuine article with an authentically ancient inscription.[62] The controversy that was mounting about the authenticity of the ossuary did not seem to register with officials at the ROM as they decided to put it on display. In fact, the display itself neglected to mention any discussion of the questionable circumstances of the ossuary's discovery and the debate surrounding its authenticity. As Keall points out, "Nowhere did it say we don't know if this is a real thing or not. No, it was just presented as [a genuine artifact]."[63] The museum display gave no indication that the James Ossuary could possibly be a fake.[64]

But in the months following the exhibition, scholarly opinion about the James Ossuary swayed to the side of doubt. After a careful scientific examination of both the ossuary and the Yehoash Inscription, another purportedly ancient artifact also owned by Oded Golan, the Israel Antiquities Authority reported their findings:

> At the conclusion of deliberations, the committee members summarized the results of their research and wrote an abstract of their findings (Appendices 8 and 9), as follows: "We, members of the committee for examination of the content and script in the Yehoash inscription and the James Ossuary (James son of Joseph brother of Jesus) conclude that to the best of our scientific judgement:
>
> A) the Yehoash inscription is a forgery
>
> B) The James Ossuary inscription is a forgery"
>
> We, the committee members for examination of the materials of the Yehoash inscription and the James Ossuary conclude that the patina on both items is forged and significantly varies from the original patina on the items.[65]

With mounting evidence that their decision to exhibit the ossuary may have been made too hastily, museum officials began to recharacterize their role in presenting it. While continuing to "stand by our opinion that the James Ossuary is not a forgery," the museum issued a public statement that claimed their primary goal was to foster public debate in the furtherance of scientific knowledge:

> The ROM exists in part to help facilitate public understanding and debate about important artifacts and specimens. We considered the James Ossuary an extraordinary opportunity to contribute to the scientific assessment of a new and controversial object by being the first museum to present it to the public, during an important gathering of biblical archaeology scholars, and by hosting a public debate among leading experts. This forms part of an ongoing process of scientific study and discovery, which many other famous artifacts have been undergoing for years.[66]

In recalling the exhibition, Alvarez acknowledged that skeptics were raising questions about the authenticity of the object from the outset. "But we weren't there to make that judgment at all," he claims. "We were there to show an object which was controversial. We weren't coming down on one side or the other." He insists that "the museum's position has always been, 'Here is an important object, it's subject to further study, much like a lot of other objects from this field, like the Shroud of Turin. It's still being debated. We have an opportunity to show it, [and] we're showing it.'"[67]

Yet, despite their claims of neutrality on the issue, ROM officials, both implicitly during the exhibition itself and in explicit statements afterward, have always maintained that the James Ossuary is an authentic first-century object with an authentic first-century inscription.[68] They wagered at the outset that this box was exactly what Hershel Shanks claimed it was: the real thing. They would have preferred no controversy at all. Instead, museum officials had to hedge their bets when their wager looked to be wrong. They did this by redefining themselves as the facilitators of debate rather than the conveyors of accepted knowledge.

It appears now that the ROM administrators may have lost their bet. More thorough investigations of the James Ossuary following its return to Israel after the exhibition in Toronto indicated that the museum may have been duped by a masterful forgery scheme. One might ask in retrospect, why would the Royal Ontario Museum stake its good reputation on a questionable item for which there was scarce reliable evidence? The answer can be found in the museum's bottom line. The survival of such institutions today relies as much on their position in the marketplace as it does on their authority as expert arbiters of culture. Yet, their need for gate receipts leaves them vulnerable to manipulations by those who promise a blockbuster exhibition.

Modern museums, from their very origins among wealthy merchants of Renaissance Italy, have been deeply embedded in the economic forces of market capitalism.[69] On the one hand, it may appear that museums operate contrary to the logic of the marketplace. They remove the objects in their collections from the normal channels of circulation that drive commodity markets. On the other hand, this removal itself participates in the logic of capitalistic exchange. As Pierre Bourdieu contends: "Practice never ceases to conform to economic calculation even when it gives every appearance of disinterestedness by departing from the logic of interested calculation (in the narrow sense) and playing for stakes that are non-material and not easily quantified."[70] By taking the objects they hold out of circulation, museums enhance the value of their collections. Through their efforts at authentication, conservation, and interpretation of selected objects, museums "are able to build for themselves a practice of consecration which allows them to accumulate economic capital."[71] This consecration transforms these objects into something worth more than money; they become the material goods of "heritage" that justify the social order and make it meaningful.[72]

Of course, consecration of objects also enhances their monetary value. This is why the James Ossuary went to a museum rather than a church or a shrine. For this particular object, the museum's show would establish its value as a worthy item of cultural heritage without removing it from the marketplace; ownership of the box itself, as well as the book, film, and image rights, remained in private hands. Thus, Golan and Shanks, along with others who stood to profit from the ossuary's fame, sought only the consecrating approval of the Royal Ontario Museum and the scholarly community, an approval that would raise the artifact's commodity value. They showed no interest at all in submitting the ossuary for religious consecration that would enhance its value in economies that have little to do with the accumulation of material capital.

But the economic benefits of the ossuary's appearance in Toronto did not accrue only to its owners and promoters. In 2002 the ROM was in dire need of a profitable show. Government support amounting to one-half of the museum's operating budget had been frozen since 1995, resulting in a significant reduction in staff.[73] With the disappointing attendance at a previous exhibition that summer, it looked to be another losing year for the ROM. Then Shanks called with his proposal to show "the most astonishing find in the history of archaeology" at the museum. It seemed like a gift—and certainly an offer that museum officials were inclined to accept enthusiastically.

A MATTER OF REPUTATION

In terms of gate receipts, there is no question that the James Ossuary proved an overwhelming success for the ROM. Admission fees during the ossuary exhibition "brought us back into the black," according to Keall.[74] He told reporter Jonathan Gatehouse that internal estimates placed the museum's profit on the show at $270,000.[75] Keall describes the James Ossuary exhibition as "a huge success in terms of the public awareness, and that we did it I think with dignity."[76] Yet in retrospect, there was a trade-off for the financial rewards. Following the Israel Antiquities Authority report and the indictment of the ossuary's owner, the ROM found itself defending the decision to bring the stone box to Toronto. The museum's good name became a matter of public debate.

Jonathan Pagis, head of the Israeli fraud investigation, describes the James Ossuary as "the fraud of the century" and believes that "reputations will suffer. And the Royal Ontario Museum's looks to be at the head of the line."[77] But local observers are more willing to excuse the museum's handling of the ossuary. Terry Donaldson thinks that the ROM had "egg on its face twice: one is the breaking of the ossuary in transit, although I think it was pretty clear that it wasn't their responsibility. But at least they were the ones that opened it up and found the thing in pieces. And then two, the significant questions about its authenticity." But he goes on to state that "the museum is a venerable Toronto and Canadian institution, so I don't think it would damage its overall reputation very much."[78] Fritz Kristbergs, a minister at a local church, remains pleased with how museum officials handled the various controversies that came with the bone box. "I think the museum did a great job," he says. "I was following it every day in the papers and the news, and I think the museum did a very good job."[79] John Marshall agrees. He surmises that "they seemed professional and careful about not being pulled into a controversy that was apart from their curatorial duty. They seemed to want to represent themselves as professional, and I think they succeeded in doing that."[80] With their pro-

A new addition was added to the ROM *in June 2007. (With permission of the Royal Ontario Museum ©* ROM*; photo credit: Brian Boyle)*

fessionalism and dignity intact, and with revenues back in the black, museum officials can claim success with the ossuary. At least in Toronto, their reputation remained without blemish.

But what about the figure of James? Has his status been sullied by this affair? Whatever one thinks about the stone box displayed at the ROM in 2002—even if it is a fake and never contained any famous bones—James still remains the brother (or half brother or cousin) of Jesus. His position is securely canonized in the Christian narrative, and despite the rational demands of modernity, religious people have no imperative to justify their traditions on verifiable material evidence. In this regard, exhibiting the James Ossuary at the ROM seems a misguided discursive attempt to reconcile the Christian tradition with the requirements of modernity; the assumption that Christians seek proof of the Gospel stories disregards the experiential force of religiosity that escapes rational justification. On the other hand, bringing the ossuary to the museum seems a perceptive understanding of the commercial potential of Jesus and his cohorts. Although they may not need proof of their story, modern Christians certainly desire experience of the sacred narrative, and the presence of a material object plucked right out of the story proves an irresistible opportunity that they are willing to pay for. The ROM helped create the commercial potential of that desire and consequently benefited from it. Indeed, capitalizing on the Christian desire for the sacred proved a lucrative endeavor.

ROM officials did not invent a scheme to fool the public, Christian or otherwise, about the burial container of a biblical character. They believed that the stone box that they exhibited once held the bones of James. From their perspective, however, the veracity of such a claim seems a bit irrelevant. More to the point, the ROM participated in a cultural event that caught the imagination of the museum-going public. They were able to support a particular origin story of Western society with a material object that connected the Christian narrative to the contemporary world. In this way, the James Ossuary, whether real or fake, played a very modern role. As an added benefit, the theatrical performance of their display generated a financial windfall for the museum.

I doubt that officials at the Royal Ontario Museum spend much time fretting over the wisdom of their decision to show the James Ossuary. With the opening of a spectacular new addition in 2007 as part of its Renaissance ROM campaign, the ROM has entered a new era of museumship. The Crystal, an angular steel-and-glass design conceived by noted architect Daniel Libeskind that contrasts dramatically with the neo-Romanesque architecture of the older museum building, represents a new image for the ROM. No longer the staid modernist institution of cultural expertise, the ROM now has new galleries that feature a more open design and allow the flexibility to accommodate innovative exhibitions. This "eloquent symbol of the ROM's growth and revitalization," in the words of the museum's chief executive officer, William Thorsell, "will provide Toronto residents and visitors with a place for contemplation, learning, and fun."[81] It will be, in short, an apt space for the cultural performances of modernity.

NOTES

Robert Edgecombe, a student of mine at Rhodes College, accompanied me to Toronto in March 2004 to help with research there. I am indebted to him for arranging and conducting interviews with several of the people quoted in this essay and also for his thoughtful ideas and suggestions as we worked together during our stay in Toronto and afterward. In addition, this work would not have been possible without the help and cooperation of staff members at the Royal Ontario Museum in Toronto, especially Ed Keall, who met with me and generously shared his collection of correspondence regarding the ossuary exhibition, and Francisco Alvarez, who gave me access to the museum's collection of media reports about the James Ossuary. Finally, Terry Donaldson of the University of Toronto kindly offered to query students and staff at the university regarding their experiences with the James Ossuary; the responses we received because of his efforts were exceptionally useful.

1. Edward Keall, personal interview with Thomas S. Bremer, Toronto, Ontario, March 5, 2004. Keall also describes his reaction to Shanks's initial call in "A Curator's Perspective," an appendix to the revised edition of *The Brother of Jesus: The Dramatic Story and Meaning of the First Archaeological Link to Jesus and His Family*, by Hershel Shanks and Ben Witherington III (San Francisco: HarperSanFrancisco, 2003), 281.

2. These meetings included the Society of Biblical Literature, the American Academy of Religion, the American Schools of Oriental Research, and Shanks's own group, the Biblical Archaeology Society.

3. Keall, interview. Keall told Jonathan Gatehouse that "Shanks was relentless . . . threatening to unveil the ossuary at the Smithsonian or New York's Metropolitan Museum unless the ROM agreed to his terms." Jonathan Gatehouse, "Cashbox," *MacLean's*, March 25, 2005, 3.

4. Keall, interview.

5. Hershel Shanks and Ben Witherington III, *The Brother of Jesus: The Dramatic Story and Meaning of the First Archaeological Link to Jesus and His Family* (San Francisco: HarperSanFrancisco, 2003), vii.

6. Keall, interview.

7. For one example of the James Ossuary's entanglement in modern discourses, see the discussion of sexuality in Ryan Byrne, "Anatomy of a Cargo Cult: Virginity, Relic Envy, and Hallowed Boxes," in this volume.

8. Steven Lavine and Ivan Karp, "Introduction: Museums and Multiculturalism," in *Exhibiting Cultures: The Poetics and Politics of Museum Display*, ed. Steven Lavine and Ivan Karp (Washington, D.C.: Smithsonian Institution Press, 1991), 7–8.

9. Keall, interview.

10. Keall gave me a copy of the text of the CNN Web version of the story that was sent to him in an e-mail.

11. Keall provided me with the two e-mails he received from Meg Beckel on October 22, 2002, the first arriving at 8:25 A.M. and the second received at 1:05 P.M. Evidently, there was a change in decision after Shanks's press conference.

12. Another overriding concern in the decision to not include the other

ossuaries was traffic flow through the exhibit. The designers were planning for large crowds with a potentially long wait to get into the room to see the ossuary. And as Suzan Sabir points out, "You make that even longer if you have more artifacts in there." Suzan Sabir, personal interview with Thomas S. Bremer and Robert Edgecombe, Toronto, Ontario, March 9, 2004.

13. Keall, interview.

14. My source for texts included in the exhibit is a document given to me by Suzan Sabir: "James Ossuary Exhibit: Final text, except for conservation item, Version: 08 November 2002."

15. Sabir, interview.

16. Ibid.

17. Francisco Alvarez, personal interview with Thomas S. Bremer, Toronto, Ontario, March 4, 2004.

18. Ibid.

19. Quoted in Gatehouse, "Cashbox," 30. Keall provided me with an e-mail from museum officials that discusses information needed for the loan of the ossuary to the museum, including its value; it lists the value of the James Ossuary at $2 million (U.S.). Gatehouse reports that Lloyd's of London insured the ossuary for $1 million (U.S.).

20. Alvarez, interview.

21. Keall provided me with a copy of the e-mail conveying the conservator's concerns. The revised version of the press release issued on July 23, 2003, is on the ROM website at <http://www.rom.on.ca/news/releases/public.php?mediakey=vhggd03048> (August 2, 2008).

22. Sabir, interview.

23. Peter Richardson, personal interview with Thomas S. Bremer and Robert Edgecombe, Toronto, Ontario, March 5, 2004.

24. John Kloppenborg, personal interview with Thomas S. Bremer, Toronto, Ontario, March 4, 2004.

25. André Lemaire, "Burial Box of James, the Brother of Jesus: Earliest Archaeological Evidence of Jesus Found in Jerusalem," *Biblical Archaeology Review* 28, no. 6 (2002): 24–33, 70.

26. John Marshall, personal interview with Thomas S. Bremer, Toronto, Ontario, March 5, 2004.

27. Ibid.

28. Joel Peters, vice president of marketing and commercial development at the ROM, confirmed for me that there were church groups that visited the James Ossuary exhibition, although the museum's privacy policy does not allow him to divulge the details of the visits.

29. Of the several people I interviewed who had been to the James Ossuary exhibition during normal visiting hours, none could recall a specific incident of

religious devotion at the museum. The comment of John Marshall, who went to the museum to see the ossuary on three different occasions, is typical: "I didn't get a sense of devotion from the people there. That might have been there, but it wasn't something that people showed each other." I also did an informal poll of security guards who happened to be on duty one morning in March 2004 when I was in the museum. Of the seven guards that I spoke with who had worked security on the James Ossuary exhibition, not a single one could remember any visitors kneeling or acting religiously. Only one recalled a few visitors who seemed to be quietly praying to themselves, but this was only on rare occasions and not a regular occurrence. Admittedly, my investigations do not approach anything like a reliable sampling, but they indicate that religious behaviors were not very common for viewers of the James Ossuary at the Royal Ontario Museum.

30. E-mail of March 10, 2004, from Glen Taylor to Terry Donaldson; subject: "Re: Help requested (James ossuary)."

31. E-mail of March 10, 2004, from "Sisi" to Terry Donaldson; no subject.

32. E-mail of March 11, 2004, from Fran Richardson to Terry Donaldson; subject: "James Ossuary."

33. *The Gathering: The Newsletter of the Church of the Redeemer* (Advent 2002), 22; copy in James Ossuary files in the Communications Office of the Royal Ontario Museum.

34. James Beverly, "Bone Box Creates a Stir," *Faith Today* (2003), 45.

35. E-mail of March 10, 2004, from I. G. Hauser to Terry Donaldson; subject: "Help requested (James ossuary)."

36. Alvarez, interview.

37. Terrence Donaldson, personal interview with Thomas S. Bremer and Robert Edgecombe, Toronto, Ontario, March 9, 2004.

38. Rev. Dr. Fritz Traugott Kristbergs, personal interview with Thomas S. Bremer and Robert Edgecombe, Toronto, Ontario, March 9, 2004.

39. Bruno Latour, *We Have Never Been Modern*, trans. Catherine Porter (Cambridge, Mass.: Harvard University Press, 1993), 10.

40. Gustavo Benavides, "Modernity," in *Critical Terms for Religious Studies*, ed. Mark C. Taylor (Chicago: University of Chicago Press, 1998), 186.

41. On the other hand, antimodern sentiments and rhetoric also constitute a significant dimension of the discourse on modernity. In the arena of religious studies, for instance, the widely influential ideas of Mircea Eliade present the modern epoch as a degradation of the human condition. See especially his theory of time and history in Mircea Eliade, *The Myth of the Eternal Return; Or, Cosmos and History*, trans. Willard R. Trask (Princeton: Princeton University Press, 1965).

42. Benavides, "Modernity," 188.

43. Ibid., 189.

44. For a brief discussion of the historical connection between museums and

modernity, see Susan M. Pearce, *Museums, Objects, and Collections: A Cultural Study* (Washington, D.C.: Smithsonian Institution Press, 1993), 1–4. Eilean Hooper-Greenhill discusses the fifteenth-century Medici Palace as "the first museum of Europe" in *Museums and the Shaping of Knowledge* (New York: Routledge, 1992), 23–77. Hooper-Greenhill goes on to study the historical development of the modern museum with other case studies.

45. Pearce, *Museums, Objects, and Collections*, 3.

46. Ibid., 4.

47. Hooper-Greenhill states that "knowledge is now well understood as the commodity that museums offer" (*Museums and the Shaping of Knowledge*, 2).

48. Pearce, *Museums, Objects, and Collections*, 233.

49. Pearce writes, "Museums are an important part of the way society makes history" (ibid).

50. Ibid., 17.

51. Pearce observes, "The process of selection lies at the heart of collecting, and as we shall see, the act of collecting is not simple; it involves both a view of inherited social ideas of the value which should (or should not) be attached to a particular object and which derive from the modern narratives [upon which museums depend], and impulses which lie at the deepest level of individual personality" (ibid., 7).

52. Hooper-Greenhill, *Museums and the Shaping of Knowledge*, 5.

53. Regarding the James Ossuary's connection to Christian relics, see Bernadette McNary-Zak, "Finding True Religion in the James Ossuary: The Conundrum of Relics in Faith Narratives," in this volume. Also see the discussion of "relic envy" in Ryan Byrne, "Anatomy of a Cargo Cult: Virginity, Relic Envy, and Hallowed Boxes," in this volume.

54. Barbara Kirshenblatt-Gimblett, *Destination Culture: Tourism, Museums, and Heritage* (Berkeley: University of California Press, 1998), 3.

55. Ibid., 7.

56. Sabir, interview.

57. Ibid.

58. Regarding the early Christian context of the James Ossuary, see Milton Moreland, "Christian Artifacts in Documentary Film: The Case of the James Ossuary," in this volume.

59. A copy of the Geological Survey report can be found in Shanks and Witherington III, *The Brother of Jesus*, 18. Jonathan Gatehouse reports that the geologists completed their study with only "a single day of tests" ("Cashbox," 3).

60. Pearce, *Museums, Objects, and Collections*, 237.

61. Regarding the early skepticism about the authenticity of the James Ossuary and its inscription, see Jonathan Reed, "Overcoming the James Ossuary and the Legacy of Biblical Archaeology," in this volume.

62. Keall, interview.

63. Ibid.

64. When I interviewed her, Sabir pointed out that they had display cases in the hallway outside of the exhibition room where visitors lined up before entering the exhibit; in these cases, according to Sabir, "we documented the media history behind the ossuary." The media articles (presumably including the article by André Lemaire in *Biblical Archaeology Review*) discussed, at least briefly, the controversy over the ossuary's authenticity. But the likelihood that visitors even noticed the articles or had an opportunity to grasp the issues at stake in the debate was slim at best.

65. Uzi Dahari, *Final Report of the Examining Committees for the Yehoash Inscription and James Ossuary*, on Israel Antiquities Authority website, <http://www.antiquities.org.il/article_Item_eng.asp?sec_id=17&sub_subj_id=185> (August 5, 2008).

66. "Royal Ontario Museum Statement: Oded Golan's arrest / James Ossuary," news release of July 23, 2003, posted on the ROM website, <http://www.rom.on.ca/news/releases/public.php?mediakey=vhggd03048> (August 3, 2008).

67. Alvarez, interview.

68. Expanding on the museum's official stance that "the James Ossuary is not a forgery," curator Keall explains his opinion more thoroughly in an essay included in the second edition of the book by Shanks and Witherington on the James Ossuary. While Keall acknowledges that he may have been "duped by an extremely clever forger," he concludes: "I have yet to be shown any clear and unequivocal scientific evidence that definitively demonstrates that the inscription is completely false" ("A Curator's Perspective," 301).

69. Pearce, *Museums, Objects, and Collections*, 235.

70. Pierre Bourdieu, *Outline of a Theory of Practice*, trans. Richard Nice (New York: Cambridge University Press, 1977), 177.

71. Pearce, *Museums, Objects, and Collections*, 236.

72. Ibid., 33.

73. Gatehouse, "Cashbox," 3.

74. Keall, interview.

75. Gatehouse, "Cashbox," 7–8.

76. Keall, interview.

77. Gatehouse, "Cashbox," 2.

78. Donaldson, interview.

79. Kristbergs, interview.

80. Marshall, interview.

81. Royal Ontario Museum press release of June 2, 2007, available on the ROM website, <http://www.rom.on.ca/news/releases/public.php?mediakey=46cdc7lafp> (August 5, 2008).

BERNADETTE McNARY-ZAK

Finding True Religion in the James Ossuary

The Conundrum of Relics in Faith Narratives

The memory of the righteous is for a blessing.
—Proverbs 10:7

An ossuary is a religious relic due to its function in a religious ritual involving the domestic care of the remains of a dead loved one by Jews and Jewish Christians in Jerusalem in the first century. Performed on the first anniversary of death, the ritual was a form of secondary burial in which the bones of the deceased were gathered from a temporary grave and deposited into an ossuary that was then placed for permanent interment in the family burial cave. For its practitioners, the ritual was intimately tied to the construction of memory. As early Christian historian John Corbett has observed, this was a social fact, for "to gather up bones was to claim kinship with the righteous dead, patriarch or Maccabean hero, saint or martyr, and paradoxically by this act to establish the one so commemorated as a friend of God."[1] A material connection to the past, a tangible reminder of a prior religious practice, and evidence of an earlier mode of religiosity, the James Ossuary afforded its viewers a way to imagine this construction of memory as a religious act nearly 2,000 years later. As denominational claims were weighed with those of the museum, the media, and the academy, Christians generally agreed that the James Ossuary was an object of importance. They disagreed, however, about its value for the present.

ENCOUNTERING AN ANCIENT OBJECT

In the midst of the controversies and debates surrounding the authenticity of the James Ossuary during and after its display in the fall of 2002, the majority of observers voiced a consistent message: the ossuary was not an object of faith. Cautionary claims and reminders of the accepted limits of the role of objects appeared widely in newsprint alongside the reports of the Israeli Antiquities Authority and others regarding the ossuary's authenticity. As one religious leader explained, "Religious artifacts can evoke feelings and memories the same way a childhood photo might evoke the connection with your family. . . . But an object doesn't create faith any more than a picture can create a family."[2] Reporter Marianne Meed Ward, author of a regular Sunday column titled "In Your Faith" for the *Toronto Sun*, offered this assessment in an interview that appeared on November 15, 2002: "Faith is not about science or history or needing proof. It's making a decision about how to live your life. Whether a box sitting in a museum actually held the bones of the brother of Jesus has very little relevance to faith."[3] A month later she wrote that "the box neither proves nor disproves the story of Jesus. But the interest it generates tells us that religion is relevant. Faith matters."[4] One observer gave this reason for his difficulty in interpreting the James Ossuary as an object of faith, explaining that there was something fundamentally absent from the ossuary that had been present with other objects encountered during his pilgrimage to Jerusalem:

> When we were in the Garden of Gethsemane the olive trees are 2,000 years old and you can visualize them actually kneeling there and being there. Essentially this did make us feel closer to Jesus because we had a communion service there and they gave us real olive wood cups as mementos. . . . At the Via Dolorosa we saw the supposed upper room where the Last Supper took place and in each of these places we had the scripture read. In Caesarea Philippi where Christ asked, "Who do you say that I am?," we read that right at the spot. We took a trip on the Sea of Galilee which was quite meaningful, too. *All of this does not compare with seeing a box.*[5]

Categorically, this observer's experiences in these places made sense because they enabled him to encounter the biblical narratives "at the site."

Through his experiences, the truthfulness of these narratives was recognizable and so confirmed and contributed to his religious worldview in an intellectual and emotional way; in contrast, as an object unfamiliar and categorically other, the ossuary was incapable of providing him similar meaning. He determined, therefore, that the ossuary "should be situated in the broader context of other archaeological finds such as the Dead Sea Scrolls, the original texts from scriptures, and now something tangible related to the death of a significant first century person."[6]

For many observers, to determine the relevance of the ossuary in these terms required serious attention to the inscription. Observers' assessments of the inscription would be complicated by the ossuary's fragmentary etiology and the debate surrounding its authenticity, contexts that would ensure a shroud of ambiguity over any claims about its significance. In an interview that appeared in *Time* magazine shortly before the ossuary was displayed, P. Kyle McCarter explained that the fact that the ossuary, as an artifact, was ripped out of context "compromises everything. We don't know where [the box] came from, so there will always be nagging doubts. Extraordinary finds need extraordinary evidence to support them."[7]

"James son of Joseph, brother of Jesus"; what was the proper identity and relationship between these three figures? As the Royal Ontario Museum (ROM) display informed visitors:

> All three names in the inscription were common in Jerusalem around this time. Of an inventory of almost 900 ossuaries, 19 carry the name of a Joseph, 10 that of a Jesus. There is also an ossuary known to have the name of Jesus son of Joseph inscribed on it. Statistically, the combination of the three names in the James ossuary increases considerably the possibility that this was James, the brother of Jesus of Nazareth. The rare reference to a brother indicates a very special relationship. But the ROM acknowledges not everyone believes that Jesus had a blood brother.[8]

Assuming authenticity, observers were left to read the inscription in the context of their own denominational perspective knowing that the truthfulness of its Christological narrative could be called into question. They read the inscription in a variety of ways.

Many observers wondered whether the ossuary challenged the Roman Catholic doctrine of the perpetual virginity of Mary. The potential re-evaluation of this doctrine was raised and discussed early on in the display.[9] Denominational publications upheld the doctrine and the lack of any contradiction by appealing to the responses of prominent scholars within the church. The *Catholic Register* printed an article in which Father Jerome Murphy O'Connor explained that "every bit of evidence is exciting. . . . If it is authentic, the only significance is that it is the earliest dated reference to Joseph, James and Jesus that we have. The only important thing is that date—*the inscription doesn't tell us anything we don't already know*."[10] One week later, reporter Marta Blocki ensured readers of the *Catholic New Times* that "Roman Catholic scholar Joseph Fitzmeyer, who represents the general response from the Roman Catholic community, requires proof that the person identified as Jesus in the text is in fact Jesus of Nazareth."[11]

Other observers required further proof regarding the identity of James. The ROM display explained that "James was the first permanent head of the Christian Church in Jerusalem. Clement, the man who replaced Peter as bishop of Rome, wrote to him as 'James, bishop of bishops, who rules Jerusalem, the holy church of the Hebrews.' He was visited in 58 CE in Jerusalem by Paul who referred to him as 'the Lord's brother.' He was sometimes referred to as James the Just."[12] Hegesippus, writing in the second century, observes that James was martyred under order of the high priest Ananus for his refusal to denounce Jesus as the Messiah. "He was pushed off the southeastern corner of the Temple wall and tumbled into the Kidron Valley, just north of Silwan. Having survived the fall, he was killed by a bystander who struck him in the head. They buried him on the spot."[13]

The death narrative of James was relevant to the interpretation of the ossuary for many Armenian Orthodox Christians, who believe that James was a stepbrother of Jesus and the traditional founder of their church. Remaining consistent with the facts of an empty ossuary and an archaeological record,[14] the church readily retains its claim that after James's death, followers built a shrine and chapel over the site where he was believed to have been buried. Tradition teaches that James's remains were later moved by necessity to the Cathedral of St. James in Jerusalem, where they are believed to remain untouched today.

Among these various groups of observers, the ossuary was defined as a material object that provided historical evidence of a funeral ritual, an act of memorial. Like other forms of archaeological evidence, it enabled a way of envisioning this religious act. If authentic, the inscription could only enhance an understanding of the function of the ossuary itself; for these observers, the inscription—apart from the box—did not generate any new meaning and, therefore, could not contribute substantively to a new way of envisioning the present.

This was not the case for all observers. In *The Brother of Jesus: The Dramatic Story and Meaning of the First Archaeological Link to Jesus and His Family*, coauthor Ben Witherington III openly disagrees with these assessments given his interpretation of the inscription's significance.

> Certainly, the consuming interest in this discovery is because of the person mentioned in the last word of the inscription—Jesus. North America, like much of the Western world, is a society in which Jesus is virtually omnipresent while at the same time the population is largely biblically illiterate. . . . The further appeal of the ossuary, I believe, is that it promises for the first time the opportunity to "touch" Jesus, to experience a physical connection with him through the inscribed burial box of his brother James, a pivotal early Christian leader who has been hidden in the shadows of history. Now, in this simple inscription, the Gospel figures of Jesus, Joseph, and James—until now known only through texts—become arrestingly tangible. In an age that demands compelling evidence for claims of faith and history, the world now has something concrete *to see, examine, reflect on, and respond to*.[15]

From this perspective, it is precisely because the ossuary is "something concrete" that it is both an object of faith and an object of history. It is telling that the same factors used by some observers to argue against the ossuary as an object of faith are advanced here to prove its religious importance. Against those who maintained an inability to experience or encounter the ossuary because of its unknown provenance or museum context, Witherington upholds the ossuary's transcendent referent: place is irrelevant in assessment of the ossuary because all that matters is written on the ossuary itself. Likewise, against those who required an authentic inscription and an uncontroversial etiology, Witherington appeals to the ossuary's ethereal call: the believer has all that is required to "touch" Jesus, to "experience a physical connection with him."

SEEING AN ANCIENT OBJECT

Despite countless fingerprints on the ossuary's glass container, observers could neither touch nor handle the object. How was it possible to produce a physical connection through sight?

As Georgia Frank has shown with regard to relics in the period of late antiquity, for many Christians the intangibility of what was known by faith could be made arrestingly tangible through sight. Visualization with the "eyes of the body" could open the "eyes of the heart" and so enable the recollection of a "presence." In this way, visualization made possible appropriation of a relic as a religious object significant to faith. Over time, the power of the "lingering gaze" of the believer to conjure a "sacred presence" would be extended to narrative as a way of understanding why words, pictures, and objects are worthy of veneration because they produce visible reminders of God.[16] Since the viewing of objects and the feelings evoked through touch were temporary and transitory, in the ancient world what pilgrims took from their encounters were the stories of their experiences; in a sense, their own stories became narrative relics to be transmitted and shared with others.[17] While their stories were grounded in the details of the biblical texts, the experiences of the individual pilgrim's journey factored into the telling. Recalling a moment of clarity or insight at a biblical site or before a religious object could conjure emotions of a deeply personal encounter. In this way, their stories gave meaning to these places and objects. We might recall the efforts of the late fourth-century pilgrim Egeria: with the biblical text as her primary guide, she writes of the emotions she felt when she walked upon the paths taken by Jesus Christ and his followers or gazed upon the site where the crucifixion occurred. By extending her endurance to reach some sites, like the summit of Mount Tabor, she envisioned participation in the biblical event and the presence of the divine.[18] Due to beliefs in the sanctity of place, encounter with the site afforded specific opportunities for Christians to exercise sensory perception for the purpose of spiritual transformation.

Witherington's statement suggests the offer of something similar: an opportunity to participate in the ossuary in a way that engaged the biblical texts anew, and so to become part of the narrative. Others encouraged modern Christians to do this by sharing their stories of encounter since, according to Southern Baptist leader Paige Patterson, the ossuary could be "enormously useful in *evangelizing* and shedding light on our understanding of the Scriptures."[19] It could also be useful in deepening this understanding, as storytellers would be guided by an ethic provided by a "resurrected" James:

> But it is James challenging us that faith must be combined with actions of love, that the way we interact with each other is evidence of belief in Jesus. James taught that perseverance matures us, that God is available to help us, that prosperity is a weak focus to strive for, that the words we speak have the power to ruin the world we live in. These convictions brought James to a violent end. If a few cracks on his supposed ossuary and the mystery that surrounds it get us talking about that, I don't think this early father of the church will mind.[20]

CLAIMING KINSHIP

Dead bodies have been a consistent source of intrigue for Christians, as stories of the early martyrs and other holy persons were crafted with neither unanimous consent nor unanimous appeal. Existing disagreement about the bodily remains of holy persons was only exacerbated in the fourth century during debates over the creedal formulation of the doctrine of the Incarnation and the imperial interests of the family of Constantine. As Byron McCane has argued, in this period the "distinction between Jewish and Christian death ritual" emerged, "when attitudes toward, and beliefs about, dead bodies became a matter of mutual self-definition"[21] and Christians "explicitly denied the impurity of the human corpse . . . and began to treat dead bodies, or parts thereof, in ways that had previously been regarded as inappropriate. . . . Christians consciously violated the social boundary of corpse impurity and brought the remains of the dead into social spaces. . . . With the rise of their public cult of martyrs, Christians welcomed the human corpse into an emerging vision of an ideal Christian society."[22] In late antiquity, claims of kinship with the righteous dead "were reflected in the rich vocabulary that expresses the relationship between believer and saint, between saint and God. A relic was thus not so much a magical object in itself, at least in the early Christian centuries, as a token of memory and affection, the outward manifestation of a blessing and the realization of a relationship with a special friend of God."[23] Its potency was determined by the beholder in the context of a worshipping community.[24]

Discourse about relics was incorporated into accounts of Christian death, embedded in the contexts of beliefs in the Incarnation and an afterlife, particularly in Christian *vita*. A brief look at two of these may help to explain the differences apparent in many observers' efforts to define the place of the ossuary in their respective Christian narrative.

In the mid-fourth century, Archbishop Athanasius of Alexandria authored *Life of Antony*, an account of the ascetic practices of an Egyptian desert monk. In a few lines found in the final portion of the work, Athanasius describes briefly Antony's death and his request to be buried in an unmarked tomb. He also relates how Antony's only possessions were distributed: Antony bequeathed his hair shirt to Athanasius and his staff to his former monastic colleague, Bishop Serapion of Thmuis. Athanasius concludes his work by exhorting his reader to tell his story to Christians and non-Christians in the hope that all persons might be affected by it.

Several decades later, in the early 380s, Bishop Gregory of Nyssa traveled to Annesi, where he was present at the death of his only sister, Macrina. In the work that bears her name, Gregory spends considerable time describing the preparation of her body for burial and the elaborate funerary procession and ritual. He explains in detail that when they prepared her body for burial, he removed her ring and gave it to one of her beloved sisters, Vetiana, as a token of Macrina's continued presence for the community of women religious; the cross Macrina wore he kept for himself.

Though both *Life of Antony* and *Life of Macrina* include death narratives, each betrays a distinct agenda. Athanasius encouraged his audiences, Christian and pagan, to incorporate into their own lives what they could from the example of Antony offered in his *Life*, since this narrative was intended to uphold and enhance an already established model of Christian piety as both exemplary and orthodox. For this reason, the largest portion of the work consists of lengthy theological discourse, put into the mouth of Antony, that is consistent with Athanasius's views. In the context of Athanasius's public involvement in the Christological debates of the fourth century, the work was intended to advance an ascetic life consistent with his statement of the doctrine of the Incarnation. To this end, encounter with the ascetic life of Antony could effect change in the reader, and the work could serve as a "guide" in the absence of its master. Athanasius's inclusion of the distribution of Antony's possessions in the work serves to heighten the significance of *his* story, of *his* word—against that of the objects and burial site—for the remembrance of Antony. The intentional widespread distribution of the work throughout the empire only fueled this end.

In contrast, Gregory's work was intended for a local audience. While he, too, was concerned that a life be honored and recalled for its exemplary piety and righteousness, to some extent he sought to preserve Macrina as a model for the members of her immediate religious community. By describing the distribution of her ring and cross and her burial rites in such length and detail, Gregory locates Macrina and her remains in a specific place; his audience knows her story and his desire to build up a shrine in the region for her honor. He intended for encounter with the relics and the narrative that explains them to confirm and enhance their spiritual understanding and to serve as evidence for what was already known about her piety and its lasting efficacy. Thus, he used his work to explain why they should establish Macrina's influence by preserving her relics and maintaining her local shrine; in this way, his story defined and situated Macrina's legacy for the local Christian community.

Observers' interpretations of the ossuary and its inscription bear a similar attempt to grapple with claims of kinship, as their storytellers controlled the elasticity of such categories and crafted tales by which, through an act of imaginative participation, ambiguity, and skepticism, were not only tolerated but, in some cases, suspended in order that the ossuary serve as a token of memory and affection in the present. Many Roman Catholic and Armenian Orthodox observers thought that the ossuary offered nothing new to their preexisting denominational narratives. Perhaps their responses demonstrate the extent to which such narratives have been internalized by adherents and the way that the explanations they contain for established doctrine and tradition have been endowed with an uncontested authenticity and authority. In both denominations, it was the narrative and not the novel object that prevailed.

For other observers, including some Protestant evangelical observers, it may have been the ossuary's implications for their narrative that triumphed, as the ossuary became "relicized" in a way akin to their early Christian predecessors. Stories of encounter with the ossuary situated the object for this end and explained how the ossuary could be experienced as an object of history that, due to the rendering of the inscription, was verification for the truth of faith. Because of the inscription, the ossuary was interpreted as a tangible connection to a sacred past—a time when "there were still people alive who knew Jesus of Nazareth"—and so required transformation of the present through the public verification of Christological claims in support of the truth of scripture. For many of these observers, the ossuary could serve as a source of new meaning in the present, whose observation was envisioned and recalled as a religious practice, an extension of religious belief.

CREATING A CHRISTIAN SYMBOL

While the co-optation and use of objects for such purposes is hardly a new phenomenon in the history of Christianity, the fact that the legitimation of the James Ossuary in this way became a predominantly Protestant evangelical effort may seem incongruous. For many of these observers, however, seeing the ossuary prompted reflection and response, as the literal meaning of the inscription made possible a tangible connection to Jesus and invited entry into the nonliteral manifestation this meaning provided of a personal and communal way of being in the present. The efficacy of the ossuary rested in its contemporary value as primary evidence for this verification.

We might consider the function of this relic impulse by looking at similar efforts made in the period of late antiquity, as the region of Palestine, already an established site of Christian pilgrimage, was transformed under the public support and imperial interest of Emperor Constantine.[25] Christian pilgrimage and the reconfiguration of the Holy Land, "a combination of biblical tourism and Christian devotion,"[26] created and defined a place for Christianity in the religious worldview in a highly commercialized and publicized way. The rise in the role and trafficking of relics paralleled the rise and power of ecclesiastics. Given that many theological controversies focused on aspects of the body of Christ, efforts to control relics were demonstrations of power in the face of increasing tension. That is to say, Christian relics were symbolic of political and religious identity.[27] Relics afforded a connection to the "land of the Bible," to the province of Palestine that "harboured the past and the future" of the Christian faith.[28] Because relics served a wide variety of private and public functions, their portability played a role in the transmission of the Christian faith throughout the empire.

Implicit in the impulse and process to define the James Ossuary as a Protestant evangelical relic are a series of assumptions about how it might serve in the present. The internal authority structures and pluralism that exists within and across these communities may have made possible the rendering of an interpretation of the inscription, and so the box, that affirms and expands their Christological narrative. As a symbol, the James Ossuary could serve as a visual embodiment of a position of Christian unity and truth.

CONCLUSION

In his article "On Relics, Forgeries, and Biblical Archaeology," Neil Asher Silberman weighs this outcome:

> So what lesson is to be learned from these recent discoveries and their disturbingly divisive aftereffects? Whether they are authentic artifacts or clever forgeries, both the James Ossuary and the Jehoash Inscription have been irreversibly transformed into *relics*. And because of their uncertain origin, they are irretrievably tainted data, lacking a proper archaeological context by which their significance might be properly assessed. Actively promoted as definitive "proof" or "evidence" in highly charged contemporary debates, their public importance has come to rest not in what they are, but what they symbolize.[29]

Hans Georg Gadamer reminds us that what makes something tangible may have little, if anything, to do with the object itself and nearly everything to do with one's effective history. In his study of interpretation with respect to objects of art, Gadamer explains that, just as an object arrives with an effective history, so, too, does the viewer-subject. He writes: "It is not that there is some autonomous object over against us which can be studied through metaphysics or ontological analysis; rather the judgment exercised by the artist in executing a work or the interpreter in evaluating a work of art is the same—the 'feeling of freedom in the play of our cognitive faculties.'"[30] Gadamer proposes that the object of art offers to the subject experience in a world in which the subject encounters the self. Encounter with the object is encounter with human experience, and so, by participating and performing in the world offered by the object of art, the subject reinterprets the effective history of the object, the effective history of the self, and the common history of the object and the subject. In this way, every encounter with the object of art is a creation entailing transformation.[31]

Some observers who approached the James Ossuary did so with their own effective history shaped, in part, by their own Christian denominational narrative; seeing the ossuary, they were engaged in an act of play with the truth claims of these narratives. The James Ossuary had arrived with an uncertain and unverifiable effective history. Though not touted as an object of faith, the ossuary was a religious object due to its function, and the ROM took care to ensure that its status was defined in terms that enhanced operative categories of religiosity.[32]

As we have seen, there was nothing self-edifying about the James Ossuary. Yet there is, perhaps, something to be said about the extent to which it was appropriated, as "relics such as this ossuary assuage a human hunger by providing a tactile connection to faith sources embedded in a distant past."[33] By interpreting its inscription in a way that facilitated the expansion of an existing Christological narrative in the present, the James Ossuary could function as a religious relic in a highly specific way for some Christians today—not in terms that marked its use in a past religious ritual, but rather in terms that identified its use as tangible evidence for doctrinal truth now. The ossuary had a potential, a power in the modern sense of its role in an act of proof. The process of defining the ossuary as a religious relic was grounded in theological concerns of the present and not the past. Time will tell whether its efficacy to this end is lasting.

NOTES

I am especially grateful to Lindsey Seifert, a student at Rhodes College, for her work during the spring 2004 semester on the denominational responses to the James Ossuary by members of the Roman Catholic and Armenian Orthodox Churches ("The James Ossuary: A Contemporary Religious Relic?," unpublished paper presented at Rhodes College on April 28, 2004).

1. John Corbett, "Relic," in *Encyclopedia of Early Christianity*, edited by E. Ferguson (Garland Publishing, 1990), 779.

2. Jeffrey Weiss, "Searching for Proof on 'Holy Ground,'" *Edmonton Journal*, August 2, 2003. Here, Weiss quotes religious leader James Stanton, the Episcopal bishop for the diocese of Dallas, Texas.

3. Mike Strobel, "Mystery Comes in a Box," *Toronto Sun*, November 15, 2002.

4. Marianne Meed Ward, "Top Religion Stories" ("In Your Faith" Sunday column), *Toronto Sun*, December 29, 2002.

5. Tom Hayes, personal interview with Thomas S. Bremer and Robert Edgecombe, Toronto, Ontario, March 7, 2004 (emphasis mine).

6. Ibid.

7. David Van Biema, "The Brother of Jesus?," *Time*, November 4, 2002, 52.

Consider also what Brian Bethune writes: "As for the box itself, its story—like seemingly every dispute in Biblical archaeology—is riddled with legal and financial implications, tenaciously held sectarian positions, and personal rivalries" ("Resurrecting James," *Maclean's*, April 21, 2003, 48). See also John Dominic Crossan and Jonathan L. Reed, *Excavating Jesus: Beneath the Stones, Behind the Texts*, rev. ed. (San Francisco: HarperSanFrancisco, 2002).

8. "James Ossuary Exhibit: Final text, except for conservation item, Version: 08 November 2002," Royal Ontario Museum document provided by Suzan Sabir, 3.

9. Bob Harvey, "James Ossuary Calls Virgin Birth into Question, Conference Told," *Gazette* (Montreal), November 24, 2002.

10. Judith Sudilovsky, "Scholars Cautious about Jesus Link," *Catholic Register*, November 10, 2002 (emphasis mine). See also Ryan Byrne, "Anatomy of a Cargo Cult: Virginity, Relic Envy, and Hallowed Boxes," in this volume.

11. Marta Blocki, "2,000-Year-Old Relic Stirs Controversy," *Catholic New Times*, November 17, 2002, 16.

12. "James Ossuary Exhibit: Final text, except for conservation item, Version: 08 November 2002," 1.

13. The observations of Hegesippus are preserved by Eusebius in his *Ecclesiastical History*, 2:4–18, 23. For treatment of this evidence, see Jodi Magness, "Ossuaries and the Burials of Jesus and James," *Journal of Biblical Literature* 124, no. 1 (2005): 121–54.

14. Yaron Z. Eliav, "The Tomb of James, Brother of Jesus, as *Locus Memoriae*," *Harvard Theological Review* 97, no. 1 (2004): 33–59. See also Lindsey Seifert, "The James Ossuary: A Contemporary Religious Relic?," unpublished paper presented at Rhodes College on April 28, 2004.

15. Hershel Shanks and Ben Witherington III, *The Brother of Jesus: The Dramatic Story and Meaning of the First Archaeological Link to Jesus and His Family* (San Francisco: HarperSanFrancisco, 2003), 91 (emphasis mine).

16. Georgia Frank, *The Memory of the Eyes: Pilgrims to Living Saints in Late Antiquity* (Berkeley and Los Angeles: University of California Press, 2000), 178. See also Peter Brown, *The Cult of the Saints* (Chicago: University of Chicago Press, 1981); Peter Brown, *Power and Persuasion in Late Antiquity* (Madison: University of Wisconsin Press, 1992); Peter Brown, *Authority and the Sacred* (Cambridge: Cambridge University Press, 1995); Claudia Rapp, " 'For Next to God, You Are My Salvation': Reflections on the Rise of the Holy Man in Late Antiquity," in *The Cult of Saints in Late Antiquity and the Middle Ages*, ed. James Howard-Johnston and Paul Anthony Hayward (Oxford: Oxford University Press, 1999), 63–81; and Jas Elsner, *Roman Eyes: Visuality and Subjectivity in Art and Text* (Princeton: Princeton University Press, 2007).

17. Georgia Frank, *The Memory of the Eyes: Pilgrims to Living Saints in Late Antiquity* (Berkeley and Los Angeles: University of California Press, 2000), 178.

See also Richard Valantasis, "Relics," in *Late Antiquity: A Guide to the Postclassical World*, ed. G. W. Bowersock, Peter Brown, and Oleg Grabar (Cambridge: Harvard University Press, 1999), 667–68.

18. John Wilkinson, *Egeria's Travels*, rev. 2nd ed. (London: Aris and Phillips, 1981).

19. Van Biema, "The Brother of Jesus?," 50 (emphasis mine).

20. Lorna Dueck, "James's Faith Contained Acts of Love," *Hamilton Spectator*, November 23, 2002.

21. Byron McCane, *Roll Back the Stone: Death and Burial in the World of Jesus* (Harrisburg, Pa.: Trinity Press International, 2003), 110.

22. Ibid., 112. On page 116, McCane writes: "The Christian dead are not impure because they are *not really dead*. They may be 'asleep' or 'at rest,' but they are part of the Christian social network and should not be separated from it."

23. Corbett, "Relic," 779.

24. Frank writes: "If detached from its worshipping community, it is void of power or significance: even Jerome conceded to his opponent Vigilantius that a relic is indeed 'a bit of powder wrapped in a costly cloth.' But Jerome also knew that the eyes of the devout could bring that bit of powder to life. For the onlookers who welcomed the prophet Samuel's relics as they were translated to Chalcedon, it was 'as if they beheld a living prophet in their midst.' Implied in this remark is that any wholeness attributed to the object is an effect of the beholder's eye. Visual perception constitutes the reality of that wholeness" (*The Memory of the Eyes*, 176).

25. On this, see E. D. Hunt, *Holy Land Pilgrimage in the Later Roman Empire, A.D. 312–460* (Oxford: Clarendon Press, 1982).

26. Ibid., 4.

27. Richard Valantasis writes: "Since ideas about relics derived primarily from a language of the body, they readily provided justification for various theological teachings. The veneration of relics thus offered a powerful and accessible idiom for articulating to ordinary believers sophisticated doctrines about the implications of Christ's life, the value of their own body, and the hope for a future bodily resurrection" ("Relics," 667).

28. Hunt, *Holy Land Pilgrimage*, 4.

29. Neil Asher Silberman, "On Relics, Forgeries, and Biblical Archaeology," SBL Forum, <http://www.sbl-site.org/publications/article.aspx?articleID=127>. See also David Samuels, "Written in Stone," *New Yorker*, April 12, 2004, 48–59.

30. Hans Georg Gadamer, *Truth and Method* (London: Sheed & Ward, 1975), 51.

31. Ibid., 102.

32. See Thomas S. Bremer, "The Brother of Jesus in Toronto," in this volume.

33. Wayne A. Holst, "The First Jewish Christian," *Globe and Mail* (Toronto), April 26, 2003 (book review of *The Brother of Jesus: The Dramatic Story and Meaning of the First Archaeological Link to Jesus and His Family*, by Hershel Shanks and Ben Witherington III).

MILTON MORELAND

Christian Artifacts in Documentary Film

The Case of the James Ossuary

INTRODUCTION

On July 4, 2003, I sat in my yard watching fireworks, enjoying food and casual conversation with my neighbors. I had moved into the neighborhood only a week prior, so this block party was a prime occasion for conversations to turn to origins and occupations. "Where are you from?" and "What do you do?" were the inevitable questions. This is a precarious moment. When I answer the occupation question, the ensuing conversation often turns to recent television documentaries about the quest for Noah's Ark, the "historical Jesus," or the Shroud of Turin. Despite the acrimonious feelings that arise within me during these discussions of made-for-TV documentaries, on this occasion I let it be known that I am an archaeologist who is interested in the origins of Christianity and early Judaism. Immediately, the conversation turned to the James Ossuary. Some neighbors were more interested than others, but the entire adult crowd was well aware of this "discovery," and at least two of my new neighbors were convinced that the ossuary was proof that Jesus was indeed the Son of God.

I was impressed by the fact that for a brief moment, at least on the minute scale of my personal experience, the ossuary had trumped the ark and the shroud in the public imagination (although I admit to having been asked about both of these topics before the night was through). In the world of "the top archaeological finds that confirm the Bible," this inscribed burial box made a rapid ascent up the chart in the minds of many

Christians and in the world of Christian publications and media. I will examine how some media and publishing outlets shaped the scholarly response to this artifact in order to sensationalize this story. The Discovery Channel documentary brought the greatest amount of attention to the ossuary, and thus the content of that film and the scholars who appear in it will be my primary focus.

With the instant popularity of the ossuary, the media raised a series of questions: Who was this James? Is this a reference to the Christian Jesus? Did Jesus really have a brother? Inevitably, scholars raised questions about the origins and authenticity of the ossuary and its inscription. These questions found their way to the front pages of newspapers around the globe; in North America, the *New York Times*, the *Los Angeles Times*, the *Toronto Globe and Mail*, the *Miami Herald*, and other papers in major cities gave significant coverage to the mysterious ossuary. Readers soon learned that, in fact, the New Testament Gospels mention that Jesus had brothers (and sisters). They also learned that this was likely a reference to Jesus of Nazareth of the Christian tradition, and that this James was very likely the person mentioned in the letters of Paul as a leader in the Christian movement of Jerusalem.

After the initial attention given to the ossuary subsided, a second wave of publicity arose in the spring of 2003—in the heart of the Lenten season—when a book and film about the ossuary were released. These projects had a significant impact on how the ossuary was presented to the public, and they claimed to provide a scholarly perspective on the ossuary's authenticity (or lack thereof). The Discovery Channel's documentary, *James: Brother of Jesus, Holy Relic or Hoax?*, was written, directed, and produced by Simcha Jacobovici. The film aired on Easter Sunday 2003 in America and worldwide in nearly seventy other countries, and over the course of the next month, it aired in eighty more countries.[1] At about the same time, HarperSanFrancisco released *The Brother of Jesus: The Dramatic Story and Meaning of the First Archaeological Link to Jesus and His Family*, a popular book authored by Hershel Shanks and Ben Witherington III (75,000 hardback copies were printed in the first run).

One of the major selling points of the documentary and the book was their portrayal of the ancient ossuary as a tangible link to Jesus. The premise was that this "physical evidence" could prove that Jesus was a historical person. Promotional material for the documentary states that the ossuary is "possibly the greatest archaeological discovery of modern times," and "if authentic, it would be the first physical evidence to prove Jesus Christ's historical existence."[2] Similarly, the subtitle of the book makes clear its intention to use the ossuary as an "archaeological link to Jesus and his family." This attempt to prove the existence of Jesus with appeal to an artifact has become an obsession in recent times.

Despite the fact that modern archaeologists do not have this as a goal, in some quarters the idea that archaeology can confirm the Bible's accuracy has never been more vibrant. And documentary films have taken a leading role in promoting the idea that the Bible can be confirmed through archaeology. By the end of the twentieth century, this genre became one of the major preoccupations of nonfiction, historically oriented television programming, and the trend does not appear to be subsiding. Many of these films and television series attempt to demonstrate the accuracy of the Bible through the analysis of artifacts and archaeological research. The role that scholars play in these documentaries is usually that of the stock "talking head"—the expert who is called on to provide analysis and interpretation.

Using archaeology to prove biblical truths is a well-established feature of the Christian tradition through the ages. Seeking a "real" piece of the Christian tradition has been a preoccupation of Christians for centuries. While the biblical-archaeology TV documentary may be the most popular venue in the modern era—and possibly the most successful venue of all time—the quest to prove the Bible's accuracy using material remains is an ancient tradition. In the history of Christianity, seeking objects that prove the truth of the Christian story has been part of the apologist's profession since at least the fourth century.

The pursuit of artifacts that authenticate the Christian story was once the goal of figures like Saint Helena, the mother of Constantine the Great. In the late 320s, the seventy-five-year-old Helena traveled over 1,400 miles from Rome to Palestine in order to discover the *real* birthplace and death place of the Roman Empire's newest deity. Tradition holds that she died at the end of that journey, but not before she had found the most sacred relic of Christendom: the *true cross*.[3] In many respects, her incredible journey set the stage for hundreds of other Christian explorers who sought their own pieces of the "true cross." Whether those relics came in the form of bones, wood, rocks, or mountains, Christian adventurers have been seeking physical proof of their faith for at least seventeen centuries. In what follows, I will pursue the idea that the development of the biblical-archaeology documentary is one of several mass media projects that now functions to authenticate faith for the observant Christian. This pursuit may now be found in the comfort of your living room, as you turn on the Discovery Channel or the National Geographic Channel and see an object that may be a tangible proof of your faith. Jacobovici's film on the James Ossuary will be placed within the history of documentary filmmaking, and his work will be taken seriously as a significant medium through which the public came to have a firsthand experience of this artifact.

A NEW MEDIUM FOR ARCHAEOLOGY AND FAITH

The rise and proliferation of the biblical-archaeology documentary reveals how powerful this film genre has become. The genre is not only powerful as a means to inform the public about the field of biblical archaeology; it also provides opportunities for viewers to associate artifacts like the ossuary with their Christian faith. In film, artifacts have a visual presence that goes beyond the experience of reading a book, often becoming props in well-choreographed reenactments. By seeing the artifact in an active role within historical reenactments, viewers are encouraged to integrate the artifact into their own ideas of Christian origins. As we will see in detail later, Jacobovici uses multiple reenactment scenes in which the ossuary plays a primary role—for example, in a fictional first-century burial cave in which it is inscribed and filled with human bones by actors playing James's family and friends. These scenes feature the ossuary as an active part of the early Christian narrative and function to solidify the idea that the ossuary is an important early Christian relic, regardless of what the "talking head" scholars in the film might be saying. Similarly, the ability of documentaries to reenact scientific tests being performed on the artifacts, and the multiple scenes that are filmed on location in exotic and even "dangerous" places, help to confirm the legitimacy of the artifact in the minds of the faithful. While not all modern Christians yearn to touch the sacred objects and be healed by their "mystic potency," there is still a strong desire to verify that faith is based on concrete realities. For many people of faith, archaeology is the key to that verification process, thus the popularity of the biblical-archaeology documentary.

I am not interested in judging this film genre as tasteful or tasteless, helpful or harmful, good or bad. Rather, I take this opportunity to examine the mass marketing of archaeology related to the Bible because it is high time that scholars pay attention to the most popular medium in which our work is presented. While traditional books, journals, and magazines reach thousands of interested readers, some form of a biblical-archaeology documentary is watched by millions of viewers each and every week. During the Easter season of 2006, approximately 4.1 million American television viewers tuned in to see *The Tomb of Jesus*, the latest version of the biblical-archaeology documentary that was produced by Jacobovici, the same person who brought us *James: Brother of Jesus*. Millions of other viewers across the globe watched the documentary as it played throughout that spring on Channel 4 in the United Kingdom, on Vision TV in Canada, and on over 100 other international channels.

I will also discuss the varied roles that scholars played in the making of the James Ossuary documentary. The increased involvement of scholars in televised venues is proportional to the popularity of documentary films. This genre has virtually replaced the book as the medium through which the public receives its information about the field of archaeology. Because more people watch television than read published archaeological reports, with the expansion of television documentaries, more people have access to archaeological information related to the Bible than ever before. Information about biblical archaeology is widely dispersed through the mass-marketed television networks. But as the venue has shifted, archaeologists have lost control over the medium through which the interested public receives archaeological information. Archaeology has become a handmaid to the filmmaker, through whom it is transported to the public.

While archaeologists and biblical scholars play significant roles in these films, the genre is not commensurate with traditional scholarly training. In many respects, the educational training of archaeologists and biblical scholars compels a scholar to spend much of his or her academic career in the painstaking and time-consuming task of writing books and articles. For those of us in the field of archaeology, our academic careers are often dependent upon the ability to produce books and articles, and writing is what we are trained and expected to do. Through years of experience, we learn the detailed process of writing, editing, indexing, and even illustrating books. While the literary medium remains vital to the academy, in recent decades documentaries have crept into the living rooms of the interested public. Scholars have played a significant role in the film genre; it is increasingly common to see scholars noting documentary film appearances in their curriculum vitae. Nevertheless, it is a medium that is both beyond the scholar's training and outside the scholar's control. Having a speaking role in a film that is edited by someone with limited background in archaeology and biblical studies is very different than writing an essay.

Filmmakers have also taken advantage of the deep divide among modern archaeologist on the issue of "archaeology and faith." Throughout the past two centuries, archaeologists have had a complicated relationship with the apologetic quest that is often found in the documentary film genre. In certain respects, the so-called field of biblical archaeology has itself refueled the ancient fires of relic discovery. While many in the field of archaeology who excavate in Israel, Jordan, Palestine, and Lebanon have been trying to distance themselves from this relic-hunting tradition and establish the science of archaeology as separate from the "archaeology of faith," one cannot deny that archaeologists remain prominent figures in the relic quest. From the earliest days of biblical archaeology, there is no doubt that many of the founders of the field were interested in providing concrete proof of "biblical truths." Those apologetic aims continue in the work of some archaeologists who think of their fieldwork as a means to prove the validity of the Bible. This divide among archaeologists is easily exploited in the documentary film genre. A filmmaker can often find two archaeologists who disagree about whether an artifact proves or disproves a biblical claim. Thus, while many modern archaeologists who excavate in the southern Levant claim that their fieldwork has nothing to do with faith, few people hear that message. Several archaeologists have attempted to file "divorce papers," claiming irreconcilable differences between scientific archaeological pursuits and theological attempts to bolster faith by appealing to artifacts.[4] The divorce proceedings have never been successful. Despite the contention that archaeology has nothing to do with faith, many Christians are more convinced than ever that new archaeological discoveries are confirming the Bible's accuracy.

The documentary film has become the major venue for attempting to prove the accuracy of the Bible. Over the past two decades, the biblical-archaeology documentary has risen quickly to the forefront of cable TV programming. Biblical archaeology is a central focus of hundreds of made-for-TV documentaries that have been featured on the History Channel, Discovery Channel, National Geographic Channel, A&E Network, Fox News Channel, PBS, CNN, CBS, NBC, and ABC. Biblical archaeology has been the major topic of three popular weekly TV documentary series:

Digging for the Truth with Josh Bernstein, *Science of the Bible* on the National Geographic Channel, and *The Naked Archaeologist* with Simcha Jacobovici. It is difficult to deny that these documentaries have become the public face of Near Eastern archaeology. There is every reason to believe that this extensive genre of filmmaking will only continue to expand.[5] The medium is escalating on a global level, as more and more cable TV providers see new types of documentary filmmaking and reality TV productions as potential cash cows in the broadcasting industry. There is little doubt that the use of archaeology to play on the hopes and fears of the faithful will continue to inspire new biblical-archaeology productions for many years to come.

THE DOCUMENTARY FILM GENRE

The documentary film has a very interesting and important history.[6] The documentary genre was developed in the early part of the twentieth century as a counterpart to the fictionalized narrative films that were intended for entertainment. The fundamental purpose of the genre was to "document" a segment of the "real world," providing information about real people, places, and events. The documentary was supposed to aim at the objective recording of the world; viewers were invited to see the lived experience of near and distant peoples and places in the comfort of the theater or, later, in their own homes.[7] For viewers who grew up watching state-supported, professionally produced documentaries on television, there is an expectation that these films will have some social value and provide a public educational service. We assume they will weigh both sides of an issue and provide a levelheaded response. As opposed to dramas, comedies, and other entertainment shows, documentaries have a traditional high level of audience trust. We expect that documentaries are not faked, staged, acted, or fictionalized.[8]

This idea of the documentary was intentionally molded by the great documentarists of the early twentieth century. For most of the past century, John Grierson and Robert Flaherty set the standard for documentary filmmakers. As teachers, producers, and directors of popular early documentaries like *Nanook of the North* (Flaherty, 1922) and *Drifters* (Grierson, 1929), they established the genre as one that would creatively—even poetically—treat "reality" or "truth" in film.[9] The documentary was intended to bring the realities of people to life in filmic versions that drew the viewer to the screen like a beautiful poem draws the reader to the page.[10] The subject might be the natural world (*Niagara Falls*), the animal kingdom (polar bears), or, most prominently in the documentary tradition, the tragedies and successes of common humans. As opposed to the fictionalized plot of the popular movie, the documentary film was to stand out as the venue for telling the truth about life in all its varied and exotic forms.

In part as a pedagogical tool of the state, the documentary genre was also crafted by television stations like the BBC and PBS as a form of cutting-edge, social journalism.[11] As Tom Mascaro explains, in the early 1960s technological advancements played a key role in the development of the genre toward investigative reporting: "The availability of lightweight 16mm film equipment enabled producers to get closer to stories and record eyewitness observations through a technique known as cinema verité, or direct cinema. A significant development was the wireless synchronizing system, which facilitated untethered, synchronized sound-film recordings."[12] Robert Drew pioneered many of the techniques that became standard features of cinema verité and the common stock of documentary films. Drew's goal was to create "a theatre without actors. It would be plays without playwrights. It would be reporting without summaries or opinion. It would be the ability to look in on peoples' lives and see a kind of truth that can only be gotten by personal experience."[13] Essential to Drew's understanding of this new genre was the idea that the camera could capture "truth." This was a central conviction of the early documentary filmmakers and a notion that is still prevalent in the minds of the viewing public: the picture does not lie, and documentary films are good venues for uncovering "truth."

With this new technology and creative energy came a boom in documentaries that provided extended investigative reports on all types of political and social concerns. From the 1960s to the early 1980s, the genre was a standard feature on the three major American networks.[14] In January 1983 David Fanning at WBGH in Boston created a documentary series that has come to represent the best of investigative journalism. As the promotional literature states, *Frontline* "has served as American public television's . . . flagship public affairs series." *Frontline* claims to be the major producer of cutting-edge journalism reports that provide "incisive documentaries covering the scope and complexity of the human experience." With support from major funders like the John D. and Catherine T.

MacArthur Foundation, *Frontline* has produced hundreds of films in the past three decades that serve to solidify the concept that documentaries are trustworthy and responsible productions, having more in common with hard-hitting news reporting than with fictionalized drama.

A quick examination of *Frontline*'s rules for their producers clarifies the key ideals that the company strives for and that many viewers have come to expect of the documentary genre. *Frontline* has eighty-four guidelines on journalistic standards and practices that stress objective, credible research and fair portrayals of the issues involved in their films.[15] For example, *Frontline* requires that its "producers . . . approach stories with an open and skeptical mind and a determination, through extensive research, to acquaint themselves with a wide range of viewpoints." Two policies further stress the need for evenhandedness: "producers will carefully examine contrary information," and "producers will give individuals or entities who are the subject of attack the opportunity to respond to those attacks." Additionally, the need to represent the views of the "actors" in the film is stated in the policies: "producers will represent fairly the words and actions of the people portrayed," and "producers will inform individuals who are the subject of an investigative interview of the general areas of questioning in advance and, if important for accuracy, will give those individuals an opportunity to check their records." Finally, the need for accuracy is paramount: "producers will try to present the significant facts a viewer would need to understand what he or she is seeing, including appropriate information to frame the program," and "producers will always be prepared to assist in correcting errors." While these policies may be idealistic, they represent the types of expectations that many viewers have for this genre, regardless of the realities.

In addition to the new energy that was pumped into the investigative-reporting documentary genre with the birth of *Frontline*, Ken Burns became the standard-bearer of historical documentaries in the 1980s.[16] He revived the idea that documentaries could provide cutting-edge investigative reporting on historical subjects. Although he was already a well established documentary filmmaker with his own production company (Florentine Films), his fame was sealed in 1990 when he completed production of the 660-minute documentary, *The Civil War*. With the financial backing of General Motors, the National Endowment for the Humanities, and PBS, Burns spent six years making the Civil War documentary (two years longer than the war itself). In the process, he redefined the genre of historical documentary for many American television viewers. In many respects, his work also provided a model for filmmakers who were interested in biblical archaeology.

Throughout the past forty years, historical documentaries have developed a very clear set of parameters and perfected many successful techniques, including the use of authoritative voice-over narration; on-camera interviews with "talking heads" (mostly sympathetic experts); well-designed shots of still photos, artwork, diagrams, maps, and charts; period music; and re-creations of historical scenes (both file footage and modern reenactments). Burns exploited the documentary ideal and created an objectified memory of the Civil War for many of his viewers. He brought the historical war to modern reality.[17]

Using the diaries and letters of dozens of war participants, often read by modern celebrities, Burns poetically blended still photographs and illustrations from the war with a soundtrack that was comprised of war-era music played on period instruments. He filmed dozens of modern historians telling stories about the war, perfecting the art of the talking-head commentator. He also used numerous scenes from the modern battlefield landscape to supplement his nineteenth-century material. From photos and soundtracks he created characters that made the audience laugh and cry. Using a swooping rostrum camera, Burns brought still photos to life. In numerous major documentary series for PBS, Burns has attempted to document American life through artistic and poetic portrayals of its individuals and institutions. In the process, he reestablished a general trust among many television viewers in the validity and value of the documentary genre. In many respects, Burns saved the documentary genre and reinvigorated the idea that television programming could be a healthy and trustworthy source of historical information. The historical documentary productions of Burns (through 2007, he had produced twenty-one documentary films) and the investigative reporting documentaries of *Frontline* have contributed a great deal to the idea that film can provide a truthful representation of reality.

We now turn our attention back to the task at hand and ask what all this has to do with the biblical-archaeology documentary and the James Ossuary. What do John Grierson, *Frontline*, and Ken Burns have to do with the Discovery Channel's *James: Brother of Jesus* documentary by Simcha Jacobovici? In what follows, I will suggest that *Frontline* and Burns set the stage for the explosion of the biblical-archaeology documentary films that we have witnessed in the past fifteen years. This explosion in Bible documentaries is riding the coattails of the renewed public interest in creative nonfiction television productions. Though one can speculate on how long the ride will last, the fact is that *Frontline* and Burns reestablished the historical and investigative documentary genres as forces to be reckoned with in modern media. Perceptive producers like Jacobovici saw this freight train rolling onto millions of television screens around the world and have taken the controls of this powerful media vehicle.

Two key components of the documentary genre have helped create the recent phenomenon. First, with *Frontline*'s rejuvenation of the investigative journalism documentary, the viewing public was enticed into believing that this film genre was trustworthy. If a film is called a documentary, a viewer tends to think of it as factually reliable. If a documentary is airing on the History Channel, an unsuspecting viewer might assume that it will provide a fairly reliable view of its subject matter. In the past two decades, there has been a wellspring of confidence in this genre that has helped spawn this biblical-archaeology documentary explosion. The second and related key component of the documentary genre that helped create the phenomenon was the idea that documentaries provide balanced and well-researched presentations of their data. Documentaries have been thought of as a medium for reasonable people to present reasonable ideas about historical and current events. The documentary is supposed to cover both sides of an issue and show no significant bias. The experts who comprise the "talking head" component of the film are supposed to be trusted authorities (like the great Memphis author and historian Shelby Foote, who spoke so gently and authoritatively in Burns's *Civil War*). Of course, most viewers have no contact with the talking heads outside of the film venue, thus they must be preconditioned to trust that these are the authorities that best represent the facts of the case. Burns and the *Frontline* producers have done an amazing job of creating a sense of trust and confidence in the worthiness of documentary spokespeople.

Similar to the work of Burns, several of the first biblical-archaeology documentaries were very well-produced and written films. In fact, the 1998 *Frontline* production of *From Jesus to Christ* might be said to be a high mark in the biblical-archaeology documentary category.[18] This four-hour documentary was produced with all the standard *Frontline* characteristics and standards. The documentary elegantly challenged some traditional components of Christian beliefs as it presented dozens of highly respected biblical scholars and archaeologists discussing their scholarship. With Professor L. Michael White serving as the principal historical consultant and editorial adviser,[19] the production team edited together an aesthetically pleasing film that won the respect of many scholars and lay viewers. The 240-minute documentary appeared first on PBS during the Lenten season of 1998 and has since appeared dozens of times on PBS networks. With the *Frontline* financial machine to back its production, the producers assembled massive amounts of new film footage and thousands of still shots of artwork that adorned the screen and kept the audience engaged. Combining a soundtrack of choir vocals and classical music, the documentary panned from beautiful sweeping shots of stained-glass panels and Renaissance Christian art to on-site footage of archaeologists discussing their recent discoveries. Scholars in churches and well-adorned campus settings discussed the history of Christian origins as medieval hymns and famous Christian artwork resonated in the background. This *Frontline* production set a high standard for narrating a story of Christianity that carefully blended sacred traditions with archaeology and scholarly reconstructions of the past. But this type of documentary is the exception rather than the rule.

A number of factors have contributed to the fact that most biblical-archaeology documentaries have much lower standards than a typical *Frontline* production. Many of these recent documentaries have relied on the viewer's good faith in the documentary genre. Increasingly, these films do not approach the quality of production that *Frontline* established. With the enlargement of cable television channels in the 1990s, there was a much greater demand for documentary programming.[20] While never comprising more than 10 percent of the overall television market, the documentary became a standard feature of several channels that generally garner about 1 percent of American television viewers (for example, the Discovery, History, and National Geographic Channels). With the increase in documentary programming came a decrease in production costs per film. Producers were expected to make an hour-long documentary for thousands of dollars rather than the hundreds of thousands that went into the production of *The Civil War* and *From Jesus to Christ*. This has led to a precipitous decline in the quality of production.

Typically, biblical-archaeology documentaries are filled with recycled stock footage of Christian Renaissance art and stained-glass panels. This artistic background is set to standard soundtracks of choir music and chants, with bland voice-over commentary and provocative interviews interspersed at just the moment the viewer is tempted to change the channel. Advances in digital camera technology and the low cost of basic editing techniques have opened the documentary floodgates, so that filmmaking is a quickly acquired skill that is open to many people in the industrialized world. Most importantly, for the biblical-archaeology film, producers have taken up a slideshow approach to the documentary. Inexperienced researchers sort through thousands of stock images in order to piece together an intriguing mix of visuals and on-site footage with no chronological rhyme or reason. The unsuspecting audience is presented with visuals, but there is usually no explanation for how the pictures on the screen fit with the voice-over narration. Footage from well-known Hollywood Bible films like *Ben-Hur* and Charlton Heston's performance of Moses in DeMille's *The Ten Commandments* are interspersed with sixteenth-century art and helicopter-flyover film footage from the Holy Land in order to produce an appropriate visual background for the poorly edited prose that is heard coming from the nonentity narrator. The goal is to present a visually attractive backdrop to a compelling narrative. The quality of scholarly content of the narrative appears to be a very low priority; the narrative content is judged primarily by its ability to keep an audience tuned to the channel. Often, every attempt is made to stir up a controversy by pairing a "conservative" Christian with a "liberal" scholar in order to stimulate the audience's attention. No doubt, the primary goal of the biblical-archaeology documentary is to sell advertising.

Biblical-archaeology documentaries also rely heavily upon the investigative-reporting documentary genre first made popular in the 1960s by television series such as CBS *Reports* (produced by Fred Friendly) and NBC *White Paper* (produced by Irving Gitlin), as well as, more recently, by PBS's *Frontline*. Most famously, the Noah's Ark story and the story of the Exodus became popular topics for these filmmakers who sought to investigate the "mysteries of the Bible." By the mid-1970s, the major television networks were already airing "investigative" documentaries that made incredible claims about archaeological discoveries that confirmed the truth of the biblical narrative. In the past thirty years, the pursuit of these claims has not subsided. As forerunners to *The Naked Archaeologist* and *Digging for the Truth*, these films have lowered the bar on investigative reporting to levels never imagined by Edward R. Morrow. While it is possible that the credulity of the television-viewing audience is limitless, one can hold out hope that this type of investigative biblical-archaeology documentary has gone to the well one too many times.

When possible, documentary producers integrate scenes of reenacted lives of biblical characters. Reenactments have become a key component of the genre. Because the filming of high-quality reenactments is more expensive than slideshow presentations of stock art images, these scenes are often cheaply produced and of very low quality. It appears that often these documentary films use reenactments that are from a stock database of file footage rather than film new reenactment scenes. Based on the increased emphasis on reenacted sequences in recent documentaries, it appears that this technique has become one of the most popular forms of representing the authenticity and importance of artifacts in the modern biblical-archaeology film. The widespread use of reenactments exemplifies the claim that the documentary genre—even from its earliest foundation—has been more of a creative venture than most documentarists openly admit.[21]

The early models of documentary filmmaking, such as *Nanook of the North* and *Drifters*, did bring the realities of life to the screen, but we now recognize that even those famous films were often staged realities. Rather than filming the "live" actions of the film's protagonist, the Eskimo Nanook was told to reenact his own life, and he was prompted to act out scenes that would work well with the general narrative that had been created by the filmmaker.[22] Not unlike contemporary "Reality TV," documentaries narrate and stage historical reenactments in such a way that they appear authentic.[23] The filmic techniques of the nonentity narrative voice and the action shot serve to draw the viewer into the world of the observed. The ultimate goal is to convince the audience that what they are seeing is real.[24] National Geographic's *Science of the Bible* program has built an entire series around this technique.[25] Combining Mel Gibson–like *Passion* reenactments with scientific investigation and commentary from noteworthy scholars and archaeologists, this series has perfected the combination of costumed reenactments sprinkled with scholarly sound bites. Reenactments of "historical events" are a primary feature of biblical-archaeology films because they bring dull artifacts to life; they connect the viewer to objects in ways that enhance the relevance of artifacts for people of faith. By showing a reenacted scene of an ancient Christian interacting with artifacts, a film provides an objectified setting for thinking of ancient material as an important feature of one's faith tradition. Documentaries contribute to the relic-making enterprise.

By using many of the techniques discussed above, the production of biblical-archaeology documentaries has captured the imagination of many television viewers. The relationship between the biblical-archaeology documentary and the Christian lay viewer has been negotiated in a variety of ways. There is no doubt that some biblical-archaeology documentaries have disputed the notion that archaeology confirms the Bible's accuracy. Careful viewers of documentary programming have seen numerous scholars and archaeologists challenge many of the precepts of the Christian faith. Documentaries have raised questions about the validity of assuming that artifacts confirm biblical truths. Nevertheless, the major relationship that has been established in this film genre between faith and archaeology is intended to affirm the Christian faith. Most of these documentaries ask stimulating questions, but in the end, they provide the viewer with rather traditional and bland results. With the proliferation of the biblical-archaeology documentary in both traditional film formats and the new weekly series on cable networks, producers have become eager to provide more titillating content in order to entice the audience to return regularly to the television trough. Relying on the good faith of the viewers to trust that the documentary genre is still sacred—one of the last television bastions for truthful reporting and historically accurate presentations—filmmakers are now beginning to press the limits of their credibility. Increasingly popular is the biblical-archaeology documentary that assumes great gullibility among its viewers. Cable programming is increasingly sponsoring documentary films that press the limits of viewer naïveté.

For example, Carsten Peter Thiede's *Quest for the True Cross* became the basis for a 2002 documentary that was produced by Mel Gibson's Icon Films for the Discovery Channel. Before his untimely death in 2004, Thiede had become famous for writing books and starring in documentaries that attempted to link artifacts from the medieval Christian tradition to the time of Jesus. With close parallels to Saint Helena, Thiede argued in this film that an ancient Christian relic—which most scholars think was one of many medieval forgeries—is truly a fragment of Jesus' *titulus crucis*, the placard on the cross placed over his head that bore the charge against him: "Jesus of Nazareth, King of the Jews." Thiede's *True Cross* film was a lucrative documentary exercise aimed at confirming a relic for the Christian faith. While the documentary promised real evidence for the historical Jesus, in actuality Thiede had only the skimpiest textual arguments to back his claim. No authoritative scientific tests had been performed; thus the viewer is left to wonder what *might* be revealed if Thiede would be allowed to date the artifact.

JAMES: BROTHER OF JESUS—THE DOCUMENTARY

Quest for the True Cross appeared on the Discovery Channel in the same year that Simcha Jacobovici was given exclusive rights by Oded Golan and Hershel Shanks to film the story of the James Ossuary. Working with Golan, an Israeli antiquities collector and the owner of the ossuary, Shanks, the editor of the *Biblical Archaeology Review* (BAR), contacted Jacobovici to produce a documentary about the ossuary.[26] Discovery Channel U.S.A. bought the rights to the film and began advertising the premiere for the 2003 Easter season. Like Thiede's *Quest*, Jacobovici prepared a documentary that claimed to have first-century evidence that could be directly tied to Jesus. These documentary projects serve as examples of films that gain profit at the expense of scholarly investigation.

By the time that Jacobovici was brought into the James Ossuary project, he was already a well-recognized and award-winning documentary filmmaker who had an interest in ancient Judaism and biblical archaeology. By 2002 he had begun working on a major documentary about the Exodus story with his more famous production partner, James Cameron. With the making of the documentary film *The Exodus Decoded*, which appeared in 2006 on the History Channel (garnering less-than-enthusiastic reviews), Jacobovici demonstrated a willingness to challenge Jewish and Christian beliefs while still maintaining core elements from the biblical narrative. In many respects, this is a pattern that is also seen in his *James: Brother of Jesus* and *Tomb of Jesus* documentaries. His films appeal to the Jewish and Christian traditions, while providing enough rash speculation and entertaining spectacle to garner the attention of the mass media.

By being able to carefully observe how the documentary film functions —what "makes it tick"—it is hoped that viewers will be better equipped to deal with the media hype that often (and increasingly) surrounds the biblical-archaeology documentary. Jacobovici's work represents a polished version of the biblical-archaeology documentary, and a careful examination of the content and techniques of his James Ossuary film should provide a helpful introduction to this wide-ranging medium. In what follows, I provide the content of a number of segments of the film in order to demonstrate how the documentary's narrative weaves its argument from many different strands of questions (both answered and unanswered), premises, and conjectures.

With his own Canadian production company and connections to deep-pocketed coproducers like James Cameron, Jacobovici has been able to integrate many of the best tricks of the documentary trade into his productions. His films thrive on professionally designed reenactments, high-tech computer animations and digital effects, and well-orchestrated interviews with legitimate and well-known scholars. In terms of the documentary film genre, Jacobovici is an award-winning professional. Yet he also considers himself an investigative reporter. Essentially, he claims to be producing investigative journalistic documentaries in the same tradition as *Frontline*. Implicitly, he has latched onto one of the key rhetorical devices of the modern documentary: the viewers themselves are required to disprove the claims made in the film. By virtue of the fact that Jacobovici makes documentaries and claims to be a journalist, many viewers will give him the benefit of the doubt and trust the claims of his films.

In the *The Lost Tomb of Jesus* and *The Exodus Decoded*, Jacobovici plays the role of an on-screen investigative reporter. He frames his documentaries in the participatory mode of filmmaking. He relies less on the nonentity narrator, opting instead to drive the narrative along by filming himself as the "reporter" who is tracking the secrets of the Bible. He is the major actor who is seen following all the clues and solving all the mysteries.[27] He stages his own objective search for the truth. Since this is also the mode he uses for the *Naked Archaeologist* series, it is not hard to see that Jacobovici has created an investigative reporter character, which has become entirely enmeshed in the persona of the filmmaker. He has become a participant in and a producer of the documentary "truth myth" that he is selling to his television audience.

As the subtitle to the film states, Jacobovici's documentary on the James Ossuary takes up the question of whether the artifact is a "holy relic or hoax." The film combines investigative journalism with the goal of providing the viewer a historical background for James, as well as an introduction to the use of ossuaries in first-century Jerusalem. It is a historical documentary that is driven by questions related to the mysteries that surround the authenticity of the ossuary and its inscription. In *James:*

Brother of Jesus, Jacobovici primarily uses a nonentity narrative voice-over to ask the probing questions. Although he does not appear as the primary investigator, he occasionally uses other "actors" to ask questions to the scholars who appear on screen. The opening of the film serves to show Jacobovici's skill in framing the documentary in the mode of investigative reporting. In the first few minutes of the film, the viewer is presented with a demonstration of many of the key elements of the documentary film genre. The film opens with a montage of footage that provides short clips of material that will appear in more detail later in the documentary. The unseen narrator states:

> In the spring of 2002 a discovery is made which some call the greatest archaeological discovery of all time. Where was it found? Others call it the greatest archaeological fraud of all time. Who's behind it? If authentic, this is the first time ever that Jesus' name appears not on parchment, but literally carved in stone. The excitement is generated by an inscription on a kind of stone coffin, an ancient bone box or ossuary. If this ossuary and the inscription on it are authentic then we will know that a man named James died about 2,000 years ago; and far more importantly, that he had a brother called Jesus. This could be the first hard archaeological proof that Jesus of Nazareth existed.[28]

Although the claim that this is possibly "the first time ever that Jesus' name appears . . . literally carved in stone" is wrong (since other previously found ossuaries also contain forms of this name), the introduction establishes the idea that this film will provide a unbiased investigation of the mysteries surrounding the ossuary. The introduction is symptomatic of the entire film: limited investigation will lead to major, unsubstantiated claims. The ossuary inscription is touted as proof that James and Jesus existed. The film immediately connects the artifact to faith. Implicitly, by authenticating the artifact, the film has the potential to authenticate faith in Jesus. In the opening narration, Jacobovici follows a well-worn path in the biblical-archaeology genre of filmmaking.

Following this titillating introduction, Jacobovici achieves a great deal in a single opening scene. Standing in a churchlike setting in the Royal Ontario Museum (ROM) and illuminated like an ancient relic, the James Ossuary is cloaked with glass and surrounded by beautifully designed walls that explain the importance and sacredness of the stone object in the center of the room. Leaning close to the glass, Hershel Shanks examines his most recent claim to fame in the midst of several dozen specially invited scholars milling around the room. The camera focuses on two other unnamed, distinguished-looking gentlemen, Professor Frank Moore Cross and Father Joseph Fitzmyer, who are being informally interviewed by Ben Witherington III. Cross speaks first, looking toward the camera and saying, "I think it is one piece. It's done beautifully. If it's forged, it's done by a genius." Then Witherington, who appears to be innocently conversing with the two men, asks: "Is there any case of a forged Jewish ossuary unless this is it? Is there any case of such a thing? I mean, who forges a Jewish ossuary?" Although Witherington's questions are not immediately answered, they establish the general tone of the film. Tough questions will be asked; the mysteries surrounding this artifact must be solved. But even in the asking of the questions, one can see the inclination of the filmmaker. While Cross is not officially introduced in the film for another thirty minutes, his distinguished presence and his clear statement at the beginning of the documentary help to establish the credibility of the artifact and the need for the faithful viewing public to take this object seriously.

This is a stunning scene to anyone who thinks seriously about what Jacobovici and his accomplices have staged in this seemingly ad hoc conversation. In a side gallery of the ROM, Jacobovici's cameras have captured Shanks and Witherington interviewing two well-respected epigraphers as they view in person the widely publicized ossuary of James for the first time. Without microscopic aid or the final results of significant scientific tests, the scholars are asked to comment on the authenticity of the ossuary that sits behind the protective glass cover. What we as viewers witness is documentary genius at work. The investigative reporter (Witherington plays the role at this point in the film) seems to ask the right question to the right people.

There is no reference to the fact that once the camera lights were dimmed and Cross had more time to study the matter, he quickly began to disassociate himself from the statement he made in the ROM that November day in 2002. Those who supported the authenticity of the inscriptions often used Cross's inconclusive statement, "If it's forged, it's done by a genius," in support of their cause. In a letter to Hershel Shanks and André Lemaire that was published on Shanks's Biblical Archaeology Society (BAS) website, Cross made it clear that he thought the ossuary inscription was, in fact, forged. He states:

> I have received Hershel Shanks's lawyerly argument for the authenticity of the James Ossuary. I regret his continued persistence in making claims for it. I am also troubled by being quoted in a fashion which makes it appear that I support its authenticity. Hershel knows that I was troubled from the beginning by the badly weathered rosettes on the ossuary, and the unweathered character of the inscription. I have declared in the past that I was sitting on the fence in the matter of its authenticity. Many can testify to this. I have also remarked that I had no paleographic objection to the inscription. It was indeed a work of great skill. The mixing of cursive and formal characters was particularly clever, a mixture found sometimes on ossuaries, and contrary to some, not evidence of two hands. However, Hershel Shanks has left out my present opinion—which he knows—an opinion I came to by my work on another Golan inscription (the Jehoash Inscription) which is a poor forgery. . . . I now stand wholly and unambiguously with those who believe the ossuary inscription to be a forgery, a good forgery, but a forgery.[29]

Without drawing attention to the growing skepticism of the inscription's authenticity or answering Witherington's questions, the film's narrator (the voice of Don Berns) then lays out the questions to be taken up in the remaining forty-eight minutes. While the screen is filled with images of an anonymous scientist in a lab looking at a tiny piece of stone through an electron scanning microscope, the narrator states, "The ossuary will be put to all the tests modern science can muster. The stone will be traced to a specific geological area. The chemistry on its surface will be analyzed." As the scientist opens another piece of lab equipment, the narrator says that "the style of writing on it will be scrutinized." And as one more person in a different setting looks through a magnifying glass at another ossuary inscription, the narrator concludes: "And if the ossuary can pass all these tests, history will be rewritten."

Much is promised in the opening two minutes of this film. The viewer is not given an explanation of how or why "history will be rewritten," but the claim certainly provokes the imagination.[30] Is the film's author suggesting that if the ossuary and its inscription are authentic, then some part of the history of Christianity will be changed? The writer plays with the hopes of the faithful Christian viewer: Is there something about this artifact that has the potential to verify my faith, to prove that Jesus was real?

Will the doubts of the faithless regarding the origins of Christianity be dismissed by this film? If the result of this film's investigation is the rewriting of history, it is left to the viewer's imagination to decide what that really means. Thus the film begins in the mode of investigative reporting and quickly promises the viewer amazing results from this quest. The film begins with qualities that remind the viewer of the traditional truth claims of the documentary film genre: this film will provide you with astounding information that could change history. The author relies on the good faith of the television viewer to trust that this film will provide a scientifically verifiable result.

Jacobovici turns next to a quick explanation of the inscription, describing the names on the ossuary and briefly explaining why "Yaʿakov" in Aramaic is actually "James" of the English language. As the ossuary inscription is highlighted on screen, the narrator states, "It reads, Yaʿakov or Jacob, which became Iacobus in Greek, Jacomus in Latin, and James in English." While this is an important point (the translation of the name will be discussed in more detail below), the narrator quickly establishes the idea that this name is none other than that of the New Testament character known as "James."

THE ROLE OF THE SCHOLAR IN *JAMES: BROTHER OF JESUS*

At that point in the film, the first headshot of a scholar appears on the screen. Professor Robert Eisenman of California State University is seen with his name and university printed across the bottom of the picture. He states, "If this is real, then this is the find of the millennium, maybe the two millennia, because this is an artifact that overarches all the artifacts. This is not someone's tongue, ear, finger, head, ankle, you know, whatever, you know, vertebrae. This is an inscription saying Jesus existed in the first century."

Scholars are used throughout the film to drive the narrative forward and interpret the meaning and importance of the ossuary. Eisenman is the first of twenty-three different scholars, museum officials, curators, scientists, archaeologists, and priests who make brief appearances throughout the film. Their statements comprise approximately 2,312 words out of about 6,157 spoken words in the film. The narrator reads another 3,160 words from a written script authored by Jacobovici. The remaining 685 words are spoken by Oded Golan and other people from the antiquities trade in Israel who are interviewed as part of the investigation into the origins of the ossuary.

Eisenman's role at this point in the film is to stimulate the idea that this is a significant artifact, one that apparently overshadows all of the other relics ("tongue, ear, finger, head, ankle") from the past 2,000 years. While Eisenman's statement is intriguing—and it is very fitting at this moment in the film—there is no recognition of the fact that Eisenman was one of the most outspoken critics of the ossuary's authenticity from the very day of the press release in October 2002. Eisenman was one of dozens of scholars who were contacted by news reporters from around the world in the fall of 2002. With the barrage of news stories, reporters immediately sought out scholars to interpret the ossuary, its inscription, and what this meant for modern Christianity. Like most of those scholars, Eisenman was very skeptical of the inscription.

As we examine the James Ossuary documentary, we have the opportunity to look in more detail at the role that several of the scholars who appear in the film played in the period leading up to and immediately following the press release. With the public announcement of the ossuary, a host of scholarly voices joined the chorus in order to produce a rather cacophonous response to the BAS's news. In retrospect, when one observes the variety of scholarly publications on "James the Just" that preceded the ossuary's unveiling, it is clear that the reaction of many scholars to the ossuary was directly based on their various preexisting reconstructions of earliest Christianity. Prior to the ossuary "discovery," the topic of "James the Just" was featured prominently in books and scholarly meetings throughout the 1990s. Scholars were involved in a lively debate about the role that James played in the origins of Christianity. Although the documentary does not shed light on the fact that scholars disagree about the role that James played in the Christian tradition, the topic was the focus of several publications and conference presentations just prior to the ossuary's coming-out party. Jacobovici also rarely discloses that many of the scholars who appear as specialists in his film were outspoken critics of the ossuary inscription's authenticity. Most of the scholars who were previously involved in discussions of "James the Just" were the very ones who were the most vocal critics of the inscription and the claim that it referred to the "James" that is mentioned in Paul's Letter to the Galatians.

In this regard, Eisenman is an interesting and enigmatic scholarly spokesperson, and his appearance in the film is worth a careful look. Prior to the announcement of the ossuary, he had written extensively about the role that James played in the origins of Christianity. His reconstruction of Christian origins is a revisionist history that has met with almost universal rejection from his scholarly peers. Eisenman's 1997 monograph, *James the Brother of Jesus*, is noteworthy, if only for its popular appeal and wide-ranging availability in bookstores in the years prior to the ossuary's promotion.[31] While his reconstruction of James and his historical methodology were met with almost universal rejection by scholars of early Judaism and Christianity, his popularity among the reading public was significant. His arguments are grounded in mysticlike interpretations of letter sequences that remind one of the amateur "Bible Code" approaches to the ancient texts that have become widely consumed of late by interested readers.[32] Many of his ideas are not new; they are grounded in the work of John Allegro, a scholar who is mentioned at the end of the Jacobovici film in another context (see below). The fact that Eisenman's 1,074-page tome was published by Penguin Books, widely distributed in bookstores across the world, and reviewed in many of the major newspapers in Israel, Europe, and the United States makes him an interesting choice as the first scholar to appear in the Jacobovici documentary.

Eisenman had a track record in garnering public attention for his scholarly ideas and writing projects. In the early 1990s, he argued vociferously that the Catholic scholars who had the publishing rights to the Dead Sea Scrolls had conspired to keep the unpublished scrolls secret due to the fact that the scrolls' contents would have had a dramatic impact on the Christian tradition. Working with Hershel Shanks and James Robinson, Eisenman coedited a two-volume facsimile edition of unpublished scroll fragments in 1992.[33] At about that same time, he also edited a book with Michael Wise, entitled *The Dead Sea Scrolls Uncovered: The First Complete Translation and Interpretation of 50 Key Documents Withheld for over 35 Years*, which was published by Penguin.[34] The fury over the slow publication of the scrolls became Eisenman's claim to fame. His theories about James and Christian origins were taken up by Michael Baigent and Richard Leigh in their best-selling book, *The Dead Sea Scrolls Deception*.[35] Thus, as an author of a popular Penguin Press book and the star of a controversial best-selling story on the Dead Sea Scrolls, Eisenman's fame may have made him a logical choice to lead off this documentary.

But Eisenman's ideas about James, and his many disparaging remarks about the inscription in the fall of 2002, complicate the issue. Eisenman's idea of "James" is not dependent on the New Testament references to this character, choosing instead to rely on a nearly numinous interpretation of the Dead Sea Scrolls for his source of information. According to Eisenman, James was the leader of the Christian group that was responsible for the Dead Sea Scrolls. James the brother of Jesus was the "Teacher of Righteousness," an appellation that appears in several texts that were found in these scrolls outside of Qumran. With this premise in mind, Eisenman has reconstructed Christian origins as a story that hinges on the controversy between James and Paul. On the one hand, James represents the passionate and persecuted follower (and brother) of Jesus who established a law-abiding community in the true spirit of Jesus' authentic teachings. On the other hand, Eisenman revives an old, stereotypical argument regarding Paul as the corruptor of the teachings of Jesus. Paul linked Jesus' Torah-centered, "true" message to the ideology of Hellenistic cults and then promulgated a new Torah-free movement that came to dominate the Christian tradition. The Dead Sea Scrolls are reinterpreted by Eisenman as artifacts from the true Jesus/James movement that was corrupted and persecuted by the likes of the Hellenizer Paul. Throughout his massive books,[36] Eisenman does not debate with modern scholars; he rejects scholarship as misguided and overly influenced by Pauline Christianity. His approach is that of the lone mystic interpreter who shows no regard for his contemporaries as he claims to uncover the mysteries of Christianity and the origins of the scrolls.

The fact that Eisenman's book was printed by Penguin and widely distributed in popular bookstores may seem surprising in light of the fact that his theories about James and the Dead Sea Scrolls cut against the grain of accepted scholarship and are often based on poorly contrived philological arguments that are convoluted and specious. His popularity, and thus his appearance at the opening of the Jacobovici film, is in part due to the fact that presses like Penguin are interested in publishing material that will appeal (and sell) to a wide reading audience. It is usually the case that a publisher looking to sell tens of thousands of copies of a book on Christian origins will turn to controversial and stimulating subject matter, regardless of the logic or plausibility of the arguments. Books published by popular presses like Penguin and Simon and Schuster on the origins of Christianity rarely represent the views of established and reputable scholars; rather, they often publish fanciful and outlandish theories that have been rejected by the learned community of the authors' peers.

When unsuspecting readers visit a local bookstore and venture into the "Religion" section, they are confronted by a mass of books with theses that few scholars would support. A reader is more likely to find a thick tome by Eisenman or Barbara Thiering than a reasonable presentation that actually interacts with the current scholarly discourse about Christian origins.[37] While it may be exciting to think that Christianity began in a way that is wildly divergent from the pictures presented in the extant early Christian literature (and many reputable scholars do disagree with the received traditions), many of the publications that pass through the labyrinth of mass marketing and end up on the shelf at the local Barnes & Noble present implausible theories that have previously been rejected by a vast majority of scholars. This is not to say that all books on Christian origins by popular presses are outlandish. But it does help explain why a thesis such as the one promoted by Eisenman is widely available to the public in venues where plausible scholarly reconstructions are often excluded. It also helps explain why Eisenman appears as the first talking-head interview in the Jacobovici film.

Despite the incredible role that Eisenman reconstructs for James in the history of early Judaism and early Christianity, when the ossuary inscription was announced, he was one of the earliest and most vociferous opponents of its authenticity and importance. The following reference to Eisenman appears in an Associated Press article titled "Burial Box Inscription Could Be Oldest Archaeological Link to Jesus," which was the first AP piece published about the ossuary: "Lemaire's claim was attacked by Robert Eisenman of California State University, Long Beach, who unlike most scholars thinks that 'Jesus' existence is a very shaky thing.' Since Eisenman is highly skeptical about New Testament history, he considers the new discovery 'just too pat. It's just too perfect.'"[38]

The *Christian Science Monitor* reported a similar statement on the following day: "Experts already disagree about the authenticity. Crossan figures it's most likely credible. But Robert Eisenman, author of *James the Brother of Jesus*, worries the inscription is too good to be true. 'It's too pat,' he says. 'Why add "Jesus" to the inscription? It's like someone wanted us to be sure.'"[39] And in the *Daily Telegraph* (Sydney, Australia), the story read, "Others, however, aren't convinced. 'It's too perfect,' says Robert Eisenman, professor of Middle East religions and archaeology at California State University. 'It's very questionable. It seems directed at the modern believer and not the people of that time.'"[40] Similarly, following the release of Jacobovici's film in 2003, Eisenman was quoted in newspaper reports about the documentary: "Robert Eisenman, a biblical archaeologist at California State University, said: 'Several things cast suspicion. The inscription is too perfect. They would never have written 'brother of Jesus' in the first century.'"[41]

Due to Eisenman's controversial theories of Christian origins, he gained the attention of popular book publishers and conspiracy theorists in the 1990s. In the media attention that was generated around the James Ossuary, he became a natural target for reporters interested in generating a scholarly response to the artifact. After all, the title of his popular book, published five years earlier, foreshadowed the inscription on the burial box. But for the purposes of the documentary, Eisenman's complicated theories about the origins of Christianity were not important. He appears only once in the film as an expert witness in this investigation. He drives Jacobovici's narrative forward by testifying to the fact that this ossuary (if real) is "an artifact that overarches all the artifacts." His statement functions to validate the importance of the investigation, regardless of the fact that he had been consistently quoted in other media outlets as the scholar who doubted the authenticity of the name "Jesus" in the inscription.

Several other scholars are similarly introduced in the next section of the film. After Eisenman, we see a reenactment scene in which a small group of costumed actors carry a body on a makeshift bed up a trail toward a cave. The voice-over narration states, "The story begins in the year 62 when a funeral procession winds its way along the Kidron Valley outside of city of Jerusalem. The funeral party consists of family members and followers of the new Jesus movement, the Jewish sect that would later become Christianity. The man being buried is none other than the person that early Christian writers called 'James the Just,' the head of the Jesus movement in Jerusalem, the brother of Jesus."

The reenactment is clearly intended to set the stage for identifying the importance of James in the Christian tradition. The reenactment also prepares the viewer for a later scene in which the bones of James are placed in an ossuary within this same cave setting. Without raising any questions about the traditions involved in the story of James—traditions that are certainly not as cut-and-dried as Jacobovici implies—the film moves quickly to establish the idea that James was an important leader in Jerusalem. Two scholars are used in an effort to drive this point home. Father Jerome Murphy-O'Connor of the Ecole Biblique in Jerusalem (with his name and title on the screen), says, "James was a Jew who became a follower of Jesus, who remained true to his Jewish faith and his Jewish observances, and who was the leader of the mother church, the church of Jerusalem during its adolescent years, its whole formative period." Murphy-O'Connor has not written extensively on James, but as a famous Catholic scholar who is well known for his books on Paul and his archaeological travel guide to Israel, he makes a brief appearance in the film in support of the idea that James was an important leader in Jerusalem.

What the viewers do not hear is that Murphy-O'Connor was also very skeptical about the importance of the inscription. Regardless of whether the inscription was authentic or not, he had joined a significant amount of scholars who responded to the BAR press release with general indifference. Many scholars were interested in the ossuary but were not impressed by the claims that this was significant for our historical reconstructions of early Christianity. The fact is that no serious scholar doubts that there were men named Yaʿakov (Jacob/James), Yoseph (Joseph), and Yeshua (Jesus) living in or around Jerusalem in the time when ossuaries were in popular use. Additionally, the New Testament Gospels provide plenty of evidence that men with these names were related as son, father, and brother. Thus, why the excitement? The ossuary inscription, if authentic, tells us nothing new. Murphy-O'Connor was referred to in a November 2002 article as follows: "Dominican Father Jerome Murphy-O'Connor, a biblical archaeologist at Ecole Biblique in Jerusalem, said that, while the researcher who studied the ossuary was a respected expert, up to 60 percent of the artifacts found in the illegal antiquities market are fake. . . . 'If it is authentic, the only significance is that it is the earliest dated reference to Joseph, James and Jesus that we have. . . . The only important thing is that date—the inscription doesn't tell us anything we don't already know.'"[42] Murphy-O'Connor's rational ideas about the lack of importance of the ossuary are not disclosed in the film; he is simply featured one time as a scholar who can further justify the significance of James.

John Painter of Charles Stuart University (name and title on screen) follows immediately with this brief statement: "And he took the church of Jerusalem through those foundational years up to the year he was executed in the year 62. From about 30 to 62, tumultuous years, the foundation years for the beginnings of Christianity; and James is number one." Painter is used as a means to push the importance of James even further. Now James becomes "number one" in Jerusalem for the thirty-two years after the death of Jesus. Painter also appears later in the film, when he states, "I don't think it is a forgery. The person who is put in this bone box, this ossuary, was James, son of Joseph, brother of Jesus. And I imagine that is likely correct. But it doesn't tell us which James, which Joseph, which Jesus: names which are pretty common in the time." In other words, Painter's statement tells us that he may be willing to accept the authenticity of the inscription, but he has serious reservations about the notion that this was the James, Joseph, and Jesus of the Gospels. Leading up to the ossuary phenomenon, Painter was one of the leading scholars on the question of the historical James, and his scholarship and role in the documentary deserve a careful look.

In contrast to the views of Eisenman, who significantly challenged the received traditions about James, Painter's work represents a more conventional, canonically bound scholarship that was also published just a few years before the ossuary announcement. His work was not the first contribution to the recent wellspring of James scholarship, but it was the most exhaustive presentation of the ancient literary evidence related to this biblical character. His presentation of James also represents a middle ground in New Testament research. Along with scholars such as Richard Bauckham (who makes a brief appearance in the film), Bruce Chilton, and Craig Evans, Painter's reconstruction of a "historical James" is part of a time-honored strain of New Testament scholarship that takes the canonical book of Acts as a fairly reliable source for reconstructing Christian origins. Painter's *Just James: The Brother of Jesus in History and Tradition* first appeared in 1997 in a series called "Studies on Personalities of the New Testament" (University of South Carolina Press) and was rereleased in 1999 in a popular paperback edition with Fortress Press.

Painter's expansive study of early Christian literature related to James is based on the premise that many later Christian ("Gnostic") traditions contain kernels of historical data about the first-century figure. He suggests that third- and fourth-century texts that discuss "James the Just" can be mined for accurate information about the historical first-century person. Painter's book is essentially a commentary on all of the references to "James" in sources such as Paul, Hegesippus, the Gnostics, and Eusebius; it seeks "to show the central role of James in the life of the earliest church."[43] By examining the stories about James, particularly the traditions related to his life and death in Jerusalem, Painter argues that James was indeed a full brother of Jesus who was the leader of the Jerusalem disciples from a very early period in the life of the church.

For Painter, this leadership role was granted to James by none other than Jesus when he made a post-resurrection appearance to his brother and told him to lead the church in Jerusalem. Although the authors of the books that were selected to be part of the New Testament canon were interested in downplaying James's importance, Painter attempts to recover James's story by a careful interpretation of later traditions. Thus, even though the Acts of the Apostles does not mention that a brother of Jesus had a leadership role in Jerusalem, Painter assumes (along with many other church historians and scholars) that the "James" who is introduced in Acts 12:17 was just this James. Similarly, Painter presupposes that all the other references to "James" that are not specifically identified as a different character have "James the brother of Jesus" as their intended subject. In so doing he is able to reconstruct a primary role for James in the history of Christianity, one that, according to Painter, was suppressed by the emerging Catholic tradition. James—the leader of Jewish Christianity in Jerusalem—was all but forgotten by the "Great Church." The details of his story can only be recovered from the variety of later sources that refer to him.

Following this logic, Painter contends that even third- and fourth-century Gnostic literature from the Nag Hammadi Library contains information about the historical James. After the Jerusalem Christian community was dispersed during the time of the Jewish Revolt, some Christian groups outside of what would eventually be known as the Catholic tradition claimed James the brother of the Lord as their founder. The *First Apocalypse of James* and the *Second Apocalypse of James* are examples of this adaptation of "Jewish-Christian" traditions to fit later Gnostic ideology. In the new Gnostic context, James was considered a spiritual brother of Jesus (not one of the twelve apostles) who received secret knowledge from Jesus prior to the Passion. Because of this special fraternal gnosis, the stories highlight the idea that the line of authority in the Christian tradition began with James, not the twelve. James was Jesus' choice as the founder of the church, and the authors of these Gnostic Christian "apocalypses" believed they had a direct line of authority that stemmed from James. In this view, "orthodox" Christianity that traced its roots to the apostles was not as authentic as the Gnostic Christian tradition that derived directly from the brother of Jesus. Additionally, Jerusalem was associated with negative powers in the universe (the Archons); when James died as a righteous martyr in the city, this led to the destruction of Jerusalem as retribution from the most-high God. Painter suggests that these stories can be used to reconstruct aspects of the life of James that were forgotten or intentionally covered up by the emerging Catholic leaders. The Gnostic stories preserve historical aspects of the life of James, including the fact that he was a follower of Jesus prior to Jesus' death. Additionally, Painter considers the story of James' martyrdom in this tradition to be dependent on an early, independent source that helps corroborate similar stories about James that are found in Josephus and Hegessipus (as quoted by Eusebius).

While Painter's study provides a very extensive presentation and interpretation of the available literary data, for our current purposes this summary of his work should serve to demonstrate why Painter was most likely selected for an appearance in the Jacobovici film. He has a strong interest in recovering a significant role for James in the founding of Christianity. Painter's James was a disciple of his brother before the Passion, he was the first leader of the Jerusalem church, and his death as a pious Jewish-Christian was a monumental occasion in the origins of the church and a low point in the Jewish-Christian tradition. Painter's major claim is that the story of the supremacy of James has often been intentionally hidden by the emerging Catholic tradition—as well as by modern scholars—because of the commanding position that Pauline Christianity has held through the centuries (an idea that he holds in common with Eisenman).

In light of Painter's historical reconstruction, it may seem odd that he was not delighted by the 2002 "discovery" of the ossuary inscription. In fact, he was a leading critic of the inscription, both on the grounds that it may not be authentic and that, even if it was, it almost certainly did not refer to the "James the brother of Jesus" who is mentioned in the New Testament. Not long after the BAS's press release, Painter's book appeared in an expanded second edition with a detailed critique of the inscription.[44] While this new edition refers to many of the questions that were raised about the authenticity of the inscription, the majority of his analysis and his rejection of the importance of the inscription is based on other factors.

Painter's foremost criticism relates to the fact that the name "James" was so rapidly adopted by the ossuary's promoters (Lemaire, Shanks, and

Witherington) as the translation of the Aramaic name "Yaʿakov" that appears on the ossuary. As noted previously, Jacobovici quickly brushes over the issue related to the use of the Latinized version of "James." But like so much of the scholarship related to the ossuary inscription, this too is a very complex issue that cannot be swept so easily under the rug. In Greek, "Jacob" appears in the Bible both in its indeclinable Semitic form (Yaʿakov) and the Hellenized declinable form (Yacobos). Traditionally, "James" has been used by English-language translators of the New Testament for all the "Jacobs" in the New Testament that have the declinable form. In the Hebrew Bible, "Yaʿakov" is simply transliterated into "Jacob" when it is found in its Semitic form. Thus, "James" has typically been used as the Christianized form of the Hebrew "Jacob." "The name in the inscription is indistinguishable from the name of the patriarch and should surely be translated as *Jacob*," argues Painter, and his point is well taken.[45] There was no reason to translate the ossuary's Aramaic "Yaʿakov" into the Latin/Christian "James." In so doing, the modern epigrapher (Lemaire) already assumed a significant link between the inscription and the New Testament figure that came to be known by the Latinized "James." Because of the combination of the three names (Jacob/James, Joseph, Jesus), the original translator of the inscription selected the name "James" because it fit the New Testament tradition. According to Painter, this is contrary to typical practice and biased towards those who want to make a direct connection between this name and the figure in the New Testament: "The translation of the ossuary inscription as 'James the son of Joseph brother of Jesus' prejudices the decision in favor of an identification with James of Jerusalem."[46]

Painter also rejects the idea that this inscription refers to James the Just on the grounds that the form of burial does not correlate with the stories about James's death and burial in the Christian tradition. Painter's reliance on the later Christian literature had led him in the first edition of the book to conclude that James had likely been buried in the traditional site in Jerusalem that is still venerated today by Armenian Christians—beneath the Church of Saint James. In the second edition of the book, he revisits the question of James's burial and explores the possibility that James's bones could have been gathered into an ossuary. After a careful examination of the literature and the various church traditions, he concludes that "the tradition provides no hint of the use of an ossuary in the burial of the brother of the Lord, and the Jacob ossuary presents its own problems that stand in the way of an identification with the brother of the Lord."[47]

A fifty-minute documentary is not a practical venue for the complex discussion that occupies eleven pages in the second edition of Painter's book. Historical and investigative television documentaries often have a very short time to provide the necessary background to the subject matter at hand. In order to move quickly to the more entertaining and mysterious parts of the story, certain "facts" have to be established promptly at the beginning of the film. As in a fifty-minute television drama such as *CSI* or *Law and Order*, the rapid establishment of a captivating storyline requires that key "facts" must be introduced without pausing to raise serious objections. As has been demonstrated in this overview of the role that scholars play in the first few minutes of the Jacobovici film, many issues have been left on the cutting-room floor. Because of the desire to quickly convince the audience that "history will be rewritten" if this investigation can authenticate the inscription, complex issues are dealt with in the most tangential way. The need to establish that James was an important figure in early Christianity led the writer to brush over the fact that the historical reconstruction of the life of James is loaded with problems. Viewers were not told about the variety of opinions regarding James's identity that are held by the experts who were interviewed in the film's opening minutes, let alone told that many scholars disagree with both Eisenman and Painter. Nor were they told at the beginning of the film that the scholars who gave the brief introductions to the importance of James either do not think that the inscription is authentic (Eisenman) or think that the inscription, even if "real," does not refer to the James of the New Testament (Painter). While the film created a dramatic opening for its storyline, it failed to account for the complex nature of the case. There is a major difference between documentary filmmaking and scholarly research.

As the film continues, the audience is officially introduced to a scholar who is much less skeptical of the artifact. Ben Witherington III of Asbury Theological Seminary appears six different times in the film (more than any other scholar). In his film appearances and in other public venues (publications, media interviews on national radio and television, and speaking engagements), Witherington was very quick to accept the inscription as authentic and to use this new "archaeological evidence" to support both his ideas of Christian origins and his modern theological beliefs. With each appearance in the film, he either defended the authenticity of the inscription or clarified some point of contention that another scholar raised. As noted previously, Witherington and Shanks coauthored *The Brother of Jesus: The Dramatic Story and Meaning of the First Archaeological Link to Jesus and His Family*, the popular HarperSanFrancisco book that was released near the time that the film premiered. The first half of the book is written by Shanks and provides an overview of the story of the discovery of the ossuary as well as a defense of its authenticity. Like the film, Shanks puts on the demeanor of an investigative reporter or a lawyer looking at the clues to a case, but there is little doubt that his goal is to establish the viability of the ossuary. For his part, Witherington proves to be the staunchest supporter of both the authenticity of the inscription and its promise to enhance the faith of modern Christians. In the introductory comments to his section of the book, Witherington makes his intentions clear:

> The further appeal of the ossuary, I believe, is that it promises for the first time the opportunity to "touch" Jesus, to experience a physical connection with him through the inscribed burial box of his brother James, a pivotal early Christian leader who has been hidden in the shadows of history. Now, in this simple inscription, the Gospel figures of Jesus, Joseph, and James—until now known only through texts—become arrestingly tangible. In an age that demands compelling evidence for claims of faith and history, the world now has something concrete to see, examine, reflect on, and respond to.[48]

While many scholars have distanced themselves from the idea that artifacts can enhance faith claims, Witherington has embraced this idea and become a primary promoter of the ossuary. In dozens of interviews in newspapers and on television, in his online blog, and during a national speaking tour in churches throughout the country, Witherington has been (to this day) an indefatigable advocate for the importance of the ossuary. In one of his most extraordinary claims, he suggested that DNA from bone fragments that were reportedly found in the ossuary (that he claimed at one time were stored in a Tupperware container in Oded Golan's apartment) could be compared to DNA taken from blood fragments on the Shroud of Turin in order to derive the DNA of Jesus' family and prove that the James in the ossuary was the brother of Jesus. For example, he made the following statement in a 2003 article that was posted in the online edition of *Christianity Today*:

> If crucifixion had been the final event in Jesus' earthly life, then it is hard to believe that 30 years later someone would be bragging on an ossuary about being related to him. The last part of the inscription reads, almost emphatically, "his brother [is] Jesus!" or "He's the brother of Jesus!" What had happened that redeemed the honor of the crucified Jesus? It was his resurrection. So, I like to say, James is in the box, and Jesus is on the box, because of the resurrection. And perhaps, if we are able to test the bone fragments of the box soon, and compare the DNA evidence to the evidence produced in the '80s about the gene string and DNA derived from the blood samples on the Shroud, we may just have a double confirmation of the artifacts I have discussed at the beginning and end of this essay. Stay tuned.[49]

It is not impossible to connect the dots between the intentions of the film and the ideological proclivities of its major scholarly resource. Witherington's first headshot interview in the documentary provides background information about the use of ossuaries in first-century Jerusalem. Interspersed with the narrator's information about ancient burial practices and Witherington's explanation of how James (and Jesus) would have been buried, reenactment scenes role across the screen. Costumed actors carefully carry a body into the tomb, lay the body on a slab, and light candles around it. Finally, a man is shown placing bones into an open ossuary that is already half full of bones. As the man places a human skull into the ossuary, the narrator states, "A year after James's burial, when his flesh had decomposed, James's family would have gathered his bones and lovingly put them into an ossuary, so that he would be ready for judgment day. It would be 2,000 years before an ossuary surfaces that at least one expert believes belonged to James." As exemplified in this sequence, throughout the film Witherington plays the role of the sympathetic scholar who provides timely commentary that supports the major goals of the documentary. The fact that he is a strong supporter of the ossuary's importance and authenticity is never mentioned in the film.

The next appearance of Witherington occurs approximately ten minutes later in the documentary, following a segment in which the question of James's relationship to Jesus is raised for debate. Richard Bauckham of the University of St. Andrews, in his only appearance in the film, begins with this brief statement: "It is quite clear that in the Gospels and other types of early Christian literature . . . there were four men who were known as the brothers of Jesus, and at least two women who were known as the sisters of Jesus. So the question is what was the exact relation of these people to Jesus? And there have been three views of this." As the viewer sees a reenactment scene of several children of varying ages playing in the courtyard of an ancient house, the narrator explains the three views: (1) in the Catholic tradition, "brother in this instance simply means 'kin.' Since Mary remained a virgin, Jesus grew up with his cousins"; (2) Orthodox tradition holds "that Joseph had a wife prior to Mary with whom he had at least six children. According to this belief, James was the oldest of the siblings and Jesus was the youngest and only son of Mary"; and (3) "Protestants contend that though Mary was a virgin at the time of Jesus' birth, she then gave birth to at least six more children. According to this view, Jesus was the oldest, taking care of his younger siblings and providing a model for them to follow."

Witherington provides the following commentary: "If you interpret this in the context of early Judaism, the probability is that Mary and Joseph would have gone on to have more children. Why wouldn't they? There was no prohibition on them doing something like that. And there was no ascetical piety in early Judaism that ordinary Jews would be practicing that would suggest, 'OK, we'll get married, but we'll just abstain from sexual relations.'" The film provides no time to explore the complex issues related to the traditions about the family of Jesus and the traditions about Mary. Witherington's comment serves as the de facto conclusion to the matter: Mary had more children, thus James was the younger brother of Jesus. His statement alludes to one of the key components of his published work on the ossuary. In *The Brother of Jesus*, Witherington provides more detailed information about his belief that this ossuary proves that James was a true brother of Jesus—verifying the stories in the New Testament Gospels. He also concludes that this discredits a belief that is sacred in the Catholic tradition: the perpetual virginity of Mary. He states: "What should be the relationship between historical evidence and church dogma in the Catholic and Orthodox traditions? If new historical evidence calls into question traditions that are based on the *Protoevangelium* of James and not on the biblical and earliest texts, then these traditions need to weigh the matter of how strongly they should hold on to certain beliefs that may not be true or vital to Christian faith. The discovery of the ossuary provides a compelling opportunity for this kind of reassessment."[50] According to Witherington, the discovery of the ossuary obliges the Catholic and Orthodox traditions to revisit their ancient beliefs and practices. Thus, while his statement in the film, "Mary and Joseph would have gone on to have more children," may seem innocent enough, there is actually a lot more to the story that remains below the surface.

In his final appearance in the film (during the thirty-seventh minute), Witherington is brought in to provide the summary statement regarding the authenticity of the inscription. His closing statement comes after several chapters in the film in which the quest for the original tomb from which the ossuary was robbed, and the scientific investigation of the artifact, are center stage. The film's narrative flows from one scholar to the next. First, Dr. Rochelle Altman provides a negative assessment of the authenticity of the name "Jesus" in the inscription. Her well-publicized idea that the first part of the inscription was authentically ancient and the second was a fake has been introduced in the film and then quickly dismissed. Although David Mevorah, curator of the Israel Museum, does not actually comment on Altman's theory, he appears next and provides part of the rationale for why Altman is incorrect in her analysis of the script. Following a reenactment scene of a first-century man carving on an ossuary with a thin metal object in a tomb lit by candles, Mevorah confidently states that ossuary inscriptions "were done by the families, by the members of the family at the event of gathering the bones." As the screen shows a reenactment of a man in a tomb gathering bones and placing them in an ossuary, he concludes, "A very emotional event, ending the mourning of a year, and therefore not professional writing in most cases." In other words, Jacobovici uses Mevorah's comment to suggest that Altman's idea that the script was by two different hands is wrong: the script was not professionally carved. Thus one should expect inconsistencies in the writing that a mourning family puts on the stone box.

Next, Baruch Halpern of the Pennsylvania State University is shown in one of his appearances in the film. For Jacobovici's purposes, Halpern represents the skeptical scholar; with each appearance, he questions some aspect of the authenticity of the inscription. In his three scenes he discusses the sophisticated nature of the antiquities market, the problematic nature of the script on the inscription, and the ease with which patina can be forged in the modern world. At this point in the film, Halpern comments on the script:

> The thing that troubles me most of all is that the inscription starts off with perfect lapidary script, perfect typewritten script, and all of a sudden that's not important anymore. Somebody took a great deal of trouble to start the inscription, and when they wrote "Jacob the son of Joseph" they did it carefully and it was important to them. All of a sudden, somewhere in the middle of the word "brother" they don't care anymore: "Oh yeah, by the way, 'the brother of Jesus.'" Where is the profit in that, except if you are trying to sell the thing somehow?

Without any further reference to the comments of Altman and Halpern, Jacobovici links onto the word "profit" in Halpern's final question and reintroduces Witherington as a witness in defense of the ossuary's authenticity. Witherington states: "There's no profit motive. There's no evidence of a forgery here, ancient or modern." As the screen shows the previously viewed film of the scholars at the ROM exhibit looking at the ossuary, Witherington continues: "And you have the great scholars, the Aramaicists like Professor Fitzmyer; you have André Lemaire, the great epigrapher; you have Frank Moore Cross, there is hardly any more distinguished figure, from Harvard, analyzing this inscription and saying, 'by one hand,' 'Herodian period Aramaic,' 'it's consistent with the period,' 'it's consistent with the Jewish burial practices,' 'it's Jerusalem limestone.' You just sorta lay out the evidence, piece after piece; it's passed all the toughest tests."

An informed viewer of the film might wonder how unbiased Witherington is in this case. With his own book contract from HarperSanFrancisco, he seems an odd choice to state that "there's no profit motive." Arguably, in the James Ossuary phenomenon, profit motives appear at every stage of the story's development: a book contract, exclusive film contract, magazine sales, exhibition of the artifact at the ROM, insurance claims, advertisement sales by the cable network, and the like. But, regardless of whether anyone profited from the ossuary, Witherington's firm statement provides the film's narrative with a summative point: the arguments against the authenticity of the inscription are, for the most part, unfounded. Witherington serves to make a complicated situation disappear by appealing to brief statements made by people in the film who have been seen supporting the case for authenticity.

The pattern that is seen with Witherington's appearances in the film—in which he makes summative statements that "solve" all the problems—continues in several other segments. For example, in a later section, Jacobovici raises the question of whether the patina from within the inscription matches the patina on the outside of the box. This is a question that was raised in the tests conducted by the Israel Antiquities Authorities after the box was confiscated from Golan in 2003. In the film, scientists of the Geological Survey of Israel test the elements in the patina with an energy dispersive spectrometer. They compare patina that was extracted from within the letter *Samekh* to material from above the letter. As the camera focuses on the scientists examining the test results, the viewer hears this conclusion from the scientists: "You see just the elements which are supposed to be in real patina. . . . No, there is nothing suspicious here."

Halpern follows with another skeptical remark: "Forging a patina is not a difficult thing. All that is involved is taking calcium carbonate, which is the main component of a patina, putting it in your blender, so that the particles are in a suspension, painting the object in question in the new incisions, you merely have to paint the new incisions because the rest of it already has calcium carbonate, and baking it for a little while. I mean faking a patina and making this inscription, you know, you could do it in a couple of hours." This time it is left to Ewa Dziadowiec and not Witherington to resolve the issue. It is unclear how the expertise of the "ceramics, stone, and glass conservator" of the ROM fits this particular research question; nor does the film explain exactly why elements in ancient patina would fluoresce differently under ultraviolet rays than modern, baked-on patina of the same basic composition. Nevertheless, Dziadowiec reports on a long-wave ultraviolet light test that was conducted on the inscription while the ossuary was at the ROM. According to the film's narrated statement, "if one followed Professor Halpern's recipe and baked faked patina on the inscription, the ultraviolet rays would pick up the new substance and make it glow." Dziadowiec follows with the summative statement that is intended to make the patina issue disappear: "We didn't find anything suspicious, everything was very clean." Pointing at the inscription on the ossuary, she concludes: "And there is an inscription which goes from here up to there, and both parts, the first part and the part with the word Jesus looks the same, looks fine." Jacobovici's narrator concludes the segment with the final word on the matter: "The science is done; the scholars have spoken."

THE ORIGINS OF THE OSSUARY

There are several other people who make appearances in the film and speak on issues related to the origins of the artifact. André Lemaire, professor at the Sorbonne in France, was the original epigrapher to study the inscription. His first role in the film follows a second showing of the reenactment scene mentioned above, in which the "family and friends" of James are seen carrying a body into a tomb, lighting candles, and then, after a time lapse, placing bones into an ossuary. The reenactment ends with the actor placing a lid onto the bone-filled box. The scene elides into a shot of Lemaire taking the lid off of the James Ossuary—a well-orchestrated transition from reenactment to "reality." The setting is not identified, but Lemaire is clearly in the apartment of Oded Golan. The scene was shot in Tel Aviv prior to the ossuary being damaged in transit to Toronto. Lemaire is introduced by the narrator as "a professor at the Sorbonne in France. He is a world-renowned specialist on first-century Aramaic inscriptions." As he sits in Golan's living room, Lemaire speaks in French with the following voice-over translation:

> The discovery of this inscription happened totally by chance. I was working for several months in Israel, and I had the opportunity of meeting several antiquities collectors. Amongst them was one collector who said to me, "I have something to show you that may interest you." We agreed to meet. I was really taken aback, astonished and surprised. You could read it quite easily, "James, son of Joseph, brother of Jesus." I looked at it carefully under a magnifying glass, and I concluded that the shapes of the letters and the grammar were legitimate.

While the screen shows a view of Lemaire looking at the inscription with a magnifying glass in his hand, he concludes: "The inscription was ancient, not modern; obviously, authentic." With this comment, the documentary takes up a series of new questions: Where and when was the ossuary purchased? From whom did Golan purchase it? From what tomb was the ossuary taken? Is the ossuary authentic? Is the inscription authentic?

Halpern provides the skeptic's view: "The fact is that there are forgers in the antiquities market, and this is a known fact. And the forgers who are most successful are professionals. They are real professionals. They are as professional as the scholars who are assessing their work." With that warning, the film focuses on the origins of the ossuary. As the screen shows Golan playing the piano in his apartment, and the soundtrack plays his piano music, the narrator states, "The man who stands most to gain from the James Ossuary is its owner, Israeli antiquities collector Oded Golan. According to Israeli law, if the ossuary was purchased after 1978 the state can confiscate it. If it was purchased before, the ossuary is his. Golan claims he bought it in the early 1970s. Some say he could not have been a collector that far back." With that opening, the documentary provides Golan a series of scenes in which he defends his legal rights to the artifact and attempts to locate the antiquities dealer from whom he bought the ossuary. Since he says he has purchased over forty ossuaries and claims to have more than 3,000 ancient artifacts in his personal collection, he is unclear as to which dealer sold him the James Ossuary.

The quest for the origins of the ossuary takes Golan to Jerusalem. The narrator sets the stage: "If Golan can figure out which dealer he bought the ossuary from, it might trace the artifact to its place of discovery, help authenticate it, and corroborate his story." With that, the viewer is introduced to two possible antiquities dealers in the Old City of Jerusalem. The first, Haj Omar el-Aruk, is very interesting, but he is unhelpful to the cause. He knows Golan, remembers selling him ossuaries, and even says (in Arabic) that the artifacts did have inscriptions on them: "Yes, there were inscriptions. I remember one; the letters had been painted in red." A translator responds, "But those inscriptions on the ossuaries that you sold to Golan, could you tell me what was written on them?" Haj Omar responds: "They looked like Hebrew, Latin, Greek, and all sorts." Finally the question is asked, "Do you know what the inscriptions said?" Haj Omar responds: "No, I don't know. I'm illiterate, even in Arabic." The narrator concludes: "The trip to the antiquities dealer is not successful. Over the years, Golan has collected some 40 ossuaries, and it is impossible to tell if the James ossuary came from Haj Omar. He now has to track down the other dealer who might have sold him the ossuary."

As often happens in Jacobovici's film-editing practices, there is an extended break in the documentary between the first search for the antiquities dealer and the second. The entire film is broken up into short two- and three-minute segments that are woven together in such a way that the various "investigations" are rarely completed in one section. In this case, there are over seventeen minutes between the antiquity dealers' scenes; several other issues are discussed before the second dealer makes an appearance. Prior to Golan's renewed search, the viewer is introduced to ten other topics:

1. The Armenian Patriarchate, Rev. Bishop Aris Shirvanian, provides details about the belief that James was first buried in the Kidron Valley before his bones were moved to the Cathedral of St. James (see discussion below).

2. Stephen Pfann discusses his hypothesis that only famous brothers were mentioned in ossuary inscriptions.

3. Witherington dismisses the notion that James was not a blood brother of Jesus, and draws his conclusion that James was a child of Mary and Joseph.

4. Dr. Shimon Ilani of the Geological Survey of Israel examines the limestone ossuary and concludes that it is from the Jerusalem area and that the soil on the ossuary is a Rendzina-type soil that is typical to the Silwan area in Jerusalem.

5. Amir Ganor, the chief investigator for the Anti-Looting Unit of the Israel Antiquities Authority, questions Golan's story about purchasing the ossuary (more details of this segment are described below).

6. The editor and staff of the BAS are seen at work on the BAR story, during which time Hershel Shanks declares, "We have a spectacular find. There is no question about it."

7. The museum is introduced, and William Thorsell of the ROM reveals the damaged ossuary to the bewildered media.

8. Witherington and Jonathan Reed each reiterate that James was important to the history of Christianity, even though he was "written out of the story" in antiquity.

9. Ewa Dziadowiec, the ROM's "expert on ceramic and stone restoration," begins piecing the ossuary back together in a lab.

10. Vincent Vertolli, the assistant curator of geology at the ROM, discusses test results on the incrustation within the ossuary that revealed phosphate on the box, thus proving that there had once been bones in the box.

Immediately following the interview with Vertolli, the film returns to a scene inside the ROM lab where the ossuary is being repaired. The narrator makes the transition back to Golan's search for the dealer: "After the tests it is clearer than ever that the box is authentic, but that doesn't mean that the inscription is also authentic. It would help to know how the ossuary suddenly appeared. What is its point of origin? Is it a modern forgery executed by cynical men carving on an ancient artifact?" The scene switches back to Golan walking down a street in the Old City of Jerusalem, and the narrator asks: "Or is it a 2,000-year-old relic, surfacing in a post-9/11 world to remind humanity of a man called James the Just?"

Without explaining the drama-filled reference to the attacks on the World Trade Center and Pentagon or their relation to the story of James, the narrator introduces the second antiquities dealer: "Golan has been trying to find the dealer who sold him the James Ossuary. He's now almost sure he knows who it was. But the dealer Golan dealt with thirty years ago is now retired. His son Jamil has taken over the shop." A conversation with Jamil ensues, during which he says that Golan had been "dealing with my father for forty years." Jamil is then asked, "Do you know how ossuaries like the James Ossuary are discovered?" Now speaking in Arabic, with a voice-over by a translator, Jamil responds:

> Sure, let me explain. When we were younger, teenagers, we used to go up to the mountains and watch how the young men who find ossuaries excavate and dig them up. You see, they enter into the tombs to find the Israelite ossuaries. They then remove the bones from them. It is interesting, sometimes the tombs have steps and sometimes there are no steps. You see, if there is a lot of work that went into building the tomb, that means it was for someone important, some kind of leader. The young men remove the stone at the entrance, but they don't enter immediately because there is no oxygen in there. They wait a little, like ten minutes, for some oxygen to seep in. Then they light candles or carry flashlights and go in. I'll show you.

With this sober description, the film returns to a tomb setting in Jerusalem for the second time. Earlier, during the seventeen-minute interlude, Amir Ganor, an antilooting investigator for the Israel Antiquities Authority, took Jacobovici and his crew into a series of tombs that Ganor believes are similar to the one from which the ossuary was stolen. Ganor suspects that the ossuary has been looted very recently from one of the many tombs in the Kidron Valley, near the village of Silwan (just southeast of the ancient Temple Mount). After being described by the narrator as "an archaeologist who packs a gun in his belt," Ganor is seen climbing into an ancient tomb. He speaks in Hebrew with a translator's voice-over: "Oded

Golan hasn't presented us with any proof backing his story that he got the James ossuary thirty years ago. In fact, it could have come from any one of the 300 illegal excavations we discover each year."

Six film segments after Ganor's allegation, the camera focuses on a white van that is driven by Jacobovici. The van follows behind a small red car driving on a winding road south of Jerusalem. The narrator brings the viewer up to date: "The journey now takes Golan into the center of the Israeli-Palestinian conflict." As an Israeli soldier with a machine gun waves Jacobovici's van past a checkpoint, the narration continues: "A no-man's zone outside Jerusalem, where suicide bombers and soldiers clash on a daily basis." Again, as the viewer follows the red car down a winding road, we hear, "Jamil doesn't know where the James Ossuary originated, but he is guessing it is from a hill some ten kilometers outside of Jerusalem, which his suppliers have been mining for ossuaries for decades. This place is a treasure trove of burial caves and tombs. Golan is here in hopes of tracing the James Ossuary to the tomb it was found in, to prove his version of the story."

Rather than deal directly with the feasibility of Ganor's charge, Jacobovici returns to the owner's explanation of the ossuary's origins and embarks on a section of the film that should disgust most ethical viewers, though that is clearly not the filmmaker's intention. As the camera pans down into a cave opening near where the cars have parked, the narrator states, "The oldest cave they find is a tomb that was in use at least 700 years prior to the time of James." A man squats inside the cave, sifting his hands through small rocks, pottery shards, and human bones. Golan also squats on the cave floor picking up ceramic objects and bones. The narrator concludes: "The James Ossuary couldn't have come from this site; here bodies were buried together after they decomposed. No attempt was made to distinguish individuals. It was much later that ossuaries came into use." After Golan explains the differences between burial practices in the Iron Age and the Early Roman Period, the camera follows Jamil into another cave, as the narrator tells more of the story: "Jamil now does his best to help his friend by figuring out where the James Ossuary originated. He pokes about first-century tombs, but finds nothing that would suggest an important figure such as the brother of Jesus." The segment ends as Jamil climbs out of a narrow tomb entry and the narrator's voice translates his words: " 'Tomb raiders always dump the bones,' he says. 'The bones make the boxes heavier and no one really wants them. Anyway they really shouldn't be removed from their graves.'" As Jamil stands and shows the camera a piece of a bone that he has brought with him from the tomb, the viewer is left with these (discouraging) words: " 'The bones are still in this tomb,' he says, 'but the ossuary is gone.'"

The question of which tomb the James Ossuary was stolen from is left unanswered. The antiquities dealer "does his best to help his friend," but in the end there is no way to know where and when the thieves or "tomb raiders" stole the ossuary, dumped the human remains from the stone coffin, and sold it to a dealer. No ethical questions are raised in the film. The "investigation" evidently supersedes basic moral questions related to issues such as the mistreatment of human remains and the marketing of stolen grave goods.

Despite the failure of this "investigation," after five more segments, approximately thirteen minutes later in the film, Jacobovici returns to the issue of origins one last time. In the forty-second minute, a segment of the film takes up the issue of how certain we can be that the "James," "Joseph," and "Jesus" on the ossuary actually refer to the characters in the New Testament. Camil Fuchs, a statistician at Tel Aviv University, provides the analysis. Factoring in "the population of Jerusalem in the relevant sixty-five-year period[;] . . . women[;] . . . infant mortality[;] . . . literacy—only families who could read and write inscribed ossuaries[;] . . . and wealth—the deceased or their loved ones had to be able to afford an ossuary," the narrator concludes: "We're now left with only 3,000 candidates called James, who like the biblical James fit the relevant criteria. When the frequency of the names 'Joseph' and 'Jesus' are factored in, we discover only three of those 3,000 had a father named Joseph and a brother named Jesus." After Fuchs notes that "there is only one ossuary other than the James Ossuary that mentions not just the deceased and his father, but the brother," the final statistical pronouncement is read: "So it seems that once one factors in the brother reference, the three possible candidates are reduced to only one. Namely: James, son of Joseph, brother of Jesus of Nazareth."

As the film returns to the reenactment scene of people taking a body into a tomb and a man putting bones in an ossuary, the narrator declares: "Scientists, scholars, statisticians all point to the same conclusion: the ossuary is arguably the greatest archaeological find of all time, the first physical evidence that Jesus existed." With that declaration, the film briefly returns to the question of origins: "There is only one part of the mystery that still needs to be solved. Oded Golan says he bought the ossuary in the early 1970s. His family and friends corroborate his story. So how, after 2,000 years, did the James Ossuary suddenly end up in Golan's hands? There is one scenario that reconciles the stories of Israeli antiquities collector Oded Golan and the tradition of the Armenian Church."

While this statement is intended to push the narrative forward into the final segment of the film, it also serves as the last declaration on the issue of whether Golan's story is true. After all the unsuccessful searches for the original tomb, Jacobovici is left with the corroboration of "family and friends." His investigation has once again concluded with a declarative statement that is not justified by the force of his argument. Rather than leave open the possibility that the issue cannot be resolved, the documentary seeks to provide a conclusive answer. This pattern is seen throughout the film as issues are introduced, briefly discussed, and definitively solved. While this may be good television, it is a recipe for failed scientific research and sloppy scholarship.

JAMES IN THE KIDRON VALLEY

The reference to "the tradition of the Armenian Church" in the previous quotation provides Jacobovici's segue to the final chapter of the film. The film concludes with what arguably is the least convincing and most farfetched content of this documentary investigation. It is a final attempt to tie up all the loose ends. The question remains: could the ossuary have come from a tomb in the Kidron Valley? If so, can that be coordinated with the traditions of the Armenians, which hold that James was first "buried in the valley where he was martyred, in a tomb complex that has come to be identified with St. James." As the camera scans the valley and focuses on the so-called tomb of Zachariah, the narrator states Jacobovici's argument: "The tomb is connected to an impressive memorial. According to the Armenian Church, there was in ancient times a chapel at the base of the memorial. In the seventh century, the Christians fled from Muslim invaders with the bones of St. James." Apparently, his theory is that the tomb of Bene Hezir—with the so-called tomb of Zechariah ("an impressive memorial") at its southern entrance (in the Kidron Valley, or what medieval pilgrims called the "Valley of Jehoshaphat")—was actually the original tomb of James where the ossuary was first interred.

The film does not appear to be interested in reporting any factual archaeological information about the famous tomb of Bene Hezir or the many other tombs in this region. The tombs in this valley just south of the Mount of Olives have been studied by archaeologists for over a century.[51] While the Hezir tomb has been called by some later Christian pilgrims (and some modern tour guides) the "tomb of St. James," it is actually a tomb complex that was built and used during the Late Hasmonean period by a known priestly family. The tomb was built and used approximately 150 years before the traditional date of James's death. The names of several individuals (priests) are inscribed on the tomb's architrave in Hebrew, along with the family name "Hezir."[52] This tomb is associated with a *nefesh* carved out of the rock hillside (the monument outside the tomb, traditionally called the tomb of Zechariah) that was left unfinished in the first century CE and was never actually used as a tomb. The tomb of Hezir's priestly family was one of the hundreds of tombs, buildings, mountains, and other sites that were associated with Hebrew prophets and Jesus' earliest followers during late antiquity and the Middle Ages.

The other major monumental tomb in the area just north of Bene Hezir is the "tomb of Absalom," the twenty-six-foot-high decorated structure that is also carved from the rocky hillside. The reference to Absalom stems from a Medieval Jewish tradition that refers to 2 Samuel 18:18. This monument was built in the time of Herod (late first century BCE). Within the monument, there is a space for two or three burials. Behind the monument is a related tomb complex within the hillside, the so-called tomb of Jehoshaphat, which dates to the same period. While Jacobovici appeals to a late Armenian tradition that associates the Hezir tomb to James, recent archaeological work actually suggests that at some point between the late fourth and seventh centuries CE, the tomb beneath the Absalom monument may have been associated with James for the first time. The story is actually much more interesting (and complex) than Jacobovici suggests; it deserves at least a brief examination.

The attribution of names to these tombs has a long and multifaceted history.[53] Besides the most prominent appellations used in the modern tourist literature (mainly associated with Absalom, Jehoshaphat, Zechariah, and the family of Hezir), the tomb complex has also been associated at different times with a diverse cast of characters. Along with occasional references to James, the names include King Uzziah, who dwelt there when he had leprosy;[54] the tombs of the prophet Isaiah and King Hezekiah;[55] the tomb of the priest Zachariah (father of John the Baptist);[56] and the tomb of Simeon (temple priest at the circumcision of Jesus according to the Gospel of Luke) and Joseph (Jesus' father).[57] Islamic traditions have identified the complex with Ubada ibn al Samit and Shaddad ibn Aws ibn Thabit al Ansari, companions of the Prophet.[58] Although the film does not mention the late date of the James tradition, it does mention the Armenian Church tradition, which suggests that a chapel and a monastery commemorating James were built in that area of the Kidron Valley. And one learns from the film that, following the Armenian tradition, the bones in the ossuary would have been removed from this tomb in the seventh century and taken to the Church of St. James inside Jerusalem, where church tradition holds that they now reside. This is first referred to in the thirteenth minute of the film by Rev. Bishop Aris Shirvanian, Armenian Patriarchate: "Originally the bones were buried in the Kidron Valley, where there was an Armenian monastery built upon his tomb. From there his relics were moved to St. James Cathedral, where they were reburied under our main altar. So, probably, the ossuary was discarded in those early centuries, before, of course, his relics were moved from his tomb to this holy site."

To substantiate this dubious historical reconstruction, which is based on a tradition about James that developed many centuries after his death, Jacobovici abandons the typical recourse to brief scholarly interviews. He depends instead on a report of an excavation by John Allegro in 1960, in which Allegro is said by the narrator to have "uncovered pillars and tombs and the remains of an ancient chapel just where the Armenians said it should be. Various artifacts were also found, which disappeared without being catalogued or reported, perhaps an ossuary was among them."

After an unsuccessful investigation of the tombs with the modern grave robbers and antiquity dealers, the film makes an altogether astounding claim about the origins of the ossuary: it was stolen from an excavation in 1960 and sold to an antiquities dealer in Jerusalem. Jacobovici asks, "Is it possible that Allegro's workers removed the James Ossuary from the tomb of St. James during Professor Allegro's dig?" The question is followed by: "We asked his widow."

With the word "RECONSTRUCTION" printed across the screen, the viewer sees Jacobovici's final reenactment. Three men recreate the robbery of the ossuary from the 1960 excavation: they carry an empty ossuary and a lid from a valley (like the Kidron Valley area) and place the objects in the back of a Mercedes Benz 250 SE. Within the reenactment sequence,

Joan Allegro (John's widow) states: "The fact was that these Bedouin were dreadfully poor. Conditions in Jordan were pretty grim at that time, and if they could make a few bucks or shekels, or whatever, of course they would. They unearthed quite a lot of domestic products. They would take them to dealers who would give them something for them, and then they would sell them on to tourists or anybody who was interested in acquiring antiquities."

As the reenactment footage shows the three men getting in the car and driving away, the narrator summarizes the assertion:

> If the James Ossuary was found on Professor Allegro's dig, it would not have drawn much attention. In fact, it probably would have been abandoned, except that it was inscribed. Ossuaries with inscriptions were worth a few dollars and were regularly brought to shops in old Jerusalem by enterprising workmen. Seven years later during the Six-Day War, old Jerusalem passed from Jordanian to Israeli hands, becoming accessible to Israeli collectors. It is entirely plausible that the James Ossuary sat for a few more years inside Jamil's father's shop, until, as Golan claims, he bought it. All the pieces seem to fit.

There are several major problems associated with Jacobovici's solution. While it is true that artifacts have been stolen from excavation sites, that detail provides no significant or verifiable information related to this case. Joan Allegro's ideas about the economic conditions of the Bedouin in 1960s Jordan also provide no serious evidence on which to build a historical reconstruction of the origins of the ossuary. Based on the fact that John Allegro sent letters to Joan while she was back in England, it is clear that she was not actually with him during the 1960 excavation.[59] Besides, the Jacobovici film already demonstrated the fact that ancient human remains and grave goods have been pilfered from the hills around Jerusalem for many decades. Since the ossuary was purchased in the antiquities market, we already know the ossuary was stolen from an ancient tomb; this information provides no confirmation of which tomb it was taken from. Allegro's information is clearly a non sequitur in this investigation.

Regardless of the problematic nature of Joan Allegro's comment, the key difficulty with deriving any historical plausibility from this story starts with the two basic components of the reconstruction. The film combines a medieval legend with unconfirmed information from a dubious 1960s excavation—a bad combination for any serious historical investigation.

The excavation in question was, in fact, a highly publicized attempt by John Allegro to recover the "treasures of the Copper Scroll." He published the controversial text from the Dead Sea Scrolls in a much-maligned Doubleday & Company book that same year. Discovered in 1952, the Copper Scroll was cut into slices and deciphered by Allegro in Manchester, England. He believed that the scroll's text was essentially a treasure map to the "deposits of sacred material, tithe and tithe vessels, as well as silver and gold and precious vessels" from the Second Temple in Jerusalem. The scroll was "intended to tell the Jewish survivors of the war then raging [around 68–70 CE] where this sacred material lay buried."[60] Allegro not only provided a literal interpretation of the text; he also argued that he had determined the locations of the hidden treasures. He quickly raised the financial means and assembled a body of volunteers for his quest. The *Daily Mail* newspaper sponsored the expedition and received regular reports from correspondent Ralph Izzard, who was sent with Allegro.[61] With the support of the Jordanian Department of Antiquities, which provided workers, transportation, and security, he targeted six sites in the region and began excavations.

The excavation in the Kidron Valley was reported by Allegro's architect and family friend Howard E. Stutchbury in the *Palestine Exploration Quarterly* in 1961.[62] Allegro's interpretation of the Copper Scroll led him to believe that the area just west of and below the tomb of Zachariah monument was one of the locations of the treasure. By the time Allegro excavated this area, the tomb complex and monuments were already well known, with modern research having begun in 1852.[63] The famous archaeologist Nahman Avigad led a scientific exploration from 1945 to 1947 and published the material related to the Kidron Valley tombs in 1954.[64] Dan Barag conducted a major reexamination of two of the tombs in 2000–2001.[65]

The published report from Allegro's excavation mainly describes the architecture of the monument. It also provides an overview of the stairs leading up to, and the chambers beneath and around, the monument. The area they excavated and cleaned was disturbed by centuries of reuse; they report finding no ossuaries or any other artifacts from the Early Roman period. In fact, their entire project appears to have been little concerned with stratigraphic analysis; they opted instead for an expedient search through the built-up debris that lay around the monument, and they cleaned a vertical façade looking for tombs behind the monument. They did find the basic architectural remains of a small building outside of the tomb of Zachariah. Although the archaeological report does not identify those remains with any time period, the film follows a modern Armenian Church account that says these remains were part of a chapel honoring James that held his bones until the Muslim conquest of Jerusalem in the seventh century.

There are numerous Christian traditions associated with the location of the tomb of James. These traditions have been ably documented, and only a brief examination of the relevant data can be pursued in this essay.[66] The stories about the tomb of James are actually much more intriguing than Jacobovici's simple solution would have one believe. For example, one interesting story is found in a tenth-century manuscript from the library of Chartres (Cod. sign. n. 125). It tells the story of the discovery of the bones of James, the brother of Jesus, in the year 351.[67] The entire episode, if historical, must be understood within the political machinations of Cyril, the bishop of Jerusalem at the time. The story tells of an anchorite monk named Epiphanius who lived in a cave in between the Mount of Olives and the Temple Mount. He had two nocturnal visions in which James told him that the place where he was sleeping was the cave in which James was buried. Cyril initially dismissed the report when told by Epiphanius of his dreams. Later, Cyril was convinced to take the story seriously by a wealthy Christian patron named Paul from Eleutheropolis (a major Roman-Byzantine city, thirty miles southwest of Jerusalem). According to the medieval hagiographical text, bones from the cave were identified as those of James, along with the bones of Simeon and Zacharias (the two priests in the Gospel of Luke who played a role in the birth stories of Jesus). According to the tradition, on December 1, 351, Cyril took the bones of James to the Church of Mount Zion, across the Kidron Valley in Jerusalem.[68]

Two additional remarks in early Christian literature support some aspects of the story. In the middle of the fourth century, there appears to have been a debate about the place of James's tomb. There was very little speculation about the tomb of James prior to the mid-fourth century and no mention of a tomb in the pilgrim literature prior to 530 CE. The few references that exist are based on the idea that there was a marker erected immediately after James's death on the Temple Mount (historically speaking, this is extremely unlikely).[69] They are based on the assumption that James was buried at the site of his martyrdom on the southeast corner of the temple. This tradition was provided ecclesial approval when it was recorded in the *History of the Church*, written by Eusebius, the bishop of Caesarea, in the early fourth century.[70] Eusebius, following Hegesippus (his late second-century source), wrote that James was stoned and buried "by the Sanctuary [of the Temple]."[71] The idea that James was buried on the Temple Mount remained the prominent belief, as this tradition is regularly found in the extant pilgrim literature.[72]

Apparently, when Cyril "discovered" James's bones across the valley floor—or, at the very least, when some veneration of James began in the area of the Mount of Olives—this did not meet with general approval. Jerome, writing in the late fourth century, knew of a new tradition and rejected it in an offhand comment, preferring instead the location on the Temple Mount made popular by Eusebius. Concerning James, he states: "And so he [James] ruled the Church of Jerusalem thirty years that is until the seventh year of Nero, and was buried near the temple from which he had been cast down. His tombstone with its inscription was well known until the siege of Titus and the end of Hadrian's reign. Some of our writers think he was buried in the Mount of Olives, but they are mistaken."[73] Jerome's rejection of the new location suggests that he may have known of Cyril's contrivance. Of course, the tombs that are sometimes thought to be connected to James are not "in the Mount of Olives," thus we must remain uncertain about both the location of the tomb in which Epiphanius was evidently sleeping and the location of the site that Jerome rejected. At the very least, Jerome was aware that a tomb was being venerated in the Mount of Olives region.

The second relevant reference in Christian literature dates to between 518 and 538 CE, when the pilgrim Theodosius wrote corroborating information about the site of the tomb. In his travel narrative, he referred to a tomb that James had built for Saint Zacharias and Saint Simeon in the Mount of Olives.[74] He says that when James died, he was also buried in that tomb. This is the earliest mention of James's tomb in a pilgrim's journal, and despite its imprecision, the reference suggests that at least within the pilgrimage tradition of the sixth century, some visitors to the city were venerating a tomb of James.[75]

If the desire to locate James's tomb in the Mount of Olives occurred as early as the middle of the fourth century, the "discovery" of James's bones would have been a political boon for Cyril, who was actively competing for power in this part of the empire.[76] It is possible that he used this miraculous discovery of the "relics" of James to enhance his episcopal see by encouraging the veneration of James (the martyr) in the new Christian empire. If Cyril did move bones into the Holy Zion Church, it should be understood within the political and religious environment in Late Antiquity in which the veneration of relics and martyrs was extremely common.

One interesting caveat in the story was recently discovered by Joe Zias, a physical anthropologist and archaeologist who has worked on numerous sites in Israel. In 2003 Zias noticed two heavily eroded inscriptions on the tomb of Absalom.[77] As previously mentioned, for centuries the tradition about this Early Roman tomb connected it to a story in 2 Samuel 18:18. David's rebellious son Absalom is said to have erected a marker to himself in the King's Valley.[78] Through the centuries, fathers have brought their sons to the monument to pelt it with stones as a ritual remembrance of Absalom's rebellion against his father. While looking at a photo of the pockmarked monument, Zias noticed very faint writing on the surface of the monument. With much painstaking work, and the help of Emile Puech, an epigrapher, Zias was able to recover two rough Greek inscriptions. They have been translated as follows: "This is the tomb of Zachariah, martyr, very pious priest, father of John"; and "Simeon who was a very just man and a very devoted old [person] and waiting for the consolation of the people." The second is a quotation from Luke 2:25 (based on a reading from the Codex Sinaiticus).[79] The inscription has been dated to the time of Cyril in the mid-fourth century. If the date is secure, this would be the earliest known reference to Zachariah and Simeon in the Kidron Valley. And most importantly for our present interests, this provides evidence that the Christians of Cyril's day were actually venerating "Absalom's Tomb" as the tomb of Zachariah, Simeon, and James, not the tomb of Zechariah—the one that is featured in the documentary, the place where Allegro excavated in 1960. This discovery, in conjunction with the fact that early Christian pilgrims referred to the legend that Zachariah, Simeon, and James were buried in the same tomb (declared by Theodosius in the sixth century), now supports the contention that the ancient debate about the tomb of James was actually focused on this monument. There is no reason to think that Zachariah, Simeon, or James were actually buried in this monumental tomb; rather, we have evidence that provides a better idea of where the Byzantine veneration may have taken place.

As Jacobovici closes his film, he returns to a view within the St. James Cathedral in Jerusalem, where priests are performing rituals. The narrator asks, "But if this reconstruction is accurate, why don't the Armenians, who claim to have the bones of James, have a tradition about his ossuary? The answer may be hiding in plain site." The camera pans to a painting of Saint James and focuses on the top of his head. With one last attempt to persuade the audience of the validity of this investigation, the film concludes with another theory: "To the left of the throne of St. James in St. James Cathedral is a seventeenth-century portrait of James, based on a twelfth-century mural. From his high vantage point, James gazes down on the worshipers below. And there, painted on his bishop's hat, is the spirit of James rising from a box, a box that is trapezoid in shape. It is an image of James rising from an ossuary."

This is indeed a major stretch of the imagination. The box appears to be a typical twelfth-century representation of a sarcophagus or coffin that was in wide use during the late Middle Ages. Like hundreds of other artistic renditions of saints and biblical figures that date to around the twelfth century, the figure is represented as rising from a typical grave on the Day of Judgment. The reference to the trapezoid shape serves as a subtle reminder of a point earlier in the film, when it was pointed out that the ossuary is not a perfect rectangle but slightly trapezoidal. But the size of the coffin in this seventeenth-century painting corresponds to the small space that is available in the oddly shaped bishop's mitre. Once again, a glamorous thesis is presented with all the attendant visuals and sound. Evidently, the twelfth-century artist—or maybe the seventeenth century artist—saw the ossuary of James and represented it in the bishop's mitre. This is the culmination of the James Ossuary investigation according to Jacobovici. A late medieval artist has proven the case? Once again, we are left to wonder about the gullibility of the audience.

CONCLUSION: "HISTORY CHANNEL MEETS *CSI*"

The Armenian story about the bones of James that Jacobovici uses in his film is similar to many other stories about relics that are repeated in churches around the Mediterranean region. The story is loosely based on historical information. It is possible that in the Middle Ages there was a "chapel" or "monastery" of James in the Kidron Valley that was associated with the Armenian Church. It is also true that a site in the valley was thought to be the burial place of James.[80] It is true that the Armenians claim to have the bones of James in their church in Jerusalem—a building that was constructed in the twelfth century on the site that they claim is the location where James was killed.[81] Like the story of Cyril's use of James's bones in the fourth century, the Armenian Church also has a story about this relic that is primarily intended to bestow religious and political privileges on the church where the sacred objects have been deposited. All of the Armenian Church traditions should be respected as interesting facets of the medieval and modern quests for authentication; they are well worth studying. But Jacobovici's general thesis is implausible. There is no credible evidence that suggests that the tomb where Allegro excavated was really the tomb of James. For that matter, neither is there credible evidence that any known tomb in the region of Jerusalem was James's. There is also no evidence that an ossuary was stolen from Allegro's excavation in 1960 and eventually sold to Golan. Instead, when we attempt to find the tomb of James—the place where the controversial ossuary was first interred—we find a series of complex and often interwoven legends that date from the fourth century to the present.

I have attempted to demonstrate that this documentary has provided an inadequate presentation of the details surrounding the "James Ossuary phenomenon." I also hope to have conveyed some of the undisclosed aspects of the story that should truly make it compelling. The often implausible nature of Jacobovici's narrative is actually overshadowed by the intriguing characters (including the modern scholars who appear in the film) and storylines that are either ignored or quickly dismissed in the film. I have taken Jacobovici's film seriously because it is clear from conversations with neighbors, students, family, and friends that much of the information they have about biblical archaeology—including their knowledge of this ossuary—is from television documentaries. A microcosmic analysis of this genre has demonstrated that there is a great difference between a documentary and a typical scholarly process.

If Jacobovici's film is typical of the genre, then the common form of presenting archaeological material related to the Bible in the documentary film medium is not commensurate with good scholarship. It is not conducive to complicated or multifaceted issues. The need to solve a mystery in less than one hour outweighs the need to fully demonstrate the complex nature of the case at hand. There is no desire or ability to thoroughly explore issues related to the provenance and date of the artifact. Scholars are used only to propel the narrative forward; there is no desire to actually disclose how they formulated their ideas. In many cases, scholars are seen suggesting ideas that may not fully correspond to their actual thoughts on the matter (for example, the use of Eisenman in this film). There is no room for the possibility that clear and persuasive answers might not be forthcoming. In fifty minutes Jacobovici, the film's producer, writer, and director, has to solve the mystery. This is not unlike the simplicity (and appeal) of a television drama. In fact, *Washington Post* television critic Lonnae O'Neal Parker provides an apt description of *James: Brother of Jesus*, which makes this very point. A part of her statement is condensed and featured on the DVD cover of the documentary: "Riveting. . . . History Channel meets *CSI*." Writing from the perspective of a television critic reviewing a show for a wide public audience, she must judge the value of watching this one-hour program. The film has met her approval; it is an appealing hour of television. The full quote is instructive.

> *James: Brother of Jesus* is the History Channel meets *CSI*. It was produced by Simcha Jacobovici, a Jewish filmmaker whose work has explored biblical themes and who won Emmys for documentaries on the Ebola virus and the child sex trade in India. The documentary calls upon academics and historians, experts in ancient Aramaic, and translators of the Dead Sea Scrolls to argue and counterargue. It introduces us to the underbelly of the Middle Eastern antiquities market—to tomb robbers and scientists who pack handguns. It is a fascinating mystery that will most especially appeal to those who require the help of science to walk by faith.[82]

After examining several of the claims that the film makes and exploring in more detail the work of several scholars who appear in the film, there is no doubt that there are many fascinating mysteries in the story of the James Ossuary. But many of the most intriguing aspects of the story have been overlooked, while the "investigation" has focused on solving the mystery in one hour or less. The mystery of whether there was a tomb of James is highly captivating. The full scientific investigation of the ossuary inscription is also instructive and rather fascinating, as are the scholarly theories about who James was and what role he played in the formation of Christianity. These are decidedly interesting topics. But in the film, most of the complex background stories are ignored, and an implausible historical reconstruction is built up as the solution to the mystery of the ossuary.

Jacobovici may have been unaware of the wonderful stories and interesting scholarship that was associated with his topic. This essay has not followed those stories down all possible paths. But the unfinished nature of the scholarly quest is a key component that distinguishes the intellectual adventure from the perfunctory nature of the modern biblical-archaeology documentary.

NOTES

1. Jim Bawden, "A Little Box with a Big History," *Starweek Magazine* (*Toronto Star*), April 19–26, 2003.

2. This statement appears on the back cover of the DVD case and was originally used in promotional material that appeared on the Discovery Channel website.

3. Jan Willem Drijvers, *Helena Augusta: The Mother of Constantine the Great and Her Finding of the True Cross* (Leiden: Brill, 1992).

4. The history of the debate is discussed in James K. Hoffmeier and Alan Millard, eds., *The Future of Biblical Archaeology: Reassessing Methodologies and Assumptions* (Grand Rapids, Mich.: Eerdmans Publishing, 2004).

5. For example, in March 2006 the president of the Discovery Channel announced that he was hiring Josh Bernstein to develop more programming on biblical archaeology for his network.

6. On the definition and popular perception of "documentary," see Dirk Eitzen, "When Is a Documentary? Documentary as a Mode of Reception," *Cinema Journal* 35, no. 1 (1995): 81–102.

7. The idea of the "documentary" as "objective history" has been critiqued by numerous scholars. For an insightful overview, see Paula Rabinowitz, "Wreckage upon Wreckage: History, Documentary, and the Ruins of Memory," *History and Theory* 32, no. 2 (1993): 119–37.

8. See the historical overview and critique of the documentary genre in Brian Winston, *Lies, Damn Lies, and Documentaries* (London: British Film Institute, 2000), 9–59.

9. Jack C. Ellis and Betsy A. McLane, *A New History of Documentary Film* (New York: Continuum, 2005), 57–76.

10. Derek Paget, *No Other Way to Tell It: Dramadoc/Docudrama on Television* (Manchester, England: Manchester University Press, 1998), 117.

11. Ellis and McLane, *A New History of Documentary Film.*

12. Thomas A. Mascaro, "Documentary," The Museum of Broadcast Communications, <http://www.museum.tv/archives/etv/D/htmlD/documentary/documentary.htm> (August 2007).

13. Richard Krolik, "Cinéma Vérité: Documentary Television, and How It Grew

with Robert Drew," *Television Quarterly* 28, no. 2 (1996): 68–75; P. J. O'Connell, *Robert Drew and Cinéma Vérité in America* (Carbondale: Southern Illinois University, 1992).

14. Thomas A. Mascaro, *Lowering the Voice of Reason: The Decline of Network Television Documentaries in the Reagan Years* (Ph.D. diss., Wayne State University, 1994).

15. *Frontline*'s policies are available on their website: <http://www.pbs.org/wgbh/pages/frontline/us/guidelines.html> (August 2007).

16. Although Burns has faced significant criticism; see the very insightful critique of Burns's historical enterprise, especially related to his film *Not for Ourselves Alone* (1999), in Vivien Ellen Rose and Julie Corley, "A Trademark Approach to the Past: Ken Burns, the Historical Profession, and Assessing Popular Presentations of the Past," *Public Historian* 25 (2003): 49–59.

17. See the reviews of the film in Robert Brent Toplin, ed., *Ken Burns's* The Civil War*: Historians Respond* (New York: Oxford University Press), 1996. The essays in Toplin's volume are mostly positive, though the reviews of this book suggested that the authors did not go far enough in their critiques of Burns's idea of history. For example, see David W. Blight, "Homer with a Camera, Our Iliad without the Aftermath: Ken Burns's Dialogue with Historians," *Reviews in American History* 25, no. 2 (1997): 351–59.

18. The documentary was produced by Marilyn Mellowes and directed by William Cran. The film has an excellent website that provides transcripts of the interviews with scholars, maps, photos, and additional information about the topic: <http://www.pbs.org/wgbh/pages/frontline/shows/religion/> (June 2007).

19. L. Michael White is the director of the Institute for the Study of Antiquity and Christian Origins in the Classics Department at the University of Texas at Austin. An interview with White about his involvement in the production of the documentary and the complex process of developing the film can be found on the *Frontline* website: <http://www.pbs.org/wgbh/pages/frontline/shows/religion/etc/behind.html> (August 2007).

20. A&E (The Arts and Entertainment Network) began in 1984 and the Discovery Channel began in 1985.

21. Jill Godmilow and Ann-Louise Shapiro, "How Real Is the Reality in Documentary Film?," *Producing the Past: Making Histories Inside and Outside the Academy, History and Theory*, special issue, 36, no. 4 (1997): 80–101.

22. For an excellent critique of Flaherty's *Nanook of the North* and other documentary films, see Jared F. Green, "This Reality Which Is Not One: Flaherty, Buñuel, and the Irrealism of Documentary Cinema," in *Docufictions: Essays on the Intersection of Documentary and Fictional Filmmaking*, ed. Gary D. Rhodes and John Parris Springer (London: McFarland & Company, 2006), 64–87.

23. The comparison is highlighted by Leigh H. Edwards in "Chasing the Real: Reality Television and Documentary Forms," in *Docufictions: Essays on the Intersection of Documentary and Fictional Filmmaking*, ed. Gary D. Rhodes and John Parris Springer (London: McFarland & Company, 2006), 253–69.

24. Gregory Currie, "Visible Traces: Documentary and the Contents of Photographs," *Journal of Aesthetics and Art Criticism* 57, no. 3 (1999): 285–97.

25. By the end of 2006, National Geographic produced ten episodes totaling 533 minutes of footage. The series was produced by James Younger.

26. The story of Jacobovici being given the exclusive rights to film the ossuary was told in several newspaper reports in 2003. See, for example, Tony Atherton, "Film Tells Dramatic Tale of St. James Ossuary," CanWest News Service, April 14, 2003.

27. The review published in the *New York Times* ("Leaning on Theory, Colliding with Faith," March 3, 2007) has an apt description by Alessandra Stanley: "*The Lost Tomb of Jesus* is enjoyable, mostly because it is scripted like a cryptology treasure hunt and centered on the Indiana Jones–like persona of Simcha Jacobovici, an Israeli-born filmmaker based in Toronto, whose recent documentary *The Exodus Decoded*, on the History Channel, argued that the Jews really did flee Egypt by parted sea. (But in 1500 BC, a century or so earlier than most scholars suggest.)"

28. I have attempted to provide an accurate description of the narration and interviews in the film, based on the DVD version that was released in 2004 by Wellspring Media, Inc.

29. "Comments of Frank Moore Cross," <http://www.biblicalarchaeology.org/bswbOOossuary_HSALFMC.asp> (June 24, 2003).

30. Jacobovici appears to be fond of the claim that history will be rewritten. The book title of Jacobovici's recent project is *The Jesus Family Tomb: The Discovery, the Investigation, and the Evidence That Could Change History*.

31. Robert Eisenman, *James the Brother of Jesus: The Key to Unlocking the Secrets of Early Christianity and the Dead Sea Scrolls* (New York: Penguin Books, 1997).

32. Michael Drosnin's *The Bible Code* (New York: Simon and Schuster, 1997) is much less sophisticated, but the basic principle of hidden messages in letter or word combinations still applies.

33. Robert H. Eisenman and James M. Robinson, *A Facsimile Edition of the Dead Sea Scrolls*, 2 vols. (Washington, D.C.: Biblical Archaeology Society, 1992).

34. Robert Eisenman and Michael Wise, *The Dead Sea Scrolls Uncovered: The First Complete Translation and Interpretation of 50 Key Documents Withheld for Over 35 Years* (New York: Penguin Books, 1993).

35. Michael Baigent and Richard Leigh, *The Dead Sea Scrolls Deception* (New York: Simon and Schuster, 1991).

36. A second volume by Eisenman on the same topic was announced in *James*

the Brother of Jesus and has now been published as *The New Testament Code: The Cup of the Lord, the Damascus Covenant, and the Blood of Christ* (London: Watkins Books, 2006).

37. Barbara Thiering has also published popular books on Jesus and the Dead Sea Scrolls. Similar to Eisenman, her conclusions and methodology are almost universally rejected by scholars in the relevant fields of study. Like Eisenman, she works with the theory that the extant Christian and Jewish literature from the first and second centuries is full of symbolic meaning that, when interpreted correctly, reveals that Jesus survived the cross, was married, had children, and divorced. Thiering's major blockbuster was published in the United States by HarperCollins (*Jesus and the Riddle of the Dead Sea Scrolls: Unlocking the Secrets of His Life Story* [New York: HarperCollins, 1992]).

38. Richard N. Ostling, "Burial Box Inscription Could Be Oldest Archaeological Link to Jesus," Associated Press, October 21, 2002.

39. Abraham McLaughlin, "Ancient 'Bone Box' May Be Earliest Link to Jesus," *Christian Science Monitor*, October 22, 2002.

40. Michael Kilian, "Not an Open or Shut Case," *Daily Telegraph* (Sydney, Australia), October 26, 2002.

41. Sally Mclean, "Did Box Contain Christ's Brother?," *Glasgow Daily Record*, April 19, 2003.

42. Judith Sudilovsky, "Scholars Cautious about Jesus Link," Catholic News Service, November 10, 2002.

43. John Painter, *Just James: The Brother of Jesus in History and Tradition* (Minneapolis: Fortress Press, 1999), 6.

44. John Painter, *Just James: The Brother of Jesus in History and Tradition*, 2nd ed. (Columbia: University of South Carolina, 2003).

45. Ibid., 271.

46. Ibid., 272.

47. Ibid., 324.

48. Hershel Shanks and Ben Witherington III, *The Brother of Jesus: The Dramatic Story and Meaning of the First Archaeological Link to Jesus and His Family* (San Francisco: HarperSanFrancisco, 2003), 91–92.

49. Ben Witherington III, "Top Ten New Testament Archaeological Finds of the Past 150 Years: How Do Shrouds, Boats, Inscriptions, and Other Artifacts Better Help Us Understand the Christ of the Ages?," *Christianity Today*, <http://www.christianitytoday.com/ct/2003/septemberweb-only/9-22-21.0.html> (September 1, 2003).

50. Shanks and Witherington, *The Brother of Jesus*, 219. *The Protoevangelium of James* is an early Christian text that discusses the miraculous births of Mary and Jesus and is considered the earliest narrative that refers to the idea that Mary was a

perpetual virgin. See Ronald F. Hock, *The Infancy Gospels of James and Thomas: With Introduction, Notes, and Original Text Featuring the New Scholars Version Translation* (Santa Rosa, Calif.: Polebridge Press, 1996).

51. The major archaeological report (written in Hebrew) is Nahman Avigad, *Ancient Monuments in the Kidron Valley* (Jerusalem: Bialik Institute, 1954).

52. The inscription reads: "This is the tomb and the monument [*nefesh*] of Alexander, Hanniah, Yo'ezer, Judah, Simon, Johanan, the sons of Joseph, son of Oved. Joseph and Eliezer sons of Hanniah—priests of the Hezir family."

53. A majority of the pilgrimage literature from which several of the attributions derive is surveyed in Félix Marie Abel, "La Sépulture de saint Jacques le Mineur," *Revue Biblique* 28 (1919): 480–99. On the more general topic of the identification of "holy" sites by Byzantine Christians, see Peter W. L. Walker, *Holy City, Holy Places? Christian Attitudes to Jerusalem and the Holy Land in the Fourth Century* (Oxford: Clarendon Press, 1990). Regarding the identification of "holy sites" during the Crusader period, see Adrian J. Boas, *Jerusalem in the Time of the Crusades: Society, Landscape, and Art in the Holy City under Frankish Rule* (London and New York: Routledge, 2001).

54. A medieval Jewish tradition based on 2 Chron. 24:20–21.

55. The Pilgrim of Bordeaux, a Christian traveler from France, traveled to Jerusalem ca. 333 CE. He left the oldest extant Christian pilgrim's chronicle of the region. He did not mention any sites associated with James. He did report that in the Valley of Jehoshaphat, before ascending the Mount of Olives, "on the left is a vineyard where is also the rock where Judas Iscariot betrayed Christ; and on the right is the palm-tree from which the children took branches and strewed them in Christ's path. Near by, about a stone's throw away, are two memorial tombs of beautiful workmanship. One of them, formed from a single rock, is where the prophet Isaiah was laid, and in the other lies Hezekiah, king of the Jews" (*Itinerarium Burdigalense*, 594–95; in John Wilkinson, *Egeria's Travels to the Holy Land: Newly Translated with Supporting Documents and Notes* [Oxford: Aris and Phillips, 2006], 31–32). More generally, see David Satran, *Biblical Prophets in Byzantine Palestine: Reassessing the* Lives of the Prophets, Studia in Veteras Testamenti Pseudipigrapha, no. 11 (Leiden: Brill, 1995).

56. Sir John Maundeville (fourteenth-century English traveler) refers to a single place where Saint James and Zacharias were buried.

57. For example, *Sæwulf* (travel narrative written in 1102) and *Arculf* (ca. 670) refer to the tombs of Simeon and Joseph (Mary's husband).

58. The Islamic attribution can be found in the work of the late tenth-century geographer from Jerusalem, Muhammad ibn Ahmad Shams al-Din Al-Muqaddasi ("Description of Syria and Palestine," *Palestine Pilgrims' Text Society*, vol. 3, 49–50).

59. The correspondence has been used recently by John and Joan Allegro's daughter to tell a sympathetic story of his life and work. See Judith Anne Brown,

John Marco Allegro: The Maverick of the Dead Sea Scrolls (Grand Rapids, Mich.: William B. Eerdmans, 2005); regarding the 1960 expedition, see 113–33.

60. John Allegro, *The Treasure of the Copper Scroll: The Opening and Decipherment of the Most Mysterious of the Dead Sea Scrolls, a Unique Inventory of Buried Treasure* (Garden City, N.Y.: Doubleday and Company, 1960), 62.

61. Brown, *John Marco Allegro*, 120.

62. Howard E. Stutchbury, "Excavations in the Kidron Valley," *Palestine Exploration Quarterly* 93 (1961): 101–13.

63. Titus Tobler, *Topographie von Jerusalem* 2 (Berlin: Reimer, 1853). A summary of the excavation activities in this area is found in Amos Kloner and Boaz Zissu, *The Necropolis of Jerusalem in the Second Temple Period*, Interdisciplinary Studies in Ancient Culture and Religion 8 (Leuven: Peeters, 2007), 241–51.

64. Avigad, *Ancient Monuments*.

65. Dan Barag, "The 2000–2001 Exploration of the Tombs of Benei Hezir and Zechariah," *Israel Exploration Journal* 53, no. 1 (2003): 78–110.

66. Most importantly, see Abel, "La Sépulture de saint Jacques le Mineur"; Yaron Z. Eliav, "The Tomb of James, Brother of Jesus, as *Locus Memoriae*," *Harvard Theological Review* 97, no. 1 (2004): 33–59; and Painter, *Just James*, 2nd ed.

67. A French translation of the text can be found in Abel, "La Sépulture de saint Jacques le Mineur." See the description and interpretation in Jan Willem Drijvers, *Cyril of Jerusalem: Bishop and City*, Supplements to Vigiliae Christianae (Leiden: Brill, 2004), 163–64. The tradition is also mentioned in L. Y. Rahmani, "Ancient Jerusalem's Funerary Customs and Tombs: Part Three," *Biblical Archaeologist* 45, no. 1 (1982): 43–53.

68. Construction of the Church of Mount Zion was undertaken in 340 CE by Maximus, bishop of Jerusalem. It was a massive structure, as is suggested by its size on the Madaba Map and in the pilgrimage reports. Destroyed by the Persians in 614, it was rebuilt in the late seventh century, only to be destroyed again in 966.

69. Regardless of any historical plausibility that scholars might attribute to the story of Hegesippus concerning the place of James's death, by 70 CE the entire temple area had been completely destroyed. It is very unlikely that any marker survived this catastrophe.

70. It should be noted that in the time of Eusebius as well as Cyril, the Episcopal see in Jerusalem was under the authority and in competition with the Bishopric of Caesarea. See Walker, *Holy City, Holy Places?*, 311–401.

71. The full story is found in Eusebius, *History of the Church*, 2.23:4–18. For a thorough discussion of the passage, see Painter, *Just James*, 2nd ed., 119–30. There is no reason to think that James ever had a tomb on the Temple Mount next to the sanctuary. The story can best be explained as part of Hegesippus's (and Eusebius's) connection of the death of James to the fall of Jerusalem.

72. Two twelfth-century pilgrim narratives explicitly mention that a "Chapel of

James" had been built in the area of the Temple Mount (not in the Kidron Valley). John of Würzburg (ca. 1165–1170, "Descriptio Terrae Sanctae") and Theodoricus (ca. 1172, "Libellus de Locis Sanctis") mention that James was buried at the site of the chapel, which, from their descriptions, must have been close to the present site of the Dome of the Chain (a small dome next to the Dome of the Rock). See John Wilkinson, Joyce Hill, and W. F. Ryan, eds., *Jerusalem Pilgrimage, 1099–1185*, Works Issued by the Hakluyt Society, 2nd ser. 167 (London: Hakluyt Society, 1988).

73. Saint Jerome, *On Illustrious Men*; in *The Fathers of the Church*, trans. Thomas P. Halton (Washington, D.C.: The Catholic University of America Press, 1999), 8.

74. *De situ Terrae sanctae*, 9; in John Wilkinson, *Jerusalem Pilgrims before the Crusade*, rev. ed. (Oxford: Aris & Phillips, 2003), 186–92. On the pilgrim travel narratives of Theodosius, see Yoram Tsafrir, "The Maps Used by Theodosius: On the Pilgrim Maps of the Holy Land and Jerusalem in the Sixth Century C.E.," *Dumbarton Oaks Papers* 40 (1986): 129–45.

75. Tsafrir doubts that the references to "the Mount of Olives" (*in monte Oliveti*) by Jerome and Theodosius are the same as the tomb locations in the Kidron Valley ("Valley of Jehoshaphat") ("The Maps Used by Theodosius," 45, n. 44).

76. Drijvers, *Cyril of Jerusalem*.

77. For useful news reports of the story, see Ben Lynfield, "New Find, Old Tomb, and Peaks at Early Christians," *Christian Science Monitor*, December 18, 2003; and Peter Nathan, "Written in Stone," *Visions: Insights and New Horizons* (Summer 2004), <http://www.vision.org/visionmedia/article.aspx?id=910> (June 2007).

78. The first known connection of Absalom to the monument is found in a twelfth-century travel narrative; see Marcus Nathan Adler, ed. and trans., *The Itinerary of Rabbi Benjamin of Tudela* (New York: Philipp Feldheim, 1907). Upon descending into the Valley of Jehoshaphat, he reports: "Here is the pillar called Absalom's Hand, and the sepulcher of King Uzziah" (37).

79. The reference to Zachariah most likely stems from a conflation of a story from Josephus with the story from the Gospel of Luke. Josephus tells of a man named Zachariah ("the son of Baris, one of the most eminent of the citizens") who was killed and thrown into the Kidron Valley ca. 70 CE, just prior to the Jewish War against Rome (Josephus, *The Jewish War*, books 3–4 [Loeb Classical Library no. 487], trans. H. St. J. Thackeray [Cambridge, Mass.: Harvard University Press, 1997], 225). Luke's story does not fit Josephus's chronology, nor does the Zacharias in Luke have any connection to the Kidron. Their names and stories were conflated at some point in late antiquity; Zachariah became a martyr whose body was thrown into the Kidron Valley.

80. The Armenian "monastery" may be suggested by John Phocas, a twelfth-century monk from the Island of Patmos. He mentions "an Iberian monk" who was living in what must have been the tomb of Absalom. The monk "shut himself up and is working out his own salvation." On the hillside next to the monk, Phocas

mentions, a few Orthodox and a large number of Armenian and Jacobite monks were living in artificial grottos (*Palestine Pilgrims' Text Society*, vol. 5, 22–23). Kevork Hintlian argues that several other medieval stories suggest Armenian connections to the Kidron Valley (*History of the Armenians in the Holy Land* [Jerusalem: St. James, 1976]).

81. For information about the Church of Saint James, see Nurith Kenaan-Kedar, "Armenian Architecture in 12th-Century Jerusalem," *Assaph Studies in Art History* 3 (1998): 77–91.

82. Lonnae O'Neal Parker, "Resurrecting Interest in Jesus's Brother," *Washington Post*, April 19, 2003.

RYAN BYRNE

Anatomy of a Cargo Cult

Virginity, Relic Envy, and Hallowed Boxes

Stabat mater dolorosa
iuxta Cistam lacrimosa,
dum pendebat Filius
—Nontraditional

WOMEN AND CHILDREN FIRST

The box reads, "Yaʿaqob son of Yosef, brother of Yeshua." The epigraph is a statement and, like most statements, is vulnerable to what Roland Barthes described as the "death of author." The James Ossuary has entered into our popular lexicon not only for what it says, but also for what its interpreters say it says. When the Royal Ontario Museum (ROM) hurriedly designed its display, the duress of time required the stagers to focus on the inscribed words. The ossuary's words, painted stark white and translated into different languages, adorned the walls encircling the central altar on which the heavily insured cargo rested. With divinized words, the box became logocentric in a way that was strangely both Derridean and Johannine at the same time. The *logos* had incarnated and received well-wishers as though it had become *sarx*. The museum exhibit itself even resembled a church.

Ever present but decorously taciturn during these proceedings was the mother of these two brothers. The suffering matron standing over the cold limestone box of her deceased son cuts an indelible image, though not nearly as indelible in Christian art as that of Mary, *mater dolorosa*, attending the crucifixion of her other son and cleansing his perforated corpse. Consequently, no one bothered to cultivate this image. Amidst the media hype and interdenominational polemics about perpetual virginity and biological fraternity, Mary had scarcely a private occasion to mourn Jacob. Of the many dimensions of historical interest the media might have chosen to emphasize, it was the sexuality of Mary on which they ultimately zeroed in; it was Mary who suffered most in the public spotlight. The publicity about the ossuary pushed buttons, especially those of Catholics and Protestants entangled in a centuries-long dispute about Mary's postpartum sex life, but they were buttons already there to be pushed.

A DISCOURSE OF VIRGINITY

The ossuary's unveiling produced chatter of equal parts elation, vitriol, and negligence. Emotions ran high, or at least higher than is customary for garden-variety, five-word Semitic inscriptions. The ossuary's toadies and detractors did not manufacture the disputes about Mary's sex life. They preexisted on a discursive switchboard principally devoted to the regulation of what Michel Foucault called biopower. Biopower determines what is private and what is public; it invents private life in a sense.[1] It concerns not only how institutions and cultures influence the body, sexuality, personhood, and the self, but also how "statements" (the units of discourse) privilege knowledge as the principal implement of control over the individual. What our culture knows (or believes it knows) about its present and ancestral proprietary interests in virginity, maternity, and femininity largely informs how surprised many were to find their hackles raised by five words inscribed in stone perhaps only a year earlier. Rear-guard modernists overlook the logocentric caveat at their peril.

When semiotician and psychoanalyst Julia Kristeva gave birth to a son in 1976, she perceived a discursive conundrum in her new experiences as a mother. For nearly two millennia, Kristeva argues, the West has incarnated the essentialism of femininity in the maternal ideal.[2] This imagined coextensivity finds purchase not only in representations (sacral, poetic, aesthetic) of the feminine as the mother, but also, more significantly, in the wholesale sublimation of woman into progenitress. While there are clear, and sadly unclear, consequences for the valuation of women on their own terms as a result of this sublimation, Kristeva is insistent that the maternal emphasis principally facilitates a fantasy, namely, "the idealization of the *relationship* that binds us to her, one that cannot be localized." Christianity had invested this fantasy in the cult of the Virgin Mary, who personified not only the maternal ideal to whom mere mortals could cleave and in whom human mothers could draw strength, but also the very "fulcrum of the humanization of the West in general and of love in particular." As a new mother, however, Kristeva could not discern a constructive discourse of maternity surviving the dilution of the cult of the Virgin Mary. Second-wave feminism had by the late 1970s driven a wedge between the once coterminous woman and mother, but it had hardly destroyed traditional acceptance of, or comfort with, the conventions of female representation.

Where was the new discourse, which would permit participants in this new landscape of diverse reproductive perspectives to discuss or measure the new femininities, maternities, and sexualities? Kristeva did not see a coherent discourse arising from the ashes of Mariology, and she found her own motherhood complicated by indescribable love for an infant "other" without a rubric to harmonize the seemingly irreconcilable instincts of selflessness and alienation. Third-wave feminism has made some attempt over the last generation to construct the kind of postvirginal discourse for which Kristeva called over thirty years ago, although many disagree whether this discourse has achieved the kind of constructive coherence she envisioned.

In "Stabat Mater," Kristeva dramatizes the bifurcation of the self, the subject in crisis, with dual essays on the historical decline of cultic Mariology and her own new psychoanalytic experiences with childbirth and motherhood after the birth of her son in 1976. She credits the splitting of her psyche to the failure of Western culture to produce a postvirginal (i.e., post-Mariological) discourse in which discussions of maternity harmonized the disjunction of body and ambition with the sudden utopian project of parenthood. With maternity no longer the preeminent sociobiological teleology imagined for Western women, there resulted an aporia informed by the collision of the Western inertia of maternal objectives and the uncharted plasticity of engendered individualization. What is fascinating about Kristeva's emphasis on Mary is the divine paradox of the virgin mother serving as the caretaker of Christendom's men and women alike, a kind of Madonna complex writ large.

Of course, the perceived need for a postvirginal discourse admits of a long-standing virginal discourse, which late modernity either dilutes or complicates. Foucault envisioned a valence for discourse that was quite different from the conventional definition in intellectual history. Rather than inferring meaning from essentialized propositions and utterances, Foucault understood these cultural "statements" as the units that established the basic parameters and rules of discourse, how we communicate and miscommunicate meaning, intention, and value. The specific "statements," which will govern the mechanics of discourse, in turn find definition in the *épistème* of the culture in question. Foucault's decision to privilege *épistème* over some surrogate framework like *Zeitgeist* highlights his observation that historically specific epistemologies accommodate organically commensurate statements: axioms, theorems, speech acts, and the like. Locutions reflect not only what we know, but also what we do not know. Disjunctions within discourse are especially noteworthy, prompting Foucault to emphasize the role of *events* as prominent statements. We find such disjunctive evidence for our long-standing discourse of virginity in three notable events and their attendant pretexts and feedback.

The First Event

In 1987, after receiving a spate of hate mail condemning her Greek textual criticism, Professor Jane Schaberg of the University of Detroit Mercy found her car engulfed in flames.[3] Schaberg had recently published a book on the infancy narratives of Jesus in which she challenged whether the canonical Greek texts indeed made a philologically unequivocal claim for Mary's virginity at the time of her son's conception.[4] The language of the Synoptic Gospels, Schaberg argued, allowed for fairly elastic interpretation with respect to the claims of virginal conception traditionalized by the Church Fathers of the Patristic period. More plausible for first-century Jewish Christian mores, and philologically consistent with the textual criticism, was an illegitimate pregnancy that engendered an etiological tautology of divine insemination accompanying the popular spread of the Jesus movement. Schaberg's book appeared at a time when New Testament scholars were particularly interested in reviewing the evidence for the historicity of the infancy narratives. And while Schaberg's thesis was narratologically controversial—it is easier to imagine a Mediterranean personality cult with a formulaic mortal/god copulation etiology in fact producing contrarian suspicions of illegitimacy than vice versa—she nevertheless took the Marian pregnancy at face value historically. One would think her book, *The Illegitimacy of Jesus*, would land her squarely in the middle of scholarly debate. In 1973 Raymond Brown, a Catholic priest and august text critic, had written a monograph dealing seriously with the ways in which modern biblical criticism required scholars to reexamine the traditional understanding of the Virgin Birth in the light of modern historiographic methods.[5] Ultimately, however, Brown concluded his study by privileging an ecumenical framework of Christological common ground in which the virginal conception took primacy over the Virgin Birth. He refused the empirical historical evidence to permit him to offer a definitive conclusion, preferring instead to shift responsibility to theologians and the ecumenical laity for open debate.

Five years later, Brown assembled a colloquium of Catholic and Protestant biblicists to examine the role of Mary in the early Christian movement, the results of which symposium produced a volume that further invigorated the historical reinvestigation of the canonical infancy narratives.[6] The results of this volume likewise threw the historical question to individual faith communities to settle the matter according to their doctrinal predilections. No matter how plausible or implausible the argument, one would think that a serious book like Schaberg's (with a defensible thesis proffered in place of an ecumenical shrug) would stimulate commensurately serious discussion among scholars. This was not the case. *The Illegitimacy of Jesus* did not generate the text-critical talk it should have within a guild ostensibly taken with that very thing. In the second edition of *The Birth of the Messiah*, Brown rejected Schaberg's proposal not on the basis of the philology (i.e., the closest thing to empirical evidence), but rather on his disbelief that the infancy narratives might bear a meaning at odds with the meaning they held for the early church.[7] Contrariwise, Schaberg did influence the thinking of Bishop John Shelby Spong, who became something of an advocate of her interpretation when he published a popular book on the Virgin Birth.[8] At the end of the day, neither Brown nor Spong critically dealt with the textual reading of *The Illegitimacy of Jesus*, which entered into the popular readership (to the extent that it was read, rather than reviled sight unseen) stigmatized as offensive, lightweight, feminist tripe. The results? Hate mail, collegial marginalization, condemnation from then-Archbishop Adam Maida, and an automobile ignited with the glow of hatred.

The Second Event

On June 30, 2006, Dutch prime minister Jan Peter Balkenende submitted the resignation of his parliamentary cabinet to Queen Beatrix, effectively bringing down the incumbent government coalition constituting the second Balkenende cabinet. The government had endured a fatal public relations disaster concerning the manner in which its minister for immigration had handled the citizenship status of Ayaan Hirsi Ali, a member of the Dutch parliament and an increasingly famous champion of women's rights and Islamic reform. Hirsi Ali, a native Somalian, applied for Dutch asylum in 1992 to escape an arranged marriage to an unfamiliar relative. In a decade's time, she had earned a master's degree and become a minor member of Balkenende's ruling coalition. Her citizenship status eventually came under scrutiny when she revealed that she had lied about her surname and age in her application for asylum. It was Hirsi Ali's controversial discussion of what she called the "virginity doctrine," however, that precipitated scrutiny of her asylum's legitimacy and a botched ministerial investigation of her citizenship. Claims of political bias ensued, and the resulting fracas damaged public perception of the government's integrity beyond repair until it imploded under withering criticism. Hirsi Ali came to prominence in the Netherlands less as a member of parliament, however, than as an outspoken critic of male proprietorship of women in Islam. She wrote political essays, gave controversial interviews about Mohammed, and cowrote a screenplay with filmmaker Theo van Gogh called *Submission: Part 1* in 2004—the same year in which *De Maagdenkooi*, her collection of essays decrying the sexual captivity of women, was published. *Submission* aired on Dutch television in 2004, depicting degraded Muslim women (with misogynistic Koranic verses on their bodies) recounting their lives to Allah.[9] The film outraged several members of the Dutch Muslim community. On November 2, 2004, a gunman murdered van Gogh in Amsterdam, impaling a note into his chest claiming that Hirsi Ali would die next. She immediately went into hiding amid a flurry of other threats.

Hirsi Ali has since extensively articulated the virginity doctrine, that is, an "obsession with mastery over the sexuality of women" as the expression of moral dogma. "The value attached to a woman's virginity is so great that it eclipses the human catastrophes and social costs that result from it," Hirsi Ali writes. Speaking of conservative Islam in particular, she draws attention to the intact hymen as the cultural determinant not only of virginity but also of the female's social worth and her family's icon of honor. The premarital rupture of the hymen, whether by accident, consensual defloration, or rape, may bring punishments ranging from expulsion or confinement to forced marriage or honor killing. Preventative measures in some cultures are equally grim: house arrest, sequestration, or female circumcision.

At the age of five, Hirsi Ali herself suffered preventative measures, restrained by her grandmother while a strange man removed her labia and clitoris with a pair of scissors. Over the objections of Hirsi Ali's more progressive parents, who were absent at the time, the grandmother oversaw the ritual to safeguard her integrity for marriage.[10]

The efforts of some countries to crack down on female circumcision have met with mixed results. Even vigilant bans do not always meet with unqualified success in some countries. "Zero tolerance against female genital mutilation will not help unless you really discuss the sexual morality on which it rests," Hirsi Ali laments. "Pretty much like the veil. You have to tackle questions such as virginity."[11] In other words, criminalization of mutilation without systemic reforms of cultural dogma will treat the symptoms of the problem with disregard for the disease, which will remain unchallenged throughout the cultural body.[12] Hirsi Ali clearly outlines a *discourse*, something indirectly prescriptive, moreover, which thrives with dire consequences underwritten by epistemic oversight or omission. What we do not talk about is not always the surest indicator of what we do not know, but what we do not talk about is often more consequential than what we do talk about.

The Third Event

In 2002 a simple limestone box cut a swath through newspaper and Internet headlines en route from a private residence in Tel Aviv to a public museum-cum-shrine in Toronto. Soon after the public unveiling of the James Ossuary, Hershel Shanks and Ben Witherington III concluded a contract with HarperSanFrancisco to pen *The Brother of Jesus*, a companion book of sorts to complement the ossuary's publicity campaign in the pages of *Biblical Archaeology Review*.[13] Shanks, the publisher of the review, wrote the first half of the book, which focused mainly on Oded Golan's purchase of the ossuary and Andre Lemaire's decipherment. Witherington, a conservative Protestant New Testament scholar at Asbury Theological Seminary, wrote the second half of the book, which introduced the biblical character of James and his significance for the early Christian movement. Witherington begins his disquisition with encomiastic words for an object that permitted Christians to experience the historical Jesus tactilely through the sensory transubstantiation; seeing the box allowed them to "touch" Jesus.[14] Toward the closing section, after somewhat careful historical examination of the significance of Jesus' nuclear family for the early Christian movement, Witherington suddenly takes occasion to explain the significance of the James discovery for modern Christianity. For Witherington, James the blood brother signifies nothing less than a victory for Protestantism over Catholicism in a dispute stretching back to the seventeenth century. This modest box of interment serves up an immodest nail in the coffin of the doctrine of Mary's perpetual virginity. "In Catholic circles, later church traditions *make* it difficult to get back to the original historical realities," he writes, "which are vital for understanding *what authentic Christianity is*."[15] Witherington offers instead a Protestant reclamation of historical reality, facilitated by this cold limestone box. Catholicism has distorted not only what Christianity originally was and who early Christian figures actually were, but it also simultaneously distorts itself as an "authentic" incarnation of Christianity. Firing a shot across the bow of Catholicism itself, Witherington indecorously implores the Vatican to reverse itself on doctrine reaffirmed as recently as the Council of Trent: "It is my understanding that the doctrine of perpetual virginity doesn't have the authority of infallibility that an ex cathedra pronouncement has in the Catholic Church, though it does have the authority of a de fidei pronouncement, that is, a declaration intrinsic to the Catholic faith. Can the matter be revisited, as have so many beliefs and practices once considered sacrosanct in the Catholic tradition?"[16]

Careful readers will appreciate the sheer oddity of such candid denominational effrontery in an ostensibly academic discussion intended to introduce a historical object to a popular readership. It is commonplace for popular publications on biblical archaeology to present facts and theories that run counter to fundamentalist readings of the biblical text. Artifacts from the biblical periods commonly sketch out new gray areas for certain faith traditions, but one would be hard-pressed to name a reputable, responsible archaeological presentation that identified denominational invalidation as the principal historical significance of an artifact. It is frankly unnecessary to do so. The occasional dissonance between archaeological discovery and textual narrative is implicitly suggestive to some as much as the occasional correlation between discovery and narrative is to others. While *The Brother of Jesus* does not explicitly claim an ecumenical or nonpartisan high ground, it is unique in this para-academic genre for its descent into an imperious theological critique of the authenticity of "church dogma in the Catholic and Orthodox traditions."[17] Witherington's historical valuation of the box is not so much its ability to recover what ancient Christianity was as much as its potential to prove what modern Christianity is not.

NOT ONLY MARY

As a devotional phenomenon and academic discipline, Mariology is almost vast enough to permit us a simple bibliographic acknowledgment of debt before proceeding to a discussion of the philology and iconography of virginity. We must tarry a bit, however, to get a sense of perspective. Partisans who see the biblical James in the James Ossuary have touted its significance as a tangible connection to the historical Jesus, definitive proof of his existence to religious communities, who ostensibly do not privilege proof over faith or evidence over belief.[18] One might assume that this box would be enough, were the inscription authentic and its original inhabitant biblical, to stir the emotions of the reticent and puritanical all by itself. But the box happened upon the tail end of a conversation spanning thousands of years, and it could not help but to chafe at the sore spots of Mariology itself.

Recounting the history of Mariology might amount to a lifetime's project.[19] Let it suffice that the infancy narratives of Matthew and Luke indicate that Mary's divine conception of Jesus during her premarital virginity[20] became an important fixture of the early Christian movement by the late first century CE. Paul's complicated promotion of chastity and discouragement of marriage in 1 Corinthians a half century earlier perhaps played some role in the acclaim for virginity among early Christians. The extent of Paul's influence during the first century (when his letters indicate disagreement with many of his correspondents) is not particularly clear, however, notwithstanding the sway his theological outlook would hold in the second to fourth centuries on the popularization of sexual stigmas, asceticism, and the eventual celibacy of clergy. The Patristic period would see the dissemination of popular apocryphal works championing the virtues of virginity not only for Mary, but also for women who aspired to purity and salvation.

In the *Protevangelium* (the *Infancy Gospel of James*), we read that Mary was divinely conceived in the womb of her mother Anna, who was not herself an antepartum virgin.[21] Mary's divine origin lays the groundwork for the eventual doctrinal establishment of the Immaculate Conception and the canonization of Anna.[22] The text also includes a relatively detailed gynecological account of the midwife and Salome both inspecting Mary to verify her virginity after the birth of Jesus. Here the text acknowledges the reader's assumption that what goes in, however its means, must come out. This emphasis on the postpartum examination is crucial to the *Protevangelium*'s aim to establish that neither human insemination nor delivery had occurred. Just as intercourse could deflower a woman, so too could the vaginal delivery of a fetus. Direction of the intrusion is irrelevant. The midwife observes no evidence for anatomical defloration after labor. What this labor consisted of and what criteria the midwife used to determine Mary's virginity are particularly relevant matters in view of the iconic status of the hymen, as previously discussed. It is preferable to discuss these criteria later in the chapter, however, within the context of Greek virginity and hymenology.

In any case, the *Protevangelium* became a cardinal document in the Catholic tradition that would eventually honor Mary as *Aeiparthenos*, the perpetual virgin, who birthed no children before or after Jesus. Whether the text's original author envisioned this perpetuity is unclear, however, especially considering that the pseudepigraphic attribution to Jacob (James) suggests an authoritative birth account from a member of the nuclear family.[23] It is nevertheless the tradition of perpetual virginity that precipitated a philological clash during the Reformation concerning the Greek reading of New Testament implications of Mary's later marital sexuality (Matthew 1:18, 25) and references to the siblings of Jesus (Matthew 13:55–56).[24] We are less concerned here with the historical, traditional, or doctrinal authenticity of the Marian pregnancy, in which this study is disinterested.[25] More pertinent is the acknowledgment of early Christianity's construction of a new discourse on virginity and sexuality, which played a major identitarian role in the customization of new theological communities. Early Mariology was a prominent component, a privileged utterance, of this discourse, but the populist ambitions of the movement's early writers concerned a vernacular aspiration toward the divine. John Chrysostom, Justin Martyr, Tertullian, Origen, Ambrose, Augustine, Athananius, Jovinian, Jerome, and the Desert Fathers all wrote extensively on sexual renunciation, but not through the lens of medieval Mariology.[26] In his magisterial volume on sexuality in the first centuries of Christianity, Peter Brown is quick to remind readers that agitation to sanitize Mary's postpartum sexuality with claims for her perpetual virginity did not materialize with any significance until the end of the Patristic period. Mary was part of the picture, but not its totality. "Even the notion of perpetual virginity, though it dazzled many writers in the late third and fourth centuries, came into clear focus only in fits and starts," Brown writes. "Above all, it never acquired the unambiguous association with specifically female chastity that it achieved in other ages, both in the pagan world and in later forms of Catholic Christianity."[27]

Scholars like Brown, Elizabeth Clark, Averil Cameron, Caroline Bynum, and David Hunter have drawn important attention to the fact that the discourse of sexual renunciation, marital purity, and divination through chastity was not simply a by-product of an early form of Christianity meditating on an appropriated pagan mother goddess, but that this discourse was a central, if not the essential, means by which Christianity articulated itself within a pagan Mediterranean world.[28] Through this discourse, Christian communities negotiated the dynamics of social restraint, the role of women, the nature of marriage, the power of artistic representation, and the manner in which they would parlay with Roman and Byzantine *Hochkultur*.[29] In other words, this discourse reflected the concerns common to cultures of many eras. More important is the fact that Christians were not unique in their own era when they pursued recategorization through sexual renegotiation. Romans, Jews, and other Mediterranean cultures produced their own distinct discourses, while simultaneously participating in a larger cross-pollinating framework.[30] Christianity did not appropriate virginity from a vacuum. That is why Foucault sees discourse as the regulated product, rather than the regulating prime mover, of epistemological "statements." Averil Cameron is correct to argue that while the infancy narratives and early Mariological impulses are not dissociable from their Greco-Roman context, it was the choice to rewrite and reshape that context that reified Christianity.[31] Is the Roman cult of the vestals, which linked the ritually guarded virginity of its female adepts to the survival of the state, so very different from the metonymous (almost hypostatic) coextensivity of sixteenth-century England and its virgin queen?[32] Yes and no. These are mutually alien cultures with mutually unintelligible epistemologies. We compare them at our peril, but at no greater peril than we compare the Christianities of late antiquity with those of the High Middle Ages, and at far less peril than medieval Christianity constructed categories of virginity, marriage, and piety through comparisons of itself with that of its ancient predecessors.[33] These comparisons have the potential to produce clarity, but only the kind of invaluable, haunting clarity that comes with the realization that the discourse under the microscope is always observed through the specula of one's own discourse.

One jarring example will illustrate the workings of this speculum. In the *Acts of Paul and Thecla*, a young Thecla renounces her marriage contract at her own mortal peril to follow the instructions of Paul, who insists on utter chastity.[34] Saved from execution on numerous occasions, Thecla follows Paul from city to city until she is finally baptized by supernatural means in a gladiatorial arena. Thecla then pursues a career in proselytizing the Gospel—a controversial issue for second-century Christianity—until she finally succumbs to old age. While the text lauds her for dying a virgin, it does not deny her sexual desires. Indeed, when we meet her, she is clinging to the window "like a spider" in hopes of catching a glimpse of Paul as he happens by her window. After Paul is imprisoned for playing Lysistrata to the city's married women, who renounce sexual relations with their husbands, Thecla visits him in his cell, kneels, and kisses the chains of his ankle fetters. All erotic ambiguity is lost when the guards remove Paul from his cell. Thecla stays, and in the sunken impression in the cell's dirt floor where he had lain, she writhes around, wallowing in his hollow. It is the tension between Thecla's adolescent sexuality and her chaste commitment to the man who inspires her that exalts the virginity. More specifically, it is the chastity standing at odds with the glory of marriage that gives the sexual renunciation a kind of sacrificial quality of martyrdom. In *De virginitate*, John Chrysostom praises the selfless choice of *parthenia* precisely because marriage and the connubial pleasures are wonderful. Such statements on virginity are distinctive in the canonical Gospels, the *Protevangelium*, *Paul and Thecla*, and *De virginitate*, reflecting the generational speed at which discourse can transform. But Thecla is special because of the role she plays in a little-known work by Methodius, a third-century Christian writer, who rewrites the map much in the way that Clark, Cameron, Bynum, and others describe. Methodius reimagines Plato's *Symposium*, recasting Socrates the philosopher with Thecla the evangelist and replacing the marvel of physical love with the ecstasy of virginity.[35] Methodius's *parthenia* is no more that of Thecla than Thecla's is that of Plato, but the specula through which each participant views the other is a tribute to the "profoundly altered ethics" of discourse taken on its own terms.[36]

THE PARTHENOS IN HER ELEMENT

The author of Matthew's prooftext for fulfillment of the biblical prophecy of a Virgin Birth is his famous citation of Isaiah 7:14.[37] Matthew's quotation obviously depends upon the Septuagint's complicated translation of Hebrew *ʿalmah* ("young woman") into Greek *parthenos* ("virgin"). This quotation contains the only attestation of the word *parthenos* in the Gospels (Matthew 1:23), which elsewhere only implies Mary's virginity with claims to divine insemination by the Holy Spirit (1:20). Upon discovery of Mary's pregnancy, Joseph himself seems to assume it is illegitimate until an angel reveals to him the preternatural manner of the conception. With the theological stakes heightened, the philological and connotative disharmony between *ʿalmah* and *parthenos* in a prophecy so pivotal to the litmus test of the Virgin Birth narrative has understandably generated more scholarly commentary than one might care to read in a lifetime. Countless text-critical articles and monographs have addressed the questionable translation in exhaustive detail, and there is little need to reinvent the wheel in this venue.[38] It is vitally important to emphasize, however, that nearly the entirety of this voluminous scrutiny of the Greek translation of Isaiah has functioned as a Christological project. In other words, the cottage industry of philological scholarship on a possibly erroneous translation owes its enthusiasm to the desire to reconcile or complicate two texts ostensibly informing the origins and nature of Jesus Christ. There is little genuine interest in Isaiah's thematic or historical context, except as it informs the Greek translation's bearing on Christian tradition. The brass tacks, whether explicit or implicit, for the paradigmatic approach are these: does the Hebrew term *ʿalmah* in fact harm or help the case for Mary's virginal conception? The intense interest is not even principally Mariological, unless one recognizes that Mariology itself is a privileged Christological heuristic. The essential ingredient of the Theotokos aggrandizement, after all, is the *theos* whom she births. If one further envisions the Mariological refinements from late antiquity to the Renaissance as the mores and utterances customizing a discourse on virginity, then it is important to acknowledge the manner in which sexual discourse also informs the "cultivated knowledge" of Christ's essence. By reiterating his asexual origins,[39] the speech acts of tradition nevertheless entrench a metaphysics of divinity framed by sexual benchmarks.[40]

The pressing question is not how the translator understood the Hebrew text, but what valence the term *parthenos* had for this translator in a Hellenistic world replete with rich connotations of the Greek word ranging from the pedestrian to the epithets of goddesses. The Christological blinders, as Ronald Troxel notes, have "preempted the normal investigation of the semantic range of a word in an author's usage and has diverted attention from features in the context signaling that the translator's center of concern lies elsewhere."[41] The Hellenistic translator who produced the Greek edition of Isaiah more than two centuries before the early Christian movement, on the other hand, did not operate through a Christological lens. The literary and religious points of reference belonged to the ambit of Hellenistic Judaism.[42] We know that the Greek rendering of Isaiah 7:14 became a point of contention between Jews and Christians during the Patristic period, but how did Jews read and understand the Greek Isaiah in the centuries before the emergence of Christianity and the prophetic birth claims of the late first century CE? The dissemination of the infancy narratives seems to divide cultural apples and oranges, which most biblicists are blithe to compare and conflate. To whatever extent Isaiah's translator believed his Hebrew *Urtext* to prophesy events beyond the translation (which I doubt), he nevertheless made lexical choices conditioned by his sense of Isaianic style, context, and cultural resonance pertinent to his own era. Had this scholar concurred with modern conventional wisdom, moreover, on the eighth-century BCE subject of the Isaianic material, then there is no reason to assume a concern on his part for the gravity of unfulfilled prophecy when choosing his words. It is the prerogative of the theologian to surmise the hand of providence in lexicology abetting true prophecy, of course, but the historical critic must work in tighter quarters.

We learn from its Massoretic attestations that the Hebrew term *ʿalmah* (*ʿalmâ*) designates a girl of marriageable age. Alternatively, modern lexica regularly render *ʿalmah* as "maiden" or "young girl." The range of connotative permutations is actually fairly wide.[43] The status of the *ʿalmah* need not etymologically preclude that she is already married (albeit eligible for divorce, hence remarriage), a widow, a slave, or a mother. The legal value placed on the *ʿalmah* in its contextual attestations seems to be the ability not just to marry but specifically to produce viable children—that is, legitimate heirs for the prospective husband. It is this value that accentuates the biological dimension of the legal status. The *ʿalmah* consequently need not be a virgin, but only fertile enough to satisfy the cardinal patrimonial criterion of a new wife. In view of the premium placed on maternal potential, the text may further qualify an *ʿalmah* as a virgin, predictably enhancing her desirability to suitors. With high infant mortality during the Iron Age, younger females had a better chance of conceiving enough children to see one or more survive into adulthood. On the other hand, an *ʿalmah* who was already a mother had demonstrated her fecundity. Notwithstanding how individual suitors prioritized virginity and proven fertility, the sexual subtext of the *ʿalmah* is never far from the surface. She is first and foremost nubile.

As a mark of distinction, biblicists have traditionally preferred Hebrew *betulah* (*betulâ*) as the technical term for virgin. The word is more malleable in reality, however, with only three of fifty-one attestations in the Hebrew Bible rendering an unequivocal meaning of *virgo intacta*.[44] In its holistic distribution, *betulah* bears similarities to the semantic range of *ʿalmah* in the sense that it more accurately designates a young female of marriageable status, albeit one likely to be a virgin in such a social location. The female ceases to be a *betulah* upon consummation of her marriage, a distinction in status borne out by the comparative Semitic evidence. Ugaritic cognate *btlt* is an epithet of the goddess Anat, whom one can only consider chaste if also willing to overlook the graphic sexual detail in which she copulates with her own brother Baal. Anat remains a *btlt* throughout her coital escapades, it would seem, as long as she does not marry; surveys of the wider Ugaritic corpus suggest that she appears content not to do so, and perforce remain a virgin.[45] Akkadian *batultu* likewise designates an "adolescent" or "nubile girl," rather than virgin.[46] As a legal term, it commonly indicates the marriageable status of a female therein betrothed.

The attested distribution of the Greek term *parthenos* includes diverse social and religious connotations. Fritz Graf ascribes to *parthenos* the principal meaning of " 'Maiden' (in the sense of an unmarried woman of marriageable age)."[47] Henry George Liddell and Robert Scott give multiple definitions under the *parthenos* entry, the first three of which occur in this order: "maiden, girl"; "virgin"; and "of unmarried women who are not virgins." For *parthen-eia* and its allomorphs, they cite terms concerning "maidens" more often than "virgins." The compound term *nothon partheneia*, moreover, refers to a "child of an unmarried woman," the latter of whom is hardly sexually inexperienced.[48] Kruse devotes no fewer than seventeen two-column pages to the meanings of *parthenos*, a small fraction of the attestations of which concern virginity.[49] Greek mythic and cultic literature identifies three Olympian goddesses as *parthenoi*: Hestia, Artemis, and obviously Athena (herself a famous product of male parthenogenesis), whose temple in her eponymous city still bears the name Parthenon. Both Athena and Artemis, like Anat at Ugarit, both keep sexual consorts but eschew marriage, the social distinction that separates *parthenoi* from *gynaikes*.[50]

Of course, one cannot initiate any discussion of the multifarious *parthenoi* or the classical rubrics of virginity without recourse to Giulia Sissa's authoritative study.[51] "Whereas the word *parthenos* tends to arouse skepticism in nonreligious interpreters and to call for cautious handling," Sissa warns, "it is not easy to capture the meaning of the abstract noun *parthenia* with a purely sociological definition."[52] Philologists tend to read literally, because (unlike the organic data of linguists) their texts are finite. Despairing of the very real vagaries of humanism conveyed across time and language, Renan accused philology of permitting its text "only one meaning."[53] Marriage signifies a crucial barrier of terminology. Beginning her exhaustive survey, Sissa notes: "Making love outside the marriage bed . . . did not result in any change in the name by which a young girl was called. She became a woman (*gyne*) only in matrimony, as the *gyne* of her husband."[54] Sissa further cites the following pertinent items: in the *Women of Trachis*, Iole is a *parthenos* while the lover of the paterfamilias until her marriage to Hyllus; Atalanta, while still an Artemisian *kore*, births a son aptly named Parthenopaeus to honor his mother's extramarital monogamy to Artemis; from Aristotle, Strabo, Ephorus, Antiochus of Syracuse, Pausanius, and other writers, we learn that mortal *parthenoi* commonly conceive and bear children, who are therefore often reckoned as bastards. On the other hand, the loss of *parthenia* could indeed indicate defloration in some contexts. Herodotus, Aelian, and Achilles Tatius describe exotic and mythic rituals to determine the sexual innocence of participants. In contrast to the nonmarital sexuality of Atalanta's *parthenia*, the carnal exploits of the Artemisian *kore* Rhodopis—although compelled by Aphrodite and the arrows of Eros—earned the wrath of Artemis, who obliterated her sworn adept. Most importantly, the Greek determination of sexual purity did not require "probative rituals," such as later hymenological inspections, but rather "mantic vision or ordeal"—hardly the stuff of scientific anatomical examination. Virginity was an invisible condition, demonstrable principally by cultic or mythic recourse. Authentic human parthenogenesis was commonplace in premarital social locations, while divine parthenogenesis was mythopoeically unexceptional.[55] Asclepius, Evadne, Ion, Telephus, and Perseus were born to virgins, a literary tradition that required Christian apologists to imagine a pre-Christian demonological campaign to obfuscate the Marian birth with rival candidates for the Isaianic prophecy.[56] What we should take away from these iterations is a healthy respect for evidentiary ambiguity and cultural diversity over the time and space of the Greek-speaking world.

> Hellenists who have studied the problems of sexuality, age groups, and rites of passage have uncovered an important fact: the Greek word *parthenos* does not unambiguously signify the perfect integrity in our word *virgin*. . . . Determined by age and marital status, virginity was thus a stage through which every woman passed on her way to full social integration. It coincided with nubility and implied proximity to as well as psychological readiness for marriage. A temporal and teleonomic notion, the word *parthenos*, we are told, simply denoted the expectant hiatus between childhood and *gamos*.[57]

The possible meanings of *parthenos* seem no less heterogeneous than their informing texts, which canvass half a millennium of cultural landscapes from Asia Minor to Syracuse. There are descriptors of nubility, that is, the potential to reproduce and suitability for marriage, as well as the rejection of marriage. Vows of *parthenia* are no less complex, as we see in the divergent cases of Atalanta and Rhodopis. Artemisian rites commonly featured choral frolicking with erotic overtones. We also see different cults of Athena and Hera serviced by residential *parthenoi* throughout the Mediterranean. *Parthenia* was also a requirement for the Pythian oracle, through whose oral and vaginal orifices divine vapor alone could pass—an intriguing prefiguration of Mary's aural insemination and childbirth of divine breath (*logoi* in both instances). *Parthenia* could preclude or complement sexual contact. Some *parthenoi* could be mothers, but none (unlike Mary) was ever a wife!

Finally, we come back to the pressing, unanswered questions. Which *parthenos* did the Hellenistic scribe have in mind when he selected the word to translate the ʿ*almah* of Isaiah 7:14? With its diverse permutations and connotations, its various cultic, mythic, literary, sexual, procreative, and marital nuances, does this *parthenos* of LXX (and its circuitous route to and through Matthew) produce an unequivocal glimpse into the mind of the translator, whose scribal training was a product of Hellenism's cultural corpora? How did Jews read this Greek text in the centuries before the infancy narratives of the early Jesus movement? And more importantly, with what caution or bravado should we tread presumptuously into the discourse governed by his epistemological reference points (whatever they were)? I think these questions are unanswered because they are unanswerable. Even the few self-aware attempts to understand the rubric of Isaiah's translator, like that of Troxel (who shuns the Christological subtext), nevertheless insist on some form of forced theological reconciliation between the Hebrew ʿ*almah* and Greek *parthenos*. But here is the rub. It has become a tautology of sorts for scholars to describe the lexical choice of *parthenos* as a mistranslation or the next best word in a language without a specific term comparable to ʿ*almah*. Given the permutations of meaning for both of these words in their native cultural environments, however, who is to say the translation is bad? Are there not available connotations of *parthenos*, which capture the essence of ʿ*almah*, regardless of how one reads the Hebrew term? Observing Renan's caveat about the larger philological picture, the translation seems innocent enough.[58] It only becomes problematic when viewed through the Marian lens.

This returns us to the matter not only of Christian readings but also Jewish readings. Of all the occurrences of ʿ*almah* in the Hebrew Bible, the Septuagint chooses *parthenos* only twice: Isaiah 7:14 and Genesis 24:43. The ʿ*almah* in question is Rebekah, whom Abraham's servant identifies as a potential wife for Isaac. Thus the Hebrew term is apt, indicating her suitability for marriage. Symmachus and Theodotion agree with Origen on the employment of *parthenos* in this instance. In the parallel Hebrew text (Genesis 24:14) foregrounding this passage, however, the MT has *na*ʿ*arah* or "young woman." Thus the servant declares that he will inquire of the *na*ʿ*arah* (v. 14) who offers him and his camels water to drink only to encounter an ʿ*almah* (v. 43) who does just that. So here we see LXX translating both *naʿarah* and ʿ*almah* as *parthenos*, which Arie van der Kooij regards as a harmonization rather than a translation of ʿ*almah*.[59] For every other attestation of ʿ*almah* in the Massoretic Text, the Septuagint uses *neanis* "girl, maiden" (Exodus 2:8; Psalms 68:26; Song of Songs 1:3; 6:8), *neotes* "youth" (Proverbs 30:19),[60] or the transliteration *alamoth* (1 Chronicles 15:20). The appearance of *parthenos* in Isaiah 7:14 is not completely exceptional, but it does run counter to LXX's preference for *neanis* elsewhere. And here the recensional variants for Isaiah 7:14 are provocative. Whereas Origen has *parthenos* in the fifth Hexaplaric column, Aquila, Symmachus, and Theodotion unanimously choose *neanis*. In view of Origen's copious source material, his decision to depart from his comparative source material suggests a theological imperative to privilege the Matthean prophecy over the textual witnesses. On the other hand, Gerhard Delling suggests that it might be Aquila, Symmachus, and Theodotion who substitute *neanis* for *parthenos* to bolster Jewish rejoinders to the early Christological appropriation of Isaianic language.[61] Do any of these lexical choices gloss religious critiques? Do any of ours when we parse virgin from mother, cousin from brother?

We should trouble ourselves immensely were we to fret over every inconsistency in the Greek lexica, not only for Hellenistic texts but also for those of any era.[62] The translator traduces, as the maxim goes. In the instance of the Hexapla's compilation, however, we observe a unique set of circumstances in the early third century CE, when the master compiler set out to establish an authoritative edition informed by the prominent recensions of his day. We do well to recall that the LXX of Origen's fifth column is Origen's LXX, constructed through an exhaustive series of rereadings, retranslations, compromises, and innovations. The word ʿ*almah* occurs only nine times in the Hebrew Bible. Four times, the standard LXX produces *neanis*, twice *parthenos*, once an omission, and twice a lexical outlier (a misreading and a transliteration). Van der Kooij makes a noteworthy but conjectural argument for the dismissal of one contrived *parthenos* (Genesis 24:43), which if so would leave us with a single *parthenos* for ʿ*almah*—the same *parthenos* cited in Matthew 1:23 to undergird the Virgin Birth prophecy, the only attestation of *parthenos* in Matthew's Gospel. Origen had before him this Hebrew term and three influential translations in agreement on *neanis*, the commonest of the Greek lexemes chosen to communicate ʿ*almah*.[63] On what basis does Origen make his choice?

By the early third century, the Virgin Birth etiology is well established. Less than a century earlier, Justin Martyr had already condemned the ancient Greek stories of parthenogenesis as preemptive demonic disinformation. In only a century's time, moreover, the early Christian movement would see the first documented rumblings for Mary's postpartum virginity. For the purposes of our curiosity alone, it is unfortunate that the earliest extant Matthean manuscripts from mid- to late third-century Oxyrinchus do not preserve the twenty-third verse of the first chapter. This is what Foucault means by *épistème* when he qualifies the gravity of cultural knowledge and/or forgetfulness as the plasma in which utterances, speech acts, and mores construct rules of discourse, be they discernable as text or invisible as *parthenia*.

HYMENOLOGIES, OR *QUA RUPTA*

Sissa's characterization of *parthenia* as an "invisible condition" may occasion pause.[64] While the Greek documentary evidence suggests either ordeal or divination as the determinant of virginity, there remains the obvious examination of the hymen or the presence of coital bleeding. The hymen, after all, serves as the traditional icon of virginity, a membranous signifier.[65] It is a matter of some dispute, however, concerning when gynecologists discovered the hymen. Ann Hanson makes a forceful argument in favor of hymen inspections by midwives.[66] To this she adds comments from the Hippocratic text *Diseases of Women*, which describes a seal or stopper at the mouth of the uterus, which in turn remains sealed until the first coital act. The first genuine departure from this Hippocratic paradigm in the extant documentary record is the gynecological treatise of Soranus of Ephesus in the second century CE, the first point at which any medical writer in classical antiquity refers to a membranous hymen.[67]

There are problems with the assumption that ancient Greek gynecology operated by the principles of hymenological midwifery when the first anatomical awareness of the hymen is not demonstrable before the second century. Hanson's argument for the midwife's gnosis about membranes unknown to gynecologists is purely conjectural; it may be so, but there are no supporting textual attestations of any hymen before this time. The Hippocratic commentary, moreover, is proof of nothing more than anatomical ignorance about the uterus, which is not in fact sealed. If anything, the description in *Diseases of Women* is an argument against familiarity with the hymen (and its location), which we now know does not plug the cervix. When Soranus finally mentions the hymen, he identifies it with the genitals at the location of penile insertion, that is, the vagina, which opening modern medicine knows the hymen to ring. Soranus further contests the folk belief that any membranous barrier transects the vagina to cause. Nor does this membrane appear during dissection, Soranus claims. In yet another exhaustive philological study of the relevant terminology, Sissa demonstrates that no conclusive evidence exists for the awareness of the hymen as a discrete anatomical unit prior to Soranus.[68] Neither Aristotle nor Galen describes the female anatomy or interprets the physiology correctly. Of course, blood could still function as a diagnostic, however subject to folklore, to determine defloration during consummation. While gynecologists and midwives alike knew that a sexually inexperienced female would likely bleed during her first act of intercourse, neither specialist could apparently say why—at least not with any anatomical accuracy. Perhaps this explains why the Greek literature suggests that the state of *parthenia* is invisible, vulnerable only to preternatural means of verification. We cannot know, just as perhaps they could not.

If hymenological gynecology represented an anachronism or, at best, a learned but minority opinion of an Ephesian medical eccentric, then how is one to read the postpartum narrative of the *Protevangelium*? What are its biological realities? The text reports that when Joseph and the midwife approach the cave where he had left Mary, they observe a mysterious cloud shrouding it, which the midwife interprets as a miracle. "Suddenly the cloud withdrew from the cave and a great light appeared inside the cave, so that her [the midwife's] eyes could not bear to look. And a little later that light receded until an infant became visible; he went and took his mother's breast."[69] The divine cloud gave way to a divine light, which receded to reveal Mary holding her baby, whom she had delivered without assistance. Without any further inspection, the midwife exclaims again that she has seen a miracle. Encountering Salome, the midwife relates her tale, to which Salome responds, "As the Lord my God lives, unless I insert my finger and examine her, I will never believe that a virgin has given birth" (19:19).

In chapter 20, the midwife instructs Mary to brace herself for a serious test. Salome inserts her finger into Mary, whereupon her hand begins to burn as punishment for her incredulity. If this probing did not depend upon a gynecologically accurate knowledge of the hymen, and therefore did not include an examination of the hymen itself, what criteria would Salome or the midwife have employed to make such a determination? Blood would not suffice, for this was not a postcoital examination. This was an inspection to determine virginity postpartum. There would be blood, but there would also be amniotic fluid, the placenta, the umbilical cord. What the examination required was physical evidence that Mary has indeed given birth vaginally. But no one had witnessed the delivery, and the text does not specify anything other than the revelation of an infant from behind a cloud and flash of blinding, divine light. The birth, like *parthenia*, is invisible. Does the text then mean to suggest that Mary did not in fact deliver Jesus vaginally or that no humoral or membranous trace of such a delivery existed? Was Jesus born in a flash of divine light, teleported into his mother's arms to preserve her *parthenia*? Even were the delivery conventionally vaginal, the text still makes a claim for Mary's purity, meaning that the passage of the fetus through the birth canal did not alter her status.

Was it fetus or *logos* that Mary delivered? There is more to this text than its contribution to the conceptual development of Mary's perpetual virginity. It also seems to inform a later Catholic tradition of *conceptio per aurem*, by which the angel Gabriel impregnates Mary with *logoi* whispered into her ear. The Annunciation is thereby literally the divine impregnation. This logistical conception deemphasizes the sexual overtones of insemination by relocating the act to the orifice farthest removed. It also permits transubstantiation (of ingress, egress, or both) while simultaneously serving poetic justice to John the Evangelist, who envisioned Christ as the tangible incarnation of the divine Word.

The art historian Leo Steinberg has charted the relationship between the maturation of the *conceptio per aurem* and the artistic depictions of the Annunciation during the fourteenth through sixteenth centuries.[70] Steinberg persuasively locates the origins of conception by divine breath in the Patristic literature. He traces the manner in which the *spiritus sanctus*, who facilitates the conception, dovetails with its literal etymology of "spirit" or "breath of air" to produce a tradition of artistic representations in which dove, spirit, breath, word, and shaft of light inseminate Mary interchangeably and sometimes simultaneously. Steinberg describes in clear language the manner in which artists made bold choices in response to challenges of presentation better serviced by poets.[71] Especially fascinating is the bizarre intersection of calculating linear exactitude with the need to express wondrous divine abstraction.

> Accustomed by perspectival practice to tracing directional lines that converged with precision, they began answering curious questions. For instance: should those heaven-sent streamers be allowed to diffuse and shed about Mary's head, or should they collect in a single beam? And this more delicate question, hardly thought of by painters until well into the Quattrocento: should a narrowly focused light bypass the Virgin's head and aim at her bosom, or should it target her womb? . . . And if the Dove, or its breath, was the procreant agent, how close should it come? Would the avian sign of the Holy Ghost forfeit its ethereality if it came nearly touching, like a tame bird? Of all Christian mysteries none demanded more tact in the telling, for surely the very purpose of ascribing the wonder of Mary's pregnancy to the breath of God was to shield an unsearchable secret from too diligent investigation. . . . They may signify the Word of his mouth, the Word tilting wombward to perform the Creator's greatest deed, his descent into his creature's condition, entering a sealed virgin womb. But by what route? To answer this question without scanting the supernatural character of the event. The Latin Church Fathers evolved their acoustical metaphor. They taught that the Virgin conceived through the ear, the right ear.[72]

And so the divine Word enters the right ear of the *virgo intacta*, who (if we read Dante correctly) delivers the Word from her womb likewise with a breath. In the *Paradiso*, Beatrice finally leads Dante to the Virgin Mary, around whom flits Gabriel, "shaped like a ring or wreath, and spinning round her, it wound and crowned her in its spinning flame."[73] He explains himself:

> I am the Angelic Love that wheels around
> the lofty ecstasy *breathed from the womb*
> in which the hostel of Our Wish was found.[74]

The aural fixation of the Church Fathers seems to have found purchase, among so many other dabs, in the words of the poet who finished his opus only nine years before Simone Martini fashioned *The Annunciation and Two Saints* in 1330 Naples. Clearly, there was something in the air. But do we dare view the *Protevangelium* knowingly through this speculum? Do the mysterious cloud, blinding light, and anatomical innocence indeed serve "to shield an unsearchable secret from too diligent investigation," as Steinberg puts it? Sadly, we cannot go there without the hymenologies of our own discourse. It is a modern Western reductionism to equate virginity with abstinence from vaginal intercourse. Indeed, one might venture to say the equation has become a speech act (or better yet, an "illocutionary act," to crib John Searle); in some circles the statement has not only translated into practice but also exposed the deniable underbelly of practice. Originating within the Southern Baptist Convention, the True Love Waits program popularized the so-called virginity pledge, which in turn inspired several parallel pledge movements in other denominations.[75] In 2005 the *Baptist Press* website claimed that "an estimated 2.5 to 3 million youth have signed cards pledging to remain sexually abstinent until marriage."[76] On one hand, the commitment of millions of young people to eschew a particular sexual act glimpses a subcultural valorization of virginity operating on the general plane of discourse. The pledge is an utterance in the literal sense, but it is also illocutionary insofar as it affirms a denial, or puts into motion ill-defined actions intended to circumnavigate defined actions. On the other hand, one would presume that what pledgers and nonpledgers alike know about the *ars erotica*, the *studia sexualis*, and the gulf between theory and practice are generationally similar. It is an assumption on our part that pledgers and nonpledgers are comparably educated on the nature, details, and medical consequences of sexual contact—an epistemological supposition about epistemologically informed lifestyle choices—which casts Foucault's discursive framework of the *épistème* into helpful, sharp relief. The central caveat of any cultural *épistème* is the charge to strip such suppositions bare so that their vectors might reveal themselves in the blue veins peeking through naked tissue. For Alfred Kinsey, this meant exposing the ubiquity of what many considered sins and crimes with voluminous profiles of praxis. Exposing sexual behaviors that transected the public facades of private life, Kinsey upended the abnormal to establish the moral neutrality of consensual adult intimacy. For Freud, whose more modest empirical observations prefigured the Kinsey reports, this meant the understanding that what conventional science considered perversion was perhaps the only yardstick of normalcy. As he cautiously observed, genital-to-genital contact had become iconic at the expense of acknowledging typical sexual practice (kissing, masturbation, oral sex, etc.) as normative forms of excitation. "Thus the extraordinarily wide dissemination of the perversions forces us to suppose that the disposition to perversions is itself of no great rarity," Freud reasoned, "but must form a part of what passes as the normal constitution."[77] These were epistemological watersheds, corrective units of discourse, as much as they were medical advances.

So let us treat with this icon on symbolic terms. The virginity pledge circumnavigates the vagina and that which lies within. There is a confluence of sexual information and disinformation between pledgers precisely as they seek to simulate intimacy with but an icon's distance between them. And it would be a mistake to conflate the pledge against iconoclasm with an undeclared pledge against intimacy. Sociologists Hannah Brückner and Peter Bearman have conducted long-term studies of the sexual histories of pledgers in the years after they made their affirmations of denial.[78] The results indicate that sexually transmitted diseases (STDs) are disproportionately higher among pledgers than nonpledgers in the same age groups. This is partly attributable to the fact that pledgers are statistically less likely to use contraceptives than nonpledgers, especially during initial sexual activity. How is it that the abstinent contracted STDs with a frequency larger than those who were not abstinent? It is fair to infer from these findings that some pledgers in fact did not keep their pledges, but we should expect a default in any sample population. Broken pledges are incidental; they do not explain the lower frequency of contraceptive use and likely related higher frequency of disease transmission. The answer may lie in Brückner and Bearman's finding that pledgers are more likely to engage in anal and oral sex than nonpledgers, presumably as a surrogate act of intimacy to avoid the vagina, thus technically fulfilling the virginity pledge.[79]

> Because virginity is often culturally linked only to vaginal sex, to preserve virginity, adolescents and young adults may engage in other sexual behaviors that involve exchange of fluid and thus salient for STD acquisition. Overall, oral sex and anal sex are prevalent behaviors in this population, most commonly in conjunction with vaginal sex. Here we consider those who have oral or anal sex without vaginal sex. Amongst those who have only oral sex and/or anal sex, pledgers are over-represented. Overall, about 3 percent of respondents reported oral sex with one or more partners but no vaginal sex. Although just

> over 2 percent of nonpledgers fall into this group, 13 [percent] of consistent pledgers and 5 percent of inconsistent pledgers do. . . . Similarly, 0.7 percent of nonpledgers report anal but no vaginal sex, compared with 1.2 percent for pledgers.[80]

This is not a matter of hypocrisy, nor is it even a matter of semantics. These alternative paths to intimacy among pledgers crisscross the domain of *iconography*, precisely because anal and oral sex are not iconoclastic. The pledge ritually reaffirms the icon, which in turn functions as a prescriptive, proscriptive governing unit of discourse. And it is a culturally specific discourse; its enveloping *épistème* only hazily iconizes the hymen as the biological marker of virginity. Modern anatomists know that the hymen may rupture under any number of physical circumstances prior to the first act of vaginal intercourse. A so-called premature rupture, then, rarely carries the stigma in the United States or Europe that it may in cultures that place iconographic emphasis on the intact hymen as prooftext for purity. So now it is not so much the hymen as the vagina itself, which has become the new inviolate seal. In the revelatory light of Hirsi Ali's experience, the *petite mort* that the virginity pledge brings this icon of old seems ever so modern. Like the paraphernalia of the cult of the Virgin Mary, it would seem, all icons are portable and changeable.

RELIC ENVY

The James Ossuary is also iconic in a vernacular sense, by which I mean it functions as an icon without the Latin. At the outset of our research project, Bernadette McNary-Zak, Tom Bremer, Milton Moreland, and I spent countless hours debating whether we thought the ossuary was a relic. It was difficult to decide with any certainty, because while it did not meet the strictest definition of relic under the Catholic rubric, admirers of the box continued to speak about it with language otherwise reserved for relics. There is a discomfort, for example, in the writing of Witherington, who is perhaps the ossuary's most ecstatic apologist. On one hand, Witherington sees in the box a demolition of Mary's perpetual virginity and, by extension, her iconic cult and so on. His denominational critique of Catholicism in *The Brother of Jesus* is thinly veiled, which complements his public statements on the church circuit. On the other hand, there is the strangest notion in Witherington's writing that imagines (or encourages) a visceral Protestant impulse to honor the ossuary as an iconic connection to Jesus.[81] His crowd-pleasing line on the stump that imagines a DNA link between the bone fragments from the ossuary and humoral stains from the Shroud of Turin resuscitates this problem of "relic." Nowhere does Witherington use that term in the book—it is a Catholic buzzword for him, one surmises—but the Catholic semantics he uses to describe and curry Protestant interest in the ossuary as a desire to touch Jesus through the box's good offices are dripping with relic envy.

> [I]n an age of visual and tactile learners, we now have a physical artifact, not just another text, to view and ponder. The effect of seeing the ossuary can be overwhelming. It was amazing to watch so many people file through the Toronto museum and stop and reflect on the significance of the ossuary. For many of them it was an unprecedented way to get in touch with their own roots and faith. The excitement about the discovery seems to lie largely in the fact that finally we can virtually touch Jesus through this name, Yeshua, on this inscription. . . . Physical objects provide a vital tactile connection with the past and with our ancestors, and this is especially so with a burial box that contained an ancient person's remains.[82]

We may compare Witherington's phenomenological observations with Georgia Frank's research on sensory perception of relics among early Christian pilgrims.[83] Late antique authors paid close attention to the empowering significance of the pilgrim's gaze at the relic, an act that many understood to facilitate a "tactile" portal to the biblical past and (for the worthy) to the divine itself.

> Underlying these efforts [to biblicize the present] is the conviction that the biblical past would become visible only to those who were capable of both seeing and responding to the sacred presence they beheld. The "eye of faith" as Christians referred to this interactive visuality, was tactile as well as visual, not just in the sense of contact but even of engagement.[84]
>
> The physical sense of sight was anything but passive in antiquity; it was a form of physical contact between the viewer and the object. For the pilgrim, that gaze extended to the sacred past. The physical sense of sight triggered the "eye of faith," which in turn perceived a past biblical event as a present reality. The tactile and aggressive characteristics of

> this gaze were grounded in ancient visuality. Sight and touch remained discrete senses, but in late-antique Christian piety their functions converged to create the conditions for a biblical realism.[85]

Did religious visitors indeed experience the burial box in this way? Perhaps the anticipation of ecstatics informs the language of the ROM's internal planning brief for the ossuary exhibit. It describes the ossuary as a "religious artifact of breathtaking significance" that "may become an object of reverence." The brief also mentions "potential for huge crowds and reverence" as a design caveat for the staging accommodations. Asked if there were anything she might have changed about the exhibit, Suzan Sabir, the ROM's exhibit manager, considered "more reverential space" to accommodate both traffic and contemplation. She recalled that it was necessary to clean the glass of the ossuary case "all the time." The design team realized that pious visitors would want to be near the ossuary. "It was amazing how many people felt the need to touch the case, rest on the case," she said, "more so than if you go into any other exhibition."[86] Most glass cases in most museums bear fingerprints from visitors for entirely irreligious reasons. The ossuary case was disproportionately smudged, but it was also disproportionately beleaguered. And yet there is always that assumption of piety, but what does that piety entail? In nearly every interview that my colleagues and I have conducted with people who visited the ossuary out of religious interest, there is a recurring assertion that, while the ossuary (if real) may complement their faith, it does not and need not validate it; Protestant faith does not depend on confirmation by physical proofs, although it may entertain them. This complicates the notion that so many thousands of people flocking to see the ossuary constitutes a pilgrimage, especially if most are unwilling to concede that the authenticity of the object bears religious significance for their faith. And while relic envy sometimes issues from the smarmiest of denominational polemicists, we have little in the way of exhibit visitors ready to concede the divine transference or biblical portal reserved for relic lore. While Sabir remembers a visitor kneeling before the case as often as once an hour, this number seems small in light of the enormous crowds. The ROM exhibit guards, however, could not recall seeing visitors perform any acts of piety of the sort that the curators anticipated in the planning brief. So why have scholars, curators, and others assumed religiosity to define and envelop public interest in the box?

RECTA RATIO AND HEAVEN'S CRATE

When it comes to spectacle, there is a thin line between belief and the suspension of disbelief. When Phineas T. Barnum placed the Feejee Mermaid on display at New York's American Museum in 1842, most visitors suspected it was a fake.[87] That was not the point, however. Museums purport to present their exhibits with authority and integrity, but they depend on the public trust.[88] Spectators come to museums, even those built on hokum, with the hope that they will be persuaded. After the Israel Antiquities Authority (IAA) determined the James Ossuary's inscription to be modern and the Israeli police charged owner Oded Golan with forgery, the ROM's reputation suffered greatly at the hands of the media, which had generated more buzz for the box than for any other archaeological discovery since the Dead Sea Scrolls.[89] The nonstop emotional chatter filling scholarly listservs after October 22, 2002, suddenly, embarrassingly went dead when the IAA's blue-ribbon panel repudiated the inscription's antiquity in the summer of 2003. There was an unquenchable desire for scholars, the penitent, and the simply curious to believe in the box's authenticity. And why not? Among the hundreds of print newspaper headlines heralding the ossuary's discovery and the fastidious coverage of its journey to and display in Toronto, the media were also pushing buttons of faith through captions such as "Hunger Is Great to See Objects Believed Close to God" (*Toronto Star*) and "People May Be Praying at Museum" (*Catholic Register*). Even ROM curator Ed Keall subtly appealed to religion when he publicized the exhibit whose public draw of 100,000 visitors saved the museum's finances and put it back in the black. "It is natural for some to treat this as a religious icon," he told one newspaper.[90] One can draw any number of parallels between the impulse of credulity toward the box and any number of similar objects of historical interest: anatomical relics or personal effects of the beatified, the True Cross, the Jesus family tomb, or the Shroud of Turin. Other discoveries surface in controlled excavations, but the instinct to biblicize them is potent. A Roman-period boat from the bottom of the Sea of Galilee is called the Jesus Boat, and it boasts its own museum in Ginnosaur on the sea's northern shore. A garden-variety cistern with remnants spanning 1,500 years of use was dubbed the Cave of John the Baptist. A Neo-Babylonian cuneiform tablet in the bowels of the British Museum contained a name arguably similar to a name in the book of Jeremiah, prompting its collator to call it the most important discovery in biblical archaeology in the last century. This unmistakable pattern shows that while the biblical significance of these objects is dubious, once someone suggests a biblical connection, then everything changes.

The most salient change is the inversion of the burden of proof. When religious partisans of the Shroud of Turin and the James Ossuary announced the direct link to biblical characters, the burden shifted to academics to disprove the biblical associations no matter how arbitrary or imaginary the initial claim. Scholars are guilty of this behavior, too, partly because of the attention drawn to objects obscure and otherwise forgettable. This behavior calls to mind the epistemic principle of *recta ratio*, which Thomas Aquinas developed to categorize the different circumstances of ignorance. The *recta ratio* is the rule of reason, which Aquinas envisioned as a kind of threshold separating intellectual humility from audacity. In his famous debt to Averroes's systematic harmonization of philosophy with theology, Aquinas interpreted reason (in the Aristotelian sense) as a gift from God necessarily compatible with faith. One does not question divinity, nor does one deny it. Those who trespass the rule of reason commit the sin of curiosity. Those who reject the rule of reason commit the sin of negligence, the deliberate ignorance of divinity. What is the proof of divinity? It is self-evident in the existence of the world, which supposes that a divine thing is not subject to scrutiny without the accompanying sin of audacity.[91]

The so-called discovery of the unprovenanced ossuary stirred such deference to the *recta ratio* that the academy abandoned its own protocols for vetting propositions of even perfunctory and banal interest. The scholarly analysis of the James Ossuary appeared in the *Biblical Archaeology Review*. Five years later, Lemaire has yet to submit an *editio princeps* to a peer-reviewed forum in accordance with every cardinal rule of scholarship. And yet the academy embraced the ossuary in late 2002 and early 2003 and invidiously castigated early detractors of the inscription's pedigree. Skeptics, be they expert epigraphers, had forsaken the *recta ratio*. Lemaire and Shanks had announced the biblical nature of the box, and those unconvinced sinners (very few in number) responded with deliberate ignorance of its self-evident divinity. Aquinas developed this device of logical disputation within the pedagogical context of the primordial thirteenth-century University of Paris, the first laboratory of the modern academy. It is unfortunately poignant to find the *recta ratio* there still. The tension, which John Michael documents, between the need to perform as cautious, professional intellectual and the visceral desire to throw in with media ecstatics aired the dirty laundry of a sequestered institution (further fractured into market and service subcultures) anxious about the diminishment of public trust.[92] Faith in ossuary, however, has produced little refuge from the anxiety of the margins.

The antiquities black market continues to circulate highly collectible items obtained from looting or produced by forgery.[93] The American Schools of Oriental Research, the Archaeological Institute of America, the American Oriental Society, and numerous other learned organizations have responded to these assaults on cultural property with new policies governing the publication of unprovenanced objects in their periodicals. Most societies with such policies either will not accept submissions with *editios princeps* of such items or enforce strict rules concerning exemptions for mitigating circumstances. The glaring exception is the Society of Biblical Literature (SBL), which has undertaken no revision of its policy on the publication of unprovenanced artifacts even in the wake of inconceivably rampant looting in Iraq, which continues apace four years after the collapse of the Hussein regime.[94] The singular feature that sets the SBL apart, of course, is the purportedly biblical character of the objects, which one might see come to press in its journals. It is disturbing enough that the SBL has greeted the enormity of worldwide concern for the ravaging of cultural property with insouciance, but its diffidence also speaks to the willingness to prioritize biblical materialism over concern for atrocities of others' craven commerce.

We come full circle with Fiji. This biblical materialism and the scholarship eager to embrace artifacts of unprovenanced origin, so long as they have biblical valence, bear a striking resemblance to the once-popular ethnographic descriptions of the cargo cults of the South Pacific.[95] In the traditional depiction, South Pacific islanders divinize the objects (some manufactured by gods) in European and American provision crates (first from ships and later dropped from planes) from exotic, unknown origins. Under the influence of European missionary work, cargoism emerged either in the late nineteenth century or the early twentieth as a syncretistic phenomenon with rituals designed to encourage the Western gods to appear with new divine cargo for their faithful adepts. Since the mid-twentieth-century ethnographies, which depicted the cults through the corrupt lens of colonial exploitation, Martha Kaplan and other anthropologists have discredited this traditional understanding of the cargo cults.[96]

Instead of primitive, isolated religions worshipping boxes that fall from the sky, cargoism neither attaches divine significance to the crates nor functions as a coherent cult in the anthropological sense. Instead, the cargo cult is an imaginary product of the exploitation of colonial people with desolate economy. The cargoism of biblical archaeology, on the other hand, is a vibrant, demonstrable cult. It divinizes boxes of unknown origin with the hope that unseen, anonymous benefactors will bring more such treasures. It sees in these precious items, inscriptions and ivories in place of tinned meat and rifles, a validation of its most ancient indigenous belief system and rituals. It is a syncretistic cult, which attempts to harmonize the mutually alien obsessions with faith and evidence. Its impulses are iconophiliac and relicophiliac, notwithstanding the rhetoric of reason and abstraction disseminated by its own modern missiologies. But Kaplan's redescriptions are also apt, because like all imagined communities, the guild is intentional about its self-construction. It performs rituals for imaginary audiences, who in turn imagine their interest in the profoundest theorems of obscurantism. And when modern villagers produce boxes from forgotten tombs to feed families impoverished by other forms of colonialism, our cult rushes to this cargo without provenance, without hesitation, and, sadly, without regret.[97]

JACOB'S EUCHARIST

Foucault's emphasis on an epistemological rubric for our understanding of discourse is crucial. Our claims to information and deniability are individual as well as collective statements of self. Claims to knowledge are inherent in the academy's insistence on absolute professional authority, even while it turns a blind eye to the disinformation surrounding the very objects on which this expertise ostensibly depends. Provenance, after all, is an *epistemic* claim to location. In homage to the primacy of knowledge and truth claims as instruments of power, Foucault identifies *confession* as the prominent cultural device that sequesters conscious from secret knowledge, private from public knowledge, and guilty from absolved knowledge.[98] The Western tradition has long vested the power to grant moral and legal clemency to its highest institutions; so sacred is the secular power to absolve by confession that not even Richard Nixon could legally pardon himself. Consider two acts of ossuarial confession, then, as a reminder that misreading is at least as important as reading in a Barthian world where all authors are dead. In the matter of Oded Golan's purchase and possession of the James Ossuary, the early press reports document his inconsistent claims about the date he purchased the box from a Jerusalem antiquities dealer. When he ultimately insisted that he had obtained the box in the early 1970s, before the 1978 Antiquities Act criminalized such purchases, Shanks asked him why he had kept such an important discovery to himself for thirty years. Golan confessed, "I didn't know the Son of God could have a brother."[99] Prior to the Biblical Archaeology Society's press conference on October 22, 2002, in Washington, D.C., Shanks produced photographs of the ossuary's inscription for epigrapher P. Kyle McCarter, the Albright Professor at the Johns Hopkins University and my *Doktorvater*, who concurred with Lemaire's reading of the inscription (although not his paleographic assessment).[100] On Thursday, October 21, the day before the press conference at which McCarter was scheduled to interpret the ossuary for reporters, he showed me photographs of the Aramaic inscription in Baltimore and asked for my impressions. I read the five words, which translated as "Yaʿaqob son of Yosef, brother of Yeshua." Taking them at face value, I was confused. They were legible characters with names typical of ossuary epitaphs, but I knew that McCarter would not bother with my opinion about anything ordinary. It seemed so very ordinary. So I finally asked him whether it was the brother reference that he found unusual. "Jacob brother of Jesus," he replied. "Jacob, as in James?" Pause. Oh, that Jacob. It is my pleasure to confess that what seemed so obvious to experts, so prosopographically irrefutable, what passed muster for *recta ratio* among partisans, had not even occurred to me until spelled out. An epigrapher had read the letters, but he did not see the handwriting on the wall. The discourse was too big, the "obvious" too Gnostic.

> The followers said to Jesus, "We know that you are going to leave us. Who will be our leader?" Jesus said to them, "No matter where you are, you are going to go to James the Just [*Iakobos pdikaios*], for whose sake heaven and earth came into being." (*Gospel of Thomas* 12)

With this language, the *Gospel of Thomas* establishes the succession of authority and the conduit to Jesus after his departure.[101] It was indeed Iakobos, the brother of Jesus, who assumed leadership of the early Christian movement in Jerusalem until his death purportedly in 62 CE. It was this same Iakobos whom the author of the *Protevangelium* invoked to authenticate the divine conceptions of both Mary and Jesus with the authority of familial familiarity. It is likewise this Iakobos, whom some apologists like Witherington have beatified anew (through a relic in all but name) to undermine the same apocryphon. That is not quite specific enough; relicization involves a meditation on remnants of the missing. Were this newly sainted Yaʿaqob of the ossuary indeed the same Iakobos of early Christian history and mystery, then it is his second martyrdom, the looting and dumping of his mortal remains, which enthusiasts have celebrated as the tangible link to Jesus. It is now the black market for whose sake heaven and earth came into being.

This hallowed, hollow box from parts unknown did not produce any sentiments that did not already lurk under the surface, however. The public dissection of the James Ossuary pushed emotional and intellectual buttons already fixed in a discourse of virginity. The modern Christian *épistème*, as we have seen, gestates within a broader cross-cultural context, which evinces powerful (and sometimes dangerous) tensions over the valuation of femininity and proprietorship of the sexual self. While this modern Western *épistème* is historically unique, as all epistemological epochs are, it nevertheless bears a genealogical debt stretching back to Mediterranean and Near Eastern statements considerably older than Christianity itself. These are worth knowing, if only to discern which emotional buttons we have fashioned for ourselves from those buttons we have inherited from the mores of antiquity. For all its media and implements of recollection, modernity (and postmodernity, some would argue) also champions an epistemic isolationism. Can mutually alien *épistèmes* produce similar discourses? There are some utterances that transect discourses across distinctive eras, which accentuate both knowledge and ignorance of "diachronic contexts." Etiologies of utterance, after all, are no less immune to the atrophy of public memory.

NOTES

1. In the first volume of *The History of Sexuality*, Foucault locates the programmatic political articulation of biopower in the Enlightenment, when advances in medicine, agricultural management, and distribution gave state apparatuses more influence over the preservation of life, leading to a profounder awareness of what "it meant to be a living species in a living world, to have a body, conditions of existence, probabilities of life, and individual and collective welfare, forces that could be modified" (M. Foucault, *The History of Sexuality*, vol. 1, *An*

Introduction [New York: Vintage, 1978], 142–43). Foucault tends to focus on biopower, as it facilitates targets and means of control, but there are interesting dividends, especially in recent history, which the trends toward individualization have produced institutional perspectives on sexuality from the unlikeliest of places. Consider the movement within post–Vatican II Catholicism to emphasize the intimacy of interpersonal relationships within marriage at the rhetorical expense of the traditional stress on procreation. Compare L. S. Cahill, "Catholic Sexual Ethics and the Dignity of the Person: A Double Message," *Theological Studies* 50 (1989): 120–50; S. A. Ross, "The Bride of Christ and the Body Politic: Body and Gender in Pre–Vatican II Marriage Theology," *Journal of Religion* 71 (1991): 345–61; and D. P. Asci, *The Conjugal Act as a Personal Act: A Study of the Catholic Concept of the Conjugal Act in the Light of Christian Anthropology* (San Francisco: Ignatius Press, 2002).

2. J. Kristeva, "Stabat Mater," in *The Kristeva Reader*, ed. T. Moi (New York: Columbia University Press, 1986), 160–86.

3. R. Wilson, "A Scholar's Conclusions about Mary Stirs Ire," *Chronicle of Higher Education*, October 6, 1993, 7.

4. J. Schaberg, *The Illegitimacy of Jesus: A Feminist Theological Interpretation of the Infancy Narratives* (San Francisco: Harper & Row, 1987).

5. R. E. Brown, *The Virginal Conception and Bodily Resurrection of Jesus* (New York: Paulist Press, 1973).

6. R. E. Brown and others, eds., *Mary in the New Testament* (Philadelphia: Fortress, 1978).

7. R. E. Brown, *The Birth of the Messiah*, rev. ed. (New York: Doubleday, 1993).

8. See J. S. Spong, *Born of a Woman: A Bishop Rethinks the Birth of Jesus* (San Francisco: HarperSanFrancisco, 1992).

9. Hirsi Ali (*Caged Virgin: An Emancipation Proclamation for Women and Islam* [New York: Free Press, 2006], xii) describes *Submission* as "a film about the relationship between the individual and God, *in particular about the individual woman* and God." She italicizes this clause, it seems, to emphasize how the film's spiritual individualization of women represented a call for the kind of sexual emancipation that more conservative strains of Islam feared enough to silence with violence.

10. A. Hirsi Ali, *Infidel* (New York: Free Press, 2007), 31–35.

11. Interview with Ayaan Hirsi Ali, National Public Radio, February 5, 2007.

12. While genital mutilation is not comparatively common in the West, the so-called virginity doctrine (an utterance of discourse) is alive and well in the familial expectation of an intact hymen on a bride's wedding night. The practice has occurred with enough frequency in the United States to spur federal criminalization with the 1996 passage of the Female Genital Mutilation Act. See A. E. White, "Female Genital

Mutilation in America: The Federal Dilemma," *Texas Journal of Women and the Law* 10 (2001): 129–208. Multicultural immigration to the West has further articulated this discourse in the form of tensions about virginity, arranged marriages, and other proprietary dimensions of female sexuality. In adopted cultures with lesser stigmas attached to promiscuity, some women take advantage of medical procedures to obfuscate hymen ruptures from accidents, athletics, or premarital intercourse. Hymenoplasty (or hymenorrhaphy) is the surgical procedure that restores the hymen to a state resembling its original intactness. The cultural valuation of virginity that pressures women to undergo hymenoplasty has expectedly engendered a debate among physicians about the ethical ramifications of the procedure. See A. Longmans, A. Verhoeff, R. Bol Raap, F. Creighton, M. van Lent, and D. D. Raphael, "Should Doctors Reconstruct the Vaginal Introitus of Adolescent Girls to Mimic the Virginal State?," *British Medical Journal* 316 (1998): 459–60; and I. Usta, "Hymenorrhaphy: What Happens behind the Gynaecologist's Closed Door?,"*Journal of Medical Ethics* 26 (2000): 217–18. Hymenoplasty is common enough in the West to indicate a widespread cultural emphasis on virginity and its verification by an inviolate hymen. Some women choose to assert authority over their bodies, lead the sexual lives of their choice, and still rejoin communities that might wince were their lifestyles not concealable by medical treatment. Under favorable circumstances, plastic surgery can even emancipate circumcised females. For a review of U.S. physicians and practices, see S. Kobrin, "Restoring Virginity Becomes Risky Business," *Women's eNews*, May 22, 2005, <http://www.womensenews.org/article.cfm/dyn/aid/2304/context/archive>; and C. Black, "Surgery That Won't Make You Look Good in This: Is 'Vaginal Rejuvenation' on the Rise? And Why Are the Procedures So Controversial?," *Florida Times-Union*, May 23, 2006. For hymenoplasties in Canada, see M. Wente, "Like a Virgin for the Very Second Time," *Toronto Globe and Mail*, April 24, 2004. Latin America and Asia both have particularly large native markets for hymen restoration, revealing the global nature of a cultural insistence on intactness as prooftext for virginity. See H. Roberts, "Reconstructing Virginity in Guatemala," *Lancet* 367 (2006): 1227–28; and V. Jaffee (trans.), "Maidenhead Revisited," *Harper's Magazine*, May 2003, 30.

13. H. Shanks and B. Witherington III, *The Brother of Jesus: The Dramatic Story and Meaning of the First Archaeological Link to Jesus and His Family* (San Francisco: HarperSanFrancisco, 2003).

14. Ibid., 91.

15. Ibid., 218 (italics mine).

16. Ibid., 218–19.

17. Ibid., 219.

18. Despite the common Protestant aversion to the need for proof to confirm commitments to faith—a pattern Bremer and McNary-Zak's research observed in dozens of interviews (see their essays in this volume)—it is clear that the media

presumed historical "proof of faith" to be the most compelling bait for readers. Compare these international headlines in the first few days following the Biblical Archaeology Society's press conference on October 22, 2002: O. Burkeman, "Box May Have First Mention of Jesus," *Guardian* (London), October 22, 2002; "Hallan una referencia arqueológica sobre Jesús," *Miami El Nuevo Herald*, October 22, 2002; "Inscription Is 'First Physical Evidence of Christ,'" *Glasgow Herald*, October 22, 2002; M. Ellis, "Burial Box 'Is Proof of Jesus,'" *Daily Mirror* (London), October 22, 2002; N. Wapshott, "Scholar Finds 'Evidence of Jesus,'" *Times* (London), October 23, 2002; M. Warren, " 'Earliest Mention' of Jesus Is Found on 1st-Century Ossuary," *Daily Telegraph*, October 23, 2002; "Un ossuaire du ler siècle ferait réference à Jésus Christ," *Le Monde* (Paris), October 24, 2002. Dozens of similar headlines filled newspaper copy and Internet sites during the same week, with practically all operating under the rhetorical assumption that the name "Yeshua" inscribed on the ossuary meant none other than the historical Jesus of Nazareth.

19. Articles and citations in the journals *Marian Studies* and *Marianum* canvass the thousands of books and articles devoted to Mariology from the Roman period to the present. The following works provide only a glimpse of pertinent bibliography: J. Pelikan, *Mary through the Centuries: Her Place in the History of Culture* (New Haven: Yale University Press, 1996); A.-J. Levine, ed., *A Feminist Companion to Mariology* (Cleveland: Pilgrim Press, 2005); E. Carroll, "A Survey of Recent Mariology," *Marian Studies* 34 (1983): 91–126; T. A. O'Meara, *Mary in Protestant and Catholic Theology* (New York: Sheed and Ward, 1966); E. A. Johnson, *Truly Our Sister: A Theology of Mary in the Communion of Saints* (New York: Continuum, 2003); D. H. du Manoir, ed., *Maria: Études sur la sainte Vierge* (Paris: Beauchesne, 1949); G. P. Corrington, *Her Image of Salvation* (Louisville, Ky.: Westminster/John Know Press, 1992); G. Miegge, *The Virgin Mary* (Philadelphia: Westminster, 1955); D. Good, ed., *Mariam, the Mother, and the Magdalen* (Bloomington: Indiana University Press, 2005); M. Jugie, *La Mort et l'Assomption de la Sainte Vierge: Etude historico-doctrinale* (Vatican City: Biblioteca Apostolica Vaticana, 1944); J. C. Anderson, "Mary's Difference: Gender and Patriarchy in the Birth Narratives," *Journal of Religion* 67 (1987): 183–202; K. Coyle, *Mary in the Christian Tradition: From a Contemporary Perspective* (Mystic, Conn.: Twenty-Third Publications, 1996); S. Benko, *The Virgin Goddess: Studies in the Pagan and Christian Roots of Mariology* (Leiden: Brill, 1993); H. Manteau-Bonamy, *La Vierge Marie et le Saint-Esprit* (Paris: Lethielleux, 1971); H. G. Anderson, J. F. Stafford, and J. A. Burgess, eds., *The One Mediator, the Saints, and Mary* (Minneapolis: Ausburg Fortress, 1992); B. Gaventa, *Mary: Glimpses of the Mother of Jesus* (Minneapolis: Fortress, 1999); S. Ben-Chorin, *Marie: un regard juif sur la mère de Jésus* (Paris: Desclée de Brouwer, 2001); J. Alfaro, "The Mariology of the Fourth Gospel: Mary and the Struggles for Liberation," *Biblical Theology Bulletin* 10 (1980): 3–16; K. Børresen, *Anthropologie médiévale et théologie mariale* (Oslo: Univeritets-forlaget, 1971); H. Graef, *Mary: A History of*

Doctrine and Devotion (Westminster, Md.: Christian Classics, 1985); H. Kürg and J. Moltmann, eds., *Mary in the Churches* (New York: Seabury, 1983); B. Bruteau, "The Blessed Virgin Mary: A Feminine Archetype for the West," *Anima* 15 (1989): 102–38; B. V. Pentcheva, *Icons and Power: The Mother of God in Byzantium* (University Park: Pennsylvania State University, 2006); and M. Vassilaki, ed., *Images of the Mother of God: Perceptions of the Theotokos in Byzantium* (Burlington, Vt.: Ashgate, 2005).

20. Or marital abstinence; one may plausibly read the Greek of Matthew to make either claim.

21. As with most early Christian documents, arguments for the date and impetus for *Protevangelium* are diverse. Some scholars see the apocryphon as a response to Celsus and/or a source text for Justin Martyr; others prefer a later date entirely. For text-critical, chronological, and thematic dimensions of the *Protevangelium*, see representative discussions and citations in R. Hock, *The Infancy Gospels of James and Thomas* (Santa Rosa: Polebridge Press, 1995); E. de Strycker, "*Protévangile*," in *Studia Evangelica III*, ed. F. Cross (Akademie Verlag, 1964), 339–59; P. van Stempvoort, "The *Protoevangelium Jacobi*, the Sources of Its Theme and Style and Their Bearing on Its Date," in *Studia Evangelica III*, ed. F. Cross (Akademie Verlag, 1964), 413–23; E. de Stryker, "Une ancienne version latine du Protévangile de Jacques avec des extraits de la Vulgate de Matthieu 1–2 et Luc 1–2," *Analecta Bollandiana* 83 (1965): 365–402; G. T. Zervos, "Dating the *Protevangelium of James*: The Justin Martyr Connection," in *SBL Seminar Papers, 1994* (Atlanta: Scholars Press, 1994), 415–34; G. T. Zervos, "An Early Non-Canonical Annunciation Story," in *SBL Seminar Papers, 1999* (Atlanta: Scholars Press, 1999), 664–91; G. T. Zervos, "Christmas with Salome," in *A Feminist Companion to Mariology*, ed. A.-J. Levine (Cleveland: Pilgrim Press, 2005); M. F. Foskett, "Virginity as Purity in the *Protevangelium of James*," in *A Feminist Companion to Mariology*, ed. A.-J. Levine (Cleveland: Pilgrim Press, 2005), 67–76; and T. Horner, "Jewish Aspects of the Protoevangelium of James," *Journal of Early Christian Studies* 12 (2004): 313–35. For sundry evidence of the cross-cultural textual resonance of *Protevangelium* beyond the Patristic period, see C. Conybeare, "Documents: Protevangelium Iacobi," *American Journal of Theology* 1 (1897): 424–42; and C. A. Patrides, "The 'Protevangelium' in Renaissance Theology and *Paradise Lost*," *Studies in English Literature, 1500–1900* 3 (1963): 19–30.

22. Recent treatments of the veneration of Anna into the medieval period include V. Nixon, *Mary's Mother: Saint Anne in Late Medieval Europe* (University Park: Pennsylvania State University Press, 2004); and K. Ashley and P. Sheingorn, eds., *Interpreting Cultural Symbols: Saint Anne in Late Medieval Society* (Athens and London: University of Georgia Press, 1990).

23. I specify the original author in view of certain text-critical red flags raised in Papyrus Bodmer V, the oldest extant manuscript of *Protevangelium*; compare

M. Testuz, *Papyrus Bodmer V: Nativité de Marie* (Cologny-Geneva: Bibliotheca Bodmeriana, 1958).

24. Witherington resuscitates this debate in connection to the brother named on the James Ossuary; compare Shanks and Witherington, *The Brother of Jesus*, 199–209.

25. For the best recent treatment of the infancy narratives and early Mariology within the Roman cultural ambit, see M. F. Foskett, *A Virgin Conceived: Mary and Classical Representations of Virginity* (Bloomington: Indiana University Press, 2002). Contrast Foskett's expansive sense of classical contexts with the traditional approach exemplified by R. E. Brown, *The Birth of the Messiah.*

26. See the relevant discussions of Ambrose's following four treatises (*De virginibus*, *De virginitate*, *De institutione virginis*, and *Exhortatio virginitatis*) in B. Ramsey, *Ambrose* (London: Routledge, 1997); J. Quasten, *Patrology*, vol. 4: *The Golden Age of Latin Patristic Literature* (Westminster, Md.: Christian Classics, 1986); and D. G. Hunter, "The Virgin, the Bride, and the Church: Reading Psalm 45 in Ambrose, Jerome, and Augustine," *Church History* 69 (2000): 281–303, esp. 285–90. For Jerome, see N. Adkin, *Jerome on Virginity: A Commentary on the* Libellus de virginitate servanda (Cambridge: Francis Cairns, 2003).

27. P. Brown, *The Body and Society: Men, Women, and Sexual Renunciation in Early Christianity* (New York: Columbia University Press, 1988), xv; see also 350–56 for Brown's discussion of Ambrose's watershed argument for perpetuity, which built largely on the work of Origen, the godfather of chastity.

28. See E. A. Clark, "The Lady Vanishes: Dilemmas of a Feminist Historian after the 'Linguistic Turn,'" *Church History* 67 (1998): 1–31; E. A. Clark, "The Uses of the Song of Songs: Origen and the Later Latin Fathers," in *Ascetic Piety and Women's Faith: Essays on Late Ancient Christianity* (Lewiston, N.Y.: Mellen, 1986), 386–427; A. Cameron, *Christianity and the Rhetoric of Empire: The Development of Christian Discourse* (Berkeley: University of California Press, 1991); A. Cameron, "Virginity as Metaphor: Women and the Rhetoric of Early Christianity," in *History as Text: The Writing of Ancient History*, ed. A. Cameron (Chapel Hill: University of North Carolina Press, 1989), 181–205; A. Cameron, "Redrawing the Map: Early Christian Territory after Foucault," *Journal of Roman Studies* 76 (1986): 266–71; C. W. Bynum, *The Resurrection of the Body in Western Christianity, 200–1336* (New York: Columbia University Press, 1995); D. G. Hunter, "Resistance to the Virginal Ideal in Late-Fourth-Century Rome: The Case of Jovinian," *Theological Studies* 48 (1987): 45–64; D. G. Hunter, "Clerical Celibacy and the Veiling of Virgins: New Boundaries in Late Ancient Christianity," in *The Limits of Ancient Christianity: Essays on Late Antique Thought and Culture in Honor of R. A. Markus*, ed. W. Klingshirn and M. Vessey (Ann Arbor: University of Michigan Press, 1999), 139–52; D. G. Hunter, "Helvidius, Jovinian, and the Virginity of Mary," *Journal of Early Christian Studies* 1 (1993): 47–71.

29. Important representative studies with pertinent bibliographies include

K. Cooper, *The Virgin and the Bride: Idealized Womanhood in Late Antiquity* (Cambridge, Mass.: Harvard University Press, 1996); K. Cooper, "Insinuations of Womanly Influence: An Aspect of the Christianization of the Roman Aristocracy," *Journal of Roman Studies* 82 (1992): 150–64; K. A. Smith, "Inventing Marital Chastity: The Iconography of Susanna and the Elders in Early Christian Art," *Oxford Art Journal* 16 (1993): 3–24; E. Perkins, *The Suffering Self: Pain and Narrative Representation in the Early Christian Era* (London: Routledge, 1995); N. Koltun-Fromm, "Sexuality and Holiness: Semitic Christian and Jewish Conceptualizations of Sexual Behavior," *Vigiliae Christianae* 54 (2000): 375–95; A. Rousselle, *Porneia: On Desire and the Body in Antiquity* (London: Blackwell, 1988); V. Burrus, "Reading Agnes: The Rhetoric of Gender in Ambrose and Prudentius," *Journal of Early Christian Studies* 3 (1995): 25–46; V. Burrus, " 'Equipped for Victory': Ambrose and the Gendering of Orthodoxy," *Journal of Early Christian Studies* 4 (1996): 461–75; R. S. Evans, *Sex and Salvation: Virginity as a Soteriological Paradigm* (Lanham, Md.: University Press of America, 2003); P. Brown, "The Notion of Virginity in the Early Church," in *Christian Spirituality: Origins to the Twelfth Century*, ed. B. McGinn, J. Meyendorff, and J. Leclerq (New York: The Crossroads Publishing Company, 1985), 427–43; B. B. Thurston, *The Widows: A Women's Ministry in the Early Church* (Minneapolis: Fortress, 1989); S. L. Davies, *The Revolt of the Widows: The Social World of the Apocryphal Acts* (Carbondale: Southern Illinois University Press, 1980); R. Gryson, *La Ministére des femmes dans l'Église ancienne* (Gemboux: Duculot, 1972); R. Gryson, *Les Origines du célibat ecclésiastique* (Gemboux: Duculot, 1970); U. Wagener, *Die Ordnung des "Hauses Gottes": Der Ort von Frauen in der Ekklesiologie und Ethik der Pastoralbriefe* (Tübingen: Mohr Siebeck, 1994); J. LaPorte, *The Role of Women in Early Christianity* (New York: Mellen, 1982); C. Methuen, "The 'Virgin Widow': A Problematic Social Role for the Early Church," *Harvard Theological Review* 90 (1997): 285–98; C. Munier, *Mariage et virginité dans l'église ancienne* (Berne: Peter Lang, 1987); J. Meyendorff, "Christian Marriage in Byzantium: The Canonical and Liturgical Tradition," *Dumbarton Oaks Papers* 44 (1990): 99–107; S. Elm, *Virgins of God: The Making of Asceticism in Late Antiquity* (Oxford: Clarendon Press, 1994); R. S. Kraemer, "The Conversion of Women to Ascetic Forms of Christianity," *Signs* 6 (1980): 298–307; A. Vööbus, *Celibacy, a Requirement for Admission to Baptism in the Early Syrian Church* (Stockholm: 1951); C. A. Frazee, "The Origins of Clerical Celibacy in the Western Church," *Church History* 57 (1988): 108–26; A. Yarbrough, "Christianization in the Fourth Century: The Example of Roman Women," *Church History* 45 (1976): 149–65; and C. Rapp, "Figures of Female Sanctity: Byzantine Edifying Manuscripts and Their Audience," *Dumbarton Oaks Papers* 50 (1996): 313, 333, 335–44.

30. The literature on sexuality in Judaism of the Greco-Roman and Rabbinic periods is enormous, but consider the fascinating range of its iterations in studies like T. Ilan, "Premarital Cohabitation in Ancient Judea: The Evidence of the

Babatha Archive and the Mishnah (*Ketubbot* 1.4)," *Harvard Theological Review* 86 (1994): 247–64; R. S. Kraemer, "Monastic Jewish Women in Greco-Roman Egypt: Philo Judaeus on the Therapeutrides," *Signs* 14 (1989): 342–70; and D. Boyarin, "Internal Opposition in Talmudic Literature: The Case of the Married Monk," *Representations* 36 (1991): 87–113.

31. Cameron, "Redrawing the Map."

32. For the Vestal cult at Rome and the logistics and significance of sexual verification, see A. Staples, *From Good Goddess to Vestal Virgins: Sex and Category in Roman Religion* (New York: Routledge, 1998); H. N. Parker, "Why Were the Vestals Virgins? Or the Chastity of Women and the Safety of the Roman State," *American Journal of Philology* 125 (2004): 563–601; and M. Beard, "The Sexual Status of Vestal Virgins," *Journal of Roman Studies* 70 (1980): 12–27. On the hypostatic association of the virgin with the state, see S. Ortner, "The Virgin and the State," *Feminist Studies* 4 (1978): 19–35; J. N. King, "Queen Elizabeth I: Representations of the Virgin Queen," *Renaissance Quarterly* 43 (1990): 30–74; and J. N. King, "The Godly Woman in Elizabethan Iconography," *Renaissance Quarterly* 38 (1985): 41–84.

33. P. Brown, *The Body and Society*, xvii–xviii. For discussions of virginity, sexual politics, and gendered ideology in medieval Christianity, see Bynum, *The Resurrection of the Body*; C. W. Bynum, "Jesus and Mother and Abbot as Mother: Some Themes in Twelfth-Century Cistercian Writing," *Harvard Theological Review* 70 (1977): 257–84; J. Bugge, *Virginitas: An Essay in the History of a Medieval Ideal* (The Hague: Martinus Nijhoff, 1975); K. Kelly, *Performing Virginity and Testing Chastity in the Middle Ages* (New York: Routledge, 2000); C. L. Carlson and A. J. Weisl, eds., *Constructions of Widowhood and Virginity in the Middle Ages* (New York: Palgrave Macmillan, 1999); R. H. Bloch, "Medieval Misogyny," *Representations* 20 (1987): 1–24; S. Salih, *Versions of Virginity in Late Medieval England* (Cambridge: Brewer, 2001); A. Bernau, R. Evans, and S. Salih, eds., *Medieval Virginities* (Toronto: University of Toronto, 2003); J. Wogan-Browne, *Saints' Lives and Women's Literary Culture c. 1150–1300: Virginity and Its Authorizations* (Oxford: Oxford University Press, 2001); M. Goodich, "The Contours of Female Piety in Later Medieval Hagiography," *Church History* 50 (1981): 20–32; and I. R. Resnick, "Marriage in Medieval Culture: Consent Theory and the Case of Joseph and Mary," *Church History* 69 (2000): 350–71. The question of discursive disjunction is in E. J. Carlson, "Clerical Marriage and the English Reformation," *Journal of British Studies* 31 (1992): 1–31. The virgin in the built environment (the landscape of visuality) is limited to iconography. Studies on the contribution of sexual ideology to architectural phenomenology includes E. B. Gamard, "Virgil/Beatrice: Remarks on Discursive Thought and Rational Order in Architecture," *Journal of Architectural Education* 48 (1995): 154–67; H. Hills, *Invisible City: The Architecture of Devotion in Seventeenth-Century Neapolitan Convents* (Oxford: Oxford University Press, 2004); E. B. Gamard, "Cities and Virgins: Female Aristocratic Convents in Early Modern

Naples and Palermo," *Oxford Art Journal* 22 (1999): 29–54; and E. B. Gamard, "Iconography and Ideology: Aristocracy, Immaculacy, and Virginity in Seventeenth-Century Palermo," *Oxford Art Journal* 17 (1994): 16–31.

34. See M. Aubin, "Reversing Romance? The *Acts of Thecla* and the Ancient Novel," in *Ancient Fiction and Early Christian Narrative*, ed. R. F. Hock, J. B. Chance, and J. Perkins (Atlanta: Scholars Press, 1998), 257–72; J. N. Bremmer, ed., *The Apocryphal Acts of Paul and Thecla* (Kampen: Kok Pharos, 1996); V. Burrus, *Chastity as Autonomy: Women in the Stories of Apocryphal Acts* (Lewiston/Queenston: Edwin Mellen, 1987); V. Burrus, "Mimicking Virgins: Colonial Ambivalence and the Ancient Romance," *Arethusa* 38 (2005): 49–88; L. Hayne, "Thecla and the Church Fathers," *Vigiliae Christianae* 48 (1994): 209–18; L. C. Boughton, "From Pious Legend to Feminist Fantasy: Distinguishing Hagiographical License from Apostolic Practice in the *Acts of Paul/Acts Thecla*," *Journal of Religion* 71 (1991): 362–83. Thecla survives in later iconographic scenes, such as the London ivory casket in the British Museum and the Pentecost sculptured altar in the Metropolitan Museum; see H. L. Kessler, "Scenes from the Acts of the Apostles on Some Early Christian Ivories," *Gesta* 18 (1979): 109–19, esp. 113; and J. Beck, "A Sculptured Altar-Piece of the Fifteenth Century," *Metropolitan Museum of Art Bulletin* 5 (1910): 133, 146–48.

35. Compare the fascinating analysis of Methodius's *Symposium* in S. Goldhill, *Foucault's Sexuality: Ancient Erotic Fiction and the History of Sexuality* (Cambridge: Cambridge University Press, 1995), 1–4, 43–45.

36. M. Foucault, *The Care of the Self* (New York: Vintage, 1986), 240.

37. The relevant context of Isaiah 7 concerns the prophet's reassurance to King Ahaz of Judah that the dynastic House of David would not perish despite growing threats to the kingdom. The narrative is set during the so-called Syro-Ephraimite War, precipitating the kingdoms of Israel and Damascus to form a joint military pact to invade Judah. Isaiah informs Ahaz that the mother of his heir has already conceived and will give birth to a son. Before the child reaches adulthood, Isaiah continues, the Assyrian Empire would conquer and depopulate both the kingdoms of Israel and Damascus. Most scholars take this reference to indicate Hezekiah, who would later succeed Ahaz on the throne in Jerusalem. Around the time of Hezekiah's childhood, both Damascus (732 BCE) and Israel (722 BCE) indeed succumbed to Assyria's hegemonic expansion into the southern Levant. Although set sometime in the 730s BCE, the Isaianic narrative's composition likely dates to the early seventh century, specifically after Sennacherib's invasion of Judah in 701 BCE. Isaiah 36–38 and 1 Kings 18–20 present roughly duplicate accounts of Sennacherib's siege of Jerusalem, during which both King Hezekiah, he of the Davidic line, and Isaiah himself feature prominently as defenders of the city. This narrative suggests strongly that the text of 1 Isaiah (chaps. 1–39) dates to a point after the historical events, which the contents purport episodically to predict and recount. The Hezekiah/Jesus dispute begins demonstrably as early as the second

century; Justin Martyr disputes Trypho's identification of Hezekiah in Isaiah 7:14 in *Dialogue with Trypho* 66.

38. Representative studies include W. Berg, "Die Identität der 'jungen Frau' in Jes 7,14.16," *Biblische Notizen* 13 (1980): 7–13; R. G. Bratcher, "A Study of Isaiah 7:14," *Bible Translator* 9 (1958): 97–126; D. Buzy, "Les machals numériques de la sangsue et de l'ʿalmah," *Revue biblique* 42 (1933): 5–13; E. W. Conrad, "The Annunciation of Birth and the Birth of the Messiah," *Catholic Biblical Quarterly* 47 (1985): 656–63; J. Coppens, "L'interprétation d'Is VII, 14 à la lumière des études les plus récentes," in *Lex tua veritas*, ed. H. Gross (Trier: Paulinus, 1961), 31–45; J. Coppens, "La mere du Sauveur à la lumière de la théologie vétérotestamentaire," *Ephemerides theologicae lovanienses* 31 (1955): 7–20; J. Coppens, "Le prophétie de l'ʿalmah," *Ephemerides theologicae lovanienses* 28 (1952): 648–78; G. Delling, "παρθενος," in *Theological Dictionary of the New Testament*, vol. 5, ed. G. Friedrich (Grand Rapids, Mich.: Eerdmans, 1967), 826–37; L. Dequeker, "Isaïe vii 14," *Vetus Testamentum* 12 (1962): 331–35; A. M. Dubarle, "La conception virginale et la citation d'Is. VII, 14 dans l'évangile de Matthieu," *Revue biblique* 85 (1978): 362–80; G. Fohrer, "Zu Jes 7,14 im Zusammenhang von Jes. 7, 10–22," *Zeitschrift für die alttestamentliche Wissenschaft* 68 (1956): 54–56; H. Gese, "Natus ex virgine," in *Probleme biblischer Theologie*, ed. H. W. Wolff (Munich: Kaiser, 1971), 73–89; C. H. Gordon, "ʿAlmah in Isaiah 7:14," *Journal of Bible and Religion* 21 (1953): 106; H. Haag, "Jes 7,14 als alttestamentliche Grundstelle der Lehre von der Viriginitas mariae," in *Das Buch des Bundes*, ed. B. Lang (Düsseldorf: Palmos, 1980), 180–86; R. Kilian, "Die Geburt des Immanuel aus der Jungfrau Jes 7,14," in *Zum Thema Jungfrauengeburt*, ed. K. S. Frank and others (Stuttgart: KBW, 1970), 9–35; H. Kruse, "Alma Redemptoris Mater," *Trierer theologische Zeitschrift* 74 (1965): 15–36; C. Lattey, "The Term ʿAlmah in Is. 7:14," *Catholic Biblical Quarterly* 9 (1947): 89–95; H. Lenhard, " 'Jungfrau' oder 'junge Frau' in Jeseja 7,14?," *Theologische Beiträge* 7 (1976): 264–67; T. Lescow, "Das Geburtsmotiv in den messianischen Weissagungen bei Jesaja und Micha," *Zeitschrift für die alttestamentliche Wissenschaft* 79 (1967): 172–207; J. Lindblom, *A Study on the Immanuel Section in Isaiah* (Lund: Gleerup, 1958); J. A. MacCulloch, "Virgin Birth," *Encyclopedia of Religion and Ethics*, vol. 12, ed. J. Hastings (New York, 1927), 623–26; E. C. B. MacLaurin, "The Canaanite Background of the Doctrine of the Virgin Mary," *Religious Traditions* 3 (1980): 1–11; W. McKane, "The Interpretation of Isaiah VII 14–25," *Vetus Testamentum* 17 (1967): 208–19; A. E. Myers, "The Use of Almah in the OT," *Lutheran Quarterly* 7 (1955): 137–40; M. Rehm, "Das Wort ʿalmâ in Is 7,14," *Biblische Zeitschrift* 8 (1964): 89–101; L. Reinke, *Die Weissagung von der Jungfrau und vom Immanuel Jes 7,14–16* (Münster: Coppenrath'sche Buchhandlung, 1848); H. Ringgren, *The Messiah in the Old Testament* (London: SCM, 1956); J. E. Steinmüller, "Etymology and Biblical Usage of *ʿAlmah*," *Catholic Biblical Quarterly* 2 (1940): 28–43; M. E. W. Thompson, "Isaiah's Sign of Immanuel," *Expository Times*

95 (1983/84): 67–71; R. Tournay, "L'Emmanuel et sa Vierge-Mère," *Revue Thomiste* 55 (1955): 249–58; M. de Tuya, "¿La profecia de la ʿAlmah (Is. 7,14), un caso de 'tipologia redaccional'?," *Studium* 24 (1984): 231–67; H. M. Wolf, "A Solution to the Immanuel Prophecy in Isaiah 7:14–8:22," *Journal of Biblical Literature* 91 (1972): 449–56; A. van der Kooij, "Die Septuaginta Jesajas als Dokument Jüdischer Exegese: Einige Notize zu LXX-Jes 7," in *Übersetzung und Deutung: Studien zu dem Alten Testament und seiner Umwelt*, ed. H. A. Brongers and others. (Nijkerk: Callenbach, 1977), 91–102; H. Cazelles, "La Septante d'Is 7,14," in *La Mère de Jésus-Christ et la communion des saints dans la liturgie*, ed. H. Cazelles and others (Rome: Centro Liturgico Vincenziano, 1986), 45–54; M. Rösel, "Die Jungfrauengeburt des endzeitlichen Immanuel," *Jahrbuch für Biblische Theologie* 6 (1991): 135–51; and R. E. Brown, *The Birth of the Messiah*, 143–53.

39. Or those of his mother in the *Protevangelium*.

40. "The virgin birth in its sanctity works as a counterpart of natural sexual activity," observes H. von Campenhausen (*The Virgin Birth in the Theology of the Ancient Church* [Naperville, Ill.: Allenson, 1964], 53).

41. R. Troxel, "Isaiah 7,14–16 through the Eyes of the Septuagint," *Ephemerides Theologicae Lovanienses* 79 (2003): 1. See also R. Troxel, *LXX-Isaiah as Translation and Interpretation: The Strategies of the Translator of the Septuagint of Isaiah* (Leiden: Brill, 2007). Troxel's work is the notable exception to the Christological rubric, inasmuch as he focuses directly on the philological Weltanschauung of the Greek Isaiah for its own merits.

42. Namely, the Jewish community of Alexandria if Aristeas's account of the LXX's origin (while highly fictionalized) passes geographic muster.

43. Compare C. Dohmen and H. Ringgren, "*ʿalmâ*," in *Theological Dictionary of the Old Testament*, vol. 11, ed. G. J. Botterweck, H. Ringgren, and H.-J. Fabry (Grand Rapids, Mich.: Eerdmans, 2000), 154–63; G. J. Wenham, "*Betûlah* 'A Girl of Marriageable Age,'" *Vetus Testamentum* 22 (1972): 326–48.

44. See further J. Bergman, H. Ringgren, and M. Tsevat, "*bᵉthûlah*," in *Theological Dictionary of the Old Testament*, vol. 2, ed. G. J. Botterweck and H. Ringgren (Grand Rapids, Mich.: Eerdmans, 1977), 338–43; Wenham, "*Betûlah* 'A Girl of Marriageable Age,'" 326–48.

45. While "Baal makes love by the thousand" to Virgin Anat, who meanwhile "is passionate and takes hold of [his] testicles," E. R. Lacheman finds it especially difficult "to suppose that the term 'virgin' (*b-t-l-t*) in Ugaritic implies the concept of chastity"; compare E. R. Lacheman, "Apropos of Isaiah 7:14," *Journal of Bible and Religion* 22 (1954): 43.

46. See *Chicago Assyrian Dictionary*, vol. 2, ed. A. L. Oppenheim and others (Chicago: Oriental Institute, 1965), 173–74.

47. F. Graf, "Parthenos," in *Brill's New Pauly: Encyclopaedia of the Ancient World*, ed. H. Cancik and others (Leiden and Boston: Leiden, 2007), 571.

48. H. G. Liddell and R. Scott, *A Greek-English Lexicon*, rev. ed. (Oxford: Clarendon, 1968), 1339.

49. G. Kruse, "Parthenos," in *Paulys Real-Encyclopädie der classischen Altertumswissenschaft*, ed. K. Ziegler and others (Waldsee: Druckenmüller Verlag, 1949), cols. 1936–65.

50. "Rather as befits mother goddesses," writes Sarah Pomeroy, "they had enjoyed many consorts. Their failure to marry, however, was misinterpreted as virginity by succeeding generations of men who connected the loss of virginity only with conventional marriage." See S. Pomeroy, *Goddesses, Whores, Wives, and Slaves: Women in Classical Antiquity* (London: Pimlico, 1975), 6. Compare the Sophoclean demarcation of status, rather than experience, in C. Segal, "Mariage et sacrifice dans les *Trachiniennes* de Sophocle," *Antiquité classique* 44 (1975): 30–53.

51. G. Sissa, *Greek Virginity* (Cambridge, Mass.: Harvard University Press, 1990).

52. Ibid., 77.

53. E. Renan, *Oeuvres complètes*, vol. 3 (Paris: Calmann-Lévy, 1947–58), 322.

54. Sissa, *Greek Virginity*, 78.

55. In *Greek Religion* (Cambridge, Mass.: Harvard University Press, 1975), even the august Walter Burkert has a rare lapse of philological circumspection in his discussion of Hephaistos's attempt to seduce Athena. Chasing Athena, the blacksmith ejaculates onto her leg, from which she flicks his semen to the ground. The earth's insemination conceives the boy Erechtheus, whom Athena raises as her son in the Parthenon, her "Maidens' Apartment" (139). "The paradox of the identity of virgin and mother," Burkert puzzles, "is something which the myth recoils from articulating" (143). It is not clear that the myth regards the coextensivity of virginity and maternity as paradoxical, however, which would explain the silence that Burkert takes for discomfort. It is true that Athena's "auxiliary" role in Erechtheus's logistical conception clearly avoids the biological entanglement of maternity, but that is not the point. Inasmuch as the terms for the biological children of *parthenoi* (*parthenios* and *parthenias*) commonly designate illegitimate offspring born out of wedlock, *parthenoi* are consequently common enough biological mothers.

56. See Sissa, *Greek Virginity*, 77–86, and citations for elaboration of these examples.

57. Sissa, *Greek Virginity*, 76. See further A. Brelich, *Paides e parthenoi* (Rome: Edizioni dell'Ateneo, 1969); and C. Calame, *Les Choeurs des jeunes filles en Grèce archaïque*, vol. 1 (Rome: Edizioni dell'Ateneo, 1977), 65. Both Brelich and Calame exhaustively tally the manifold *social* circumstances in which a young woman might come to acquire the designation *parthenos*.

58. The contextual Greek translation of the larger Isaianic text is very literal, after all, as Troxel persuasively notes; see "Isaiah 7,14–16." His attempt to explain the superfluous *agathon e kakov* in LXX (Isaiah 7:16), however, is unnecessary and

belabored. Troxel occupies most of his presentation with the construction of a theological/conceptual rationale for the translator's frame of mind. I should have thought the Qumran manuscript variants, especially vis-à-vis LXX and the MT, would indicate the probability of a variant Hebrew *Vorlage* by logical parsimony.

59. Van der Kooij, "Die Septuaginta Jesajas als Dokument Jüdischer Exegese," 97.

60. LXX misrenders this passage terribly, but then we should note that the Greek translation of Proverbs depends on a Hebrew text at great variance with the MT.

61. Delling, "παρθενος," 833.

62. I call attention to the standard *apologias* in each new translation of Plato or Homer, whose new conservators formulaically disclaim and defend their departures in the pursuit of clarity or sensibility, irrespective of cultural valence; they may also deny any departures whatsoever. See the parade example of Allan Bloom's philosophical preface to *The Republic of Plato*, 2nd ed. (New York: BasicBooks, 1991), xi–xxiv.

63. The attempt to harmonize Matthew's discord with the Hebrew of Isaiah through selective fidelity to the textual witnesses hardly ceased with Origen. Franz Delitzsch's modern Hebrew translation of the New Testament does not in fact translate the Greek of Matthew 1:23, which quotes the problematic LXX; rather, he ignores the Greek of both LXX and Matthew and instead inserts the Massoretic Hebrew of Isaiah 7:14 (*hinnê haʿalmâ harâ wᵉyoledet ben*), giving modern Hebrew readers the false impression that the author of Matthew consulted and accurately quoted the original Hebrew. This bait and switch circumnavigates the famous incongruity between Isaiah's Hebrew and Matthew's Greek, but it ironically strips Matthew of any attestation of the word "virgin." Since his translation predated the work of Eliezer Ben-Yehuda to systematize modern spoken Hebrew, Delitzsch constructed his own hodgepodge of biblical and Rabbinic Hebrew with the aim to supply a product readable to nineteenth-century Jews conversant with traditional texts. Modern idiomatic interpolations thus stood side by side with Massoretic substitutions for Greek quotations of prophecy in the LXX. "Das hebr. Neue Testament sollte nicht den Juden den talmudischer Zeit, sondern der Gegenwart Christum verkündigen," explains Gustav Dalman in "Das Hebräische Neue Testament von Franz Delitzsch," *Hebraica* 9 (1893): 229. It is clear, then, that the philological liberties taken with the translation served the religious imperatives of evangelization as much as the need for a user-friendly text, and at the expense, moreover, of Delitzsch's otherwise objective standards of scholarly text criticism. Beginning in 1838, Delitzsch had begun to agitate for an intelligible Hebrew translation of the New Testament, which might supersede the edition first published in 1817 by the London Society for Promoting Christianity among the Jews. According to Dalman, Delitzsch's editorial successor, the endeavor was galvanized by their shared "Interesse für die Evangelisierung der Juden"; see

Dalman, "Das Hebräische Neue Testament," 227. Inchoate editions of 2,500 copies began to appear in 1877. By 1890, however, Delitzsch's declining health compelled him to entrust the finalization of the translation to younger colleagues, notably Dalman, who completed the final version of the opus. Delitzsch died later that same year, but not before he lived to see the publication of ten editions and 44,230 copies; see Dalman, "Das Hebräische Neue Testament," 231. His Hebrew New Testament has since enjoyed numerous reprintings by diverse proselytizing societies, including the British and Foreign Bible Society (now the Bible Society), the Society for Distributing Hebrew Scriptures, and Hope of Israel Publications, which republished the translation as recently as 2003.

64. Sissa, *Greek Virginity*, 83.

65. In Judaism, the Halakhic literature does discuss the perforation of the hymen, but measures vary with the circumstances. A female may retain her virginity if she can show that her hymen ruptured by nonsexual means. A divorcée may reclaim her legal virginity upon dissolution of the marriage. Female victims of rape lose their virginity only after the age of three. Contrary to popular opinion, there are no Talmudic prescriptions for the inspection of blood on connubial bed sheets to certify the bride's premarital chastity. See L. I. Rabinowitz, "Virgin, Virginity," in *Encyclopaedia Judaica*, vol. 16, ed. C. Roth and others (New York and Jerusalem: Macmillan and Keter, 1971), 162.

66. A. E. Hanson, "The Medical Writers' Woman," in *Before Sexuality: The Construction of Erotic Experience in the Ancient Greek World*, ed. D. M. Halperin, J. J. Winkler, and F. I. Zeitlin (Princeton: Princeton University Press, 1990), 309–38; and A. E. Hanson, "Obstetrics in the *Hippocratic Corpus* and Soranus," *Forum: Trends in Experimental and Clinical Medicine* 4 (1994): 93–110. For modern logistics of compulsory hymen inspection in Turkey, see E. Gürsoy and G. Vural, "Nurses' and Midwives' Views on Approaches to Hymen Examination," *Nursing Ethics* 10 (2003): 485–96.

67. Compare A. E. Hanson and M. H. Green, "Soranus of Ephesus: *Methodicorum princeps*," *Aufstieg und Niedergang der römischen Welt* 37 (1994): 984–1075; and J. R. Pinault, "The Medical Case for Virginity in the Early Second Century C.E.: Soranus of Ephesus, *Gynecology* 1.31," *Helios* 19 (1992): 123–39.

68. See Sissa, *Greek Virginity*, 1–5, 105–23; and G. Sissa, "Maidenhood without Maidenhead: The Female Body in Ancient Greece," in *Before Sexuality: The Construction of Erotic Experience in the Ancient Greek World*, ed. D. M. Halperin, J. J. Winkler, and F. I. Zeitlin (Princeton: Princeton University Press, 1990), 339–64.

69. *Protevangelium*, 19:15–16; translation by R. F. Hock in *The Complete Gospels*, ed. R. J. Miller (Sonoma, Calif.: Polebridge Press, 1992).

70. L. Steinberg, "'How Shall This Be?' Reflections on Filippo Lippi's *Annunciation* in London, Part I," *Artibus et Historiae* 8 (1987): 25–44.

71. Some artists incorporated natural phenomena with forced perspective to

answer the challenge of how best to depict the inscrutable. Consider examples like the *Annunciation* fresco, which Titian created for the Malchiostro Chapel of the Treviso Cathedral in 1519. Mary receives the incarnation through a shaft of light from the upper right-hand side, but Titian does not depict the light's origin in the painting. Rather, he places the fresco in the chapel to the lower left of the only source of illumination in the room: two windows to the upper right of the image. This permits sunlight to streak through the windows in such a way that it beams into the fresco aligned with the divine light of the Annunciation. Compare D. Rosand, "Titian's Light as Form and Symbol," *Art Bulletin* 57 (1975): 58–64, esp. 59–61.

72. Steinberg, " 'How Shall This Be?,' " 26.

73. From John Ciardi's untouchable translation of *Paradiso* 23; see Dante Alighieri, *The Divine Comedy*, trans. J. Ciardi (New York: New American Library, 1970), 800.

74. Dante, *Divine Comedy*, 801 (italics mine).

75. Compare the explanatory literature of True Love Waits at its website (<http://www.lifeway.com/tlw/>) and that of the derivative movement Silver Ring Thing (<http://www.silverringthing.com/home.asp>).

76. *Baptist Press*, February 14, 2005; compare <http://www.bpnews.net/bpnews.asp?ID=20143>.

77. S. Freud, *Three Essays on the Theory of Sexuality* (New York: BasicBooks, 1962), 37.

78. See H. Brückner and P. Bearman, "After the Promise: The STD Consequences of Adolescent Virginity Pledges," *Journal of Adolescent Health* 36 (2005): 271–78; and P. Bearman and H. Brückner, "Promising the Future: Abstinence Pledges and the Transition to the First Intercourse," *American Journal of Sociology* 106 (2001): 859–912.

79. Unprotected sexual contact in particular is pertinent, although not definitively explanatory. Companion to the higher frequency of anal and oral sex among pledgers is the lower frequency of prophylactic use among them. Brückner and Bearman ("After the Promise," 276) write: "The combination of low condom use and over-representation of pledgers provides some support for the hypothesis that this behavioral pattern is associated with greater than expected STD acquisition among pledgers, although the numbers are small and provide an insufficient basis from which to make inference."

80. Brückner and Bearman, "After the Promise," 276.

81. Shanks and Witherington, *The Brother of Jesus*, 91–92, 220.

82. Ibid., 220.

83. G. Frank, *The Memory of the Eyes: Pilgrims to Living Saints in Christian Late Antiquity* (Berkeley: University of California Press, 2000).

84. Ibid., 173.

85. Ibid., 133.

86. Interview with Suzan Sabir in Toronto, March 4, 2004.

87. See S. C. Levi, "P. T. Barnum and the Feejee Mermaid," *Western Folklore* 36 (1977): 149–54.

88. See the informative essays in J. Cuno, ed., *Whose Muse? Art Museums and the Public Trust* (Princeton: Princeton University Press, 2004).

89. Note the subtitle of Z. Singer, "Ossuary Dealer Accused of Forgery: He Seemed Honest: ROM," *National Post*, July 23, 2003; see also C. Hume, "ROM defends Decision to Display Ossuary," *Toronto Star*, June 19, 2003.

90. M. Swan, "People May Be Praying at Museum," *Catholic Register*, November 2002.

91. See Thomas Aquinas, *On Evil* (Oxford: Oxford University Press, 2003), 8c. I am indebted to my initial reading of A. Maierù, *University Training in Medieval Europe* (Leiden: Brill, 1994), 4.

92. J. Michael, *Anxious Intellects: Academic Professionals, Public Intellectuals, and Enlightenment Values* (Durham, N.C.: Duke University Press, 2000). See also D. La Capra, "The University in Ruins?," *Critical Inquiry* 25 (1998): 32–55.

93. For descriptions of the illicit trade in antiquities and discussions of the status of cultural property, see N. Brodie and C. Renfrew, "Looting and the World's Archaeological Heritage: The Inadequate Response," *Annual Review of Anthropology* 34 (2005): 343–61; R. Atwood, *Stealing History: Tomb Raiders, Smugglers, and the Looting of the Ancient World* (New York: St Martin's Griffin, 2004); C. Renfrew, *Loot, Legitimacy and Ownership* (London: Duckworth, 2000); R. Skeates, *Debating the Archaeological Heritage* (London: Duckworth, 2000); N. Brodie, J. Doole, and C. Renfrew, *Trade in Illicit Antiquities* (Cambridge: McDonald Institute, 2001); K. F. Gibbon, *Who Owns the Past? Cultural Policy, Cultural Property, and the Law* (New Brunswick: Rutgers University Press, 2005); P. Watson and C. Todeschini, *The Medici Conspiracy: The Illicit Journey of Looted Antiquities* (New York: Public Affairs, 2006); P. M. Messenger, ed., *The Ethics of Collecting Cultural Property* (Albuquerque: University of New Mexico Press, 1989); J. Carman, *Against Cultural Property: Archaeology Heritage and Ownership* (London: Duckworth, 2005); M. Bogdanos, "The Casualties of War: The Truth about the Iraq Museum," *American Journal of Archaeology* 109 (2005): 477–526.

94. For the aftermath in Iraq, see M. Bogdanos, *Thieves of Baghdad* (New York: Bloomsbury, 2005); and M. Polk and A. M. H. Schuster, eds., *The Looting of the Iraq Museum, Baghdad: The Lost Legacy of Ancient Mesopotamia* (New York: Abrams, 2005). Dr. Francis Deblauwe maintains a website with voluminous coverage and bibliography on the traffic in looted antiquities during the U.S. occupation of Iraq; see <http://iwa.univie.ac.at/>.

95. Literature on the traditional, outdated ethnographic models includes R. M. Berndt, "A Cargo Movement in the Eastern Highlands of New Guinea," *Oceania* 13

(1952): 40–65; K. Burridge, *Mambu: A Melanesian Millennium* (London: Routledge, 1960); G. Cochrane, *Big Men and Cargo Cults* (Oxford: Clarendon, 1970); E. F. Hanneman, "Le Culte du Cargo en Nouvelle-Guinée," *Le monde non Chretién* (N.S., 1948) 937–62; T. G. Harding, "A History of Cargoism in Sio, North-east New Guinea," *Oceania* 38 (1967): 1–23; P. Lawrence, *Road Belong Cargo* (Manchester and Melbourne: Melbourne University Press, 1964); and F. Steinbauer, *Melanesian Cargo Cults* (Sainta Lucia: University of Queensland Press, 1979). The older view of cargoism surprisingly turns up in enlightened historical work on religion like that of J. Z. Smith, *Imagining Religion: From Babylon to Jonestown* (Chicago: University of Chicago Press, 1982), 90–101.

96. M. Kaplan, *Neither Cargo nor Cult: Ritual Politics and the Colonial Imagination in Fiji* (Durham: Duke University Press, 1995).

97. In light of the depressed economy and infrastructure in the West Bank, Salah H. al-Houdalieh paints a gloomy portrait of the dependence of some Palestinian villages on the income derived from looting artifacts; see S. H. al-Houdalieh, "The Destruction of Palestinian Archaeological Heritage: Saffa Village as a Model," *Near Eastern Archaeology* 69 (2006): 102–12.

98. Foucault, *The History of Sexuality*, 58–67.

99. Shanks and Witherington, *The Brother of Jesus*, 84.

100. Compare ibid., 15.

101. From the Coptic translation of M. Meyer, *The Gospel of Thomas: The Hidden Sayings of Jesus* (San Francisco: HarperSanFrancisco, 1992), 27, 73–74. (Bracketed Coptic mine.)

JONATHAN L. REED

Overcoming the James Ossuary and the Legacy of Biblical Archaeology

Like the other archaeologists and biblical scholars, I had to see *the greatest archaeological discovery ever* on display in the Royal Ontario Museum (ROM). We were in Toronto for the 2002 annual meetings of the American Schools of Oriental Research and Society of Biblical Literature, and we all made the pilgrimage. Coming up the stairs from the Toronto Transit Commission's metro station, I saw a throng of people and darted to queue at the end of a line snaking around the corner from the museum's entrance. Hoping that tickets were still available, I began to notice a surprising number of children and families around me. After the line inched around the corner, I was even more surprised. I was not in line for the James Ossuary, but for the McLaughlin Planetarium's feature exhibit on *The Lord of the Rings*. That latter exhibit's sign boasted "artifacts from New Line Cinema's blockbuster film," and the children were there for artifacts of magical fantasy. As it turned out, after I skipped that line for the museum's entrance, I was there for an artifact of archaeological fantasy.

Inside the ROM, upstairs in the Mediterranean World Features Exhibitions and behind Plexiglas, was the Jewish burial box, or ossuary, whose twenty-letter Aramaic inscription had momentarily made it "the most important archaeological discovery of Christianity." The inscription read "James son of Joseph, brother of Jesus." Dating to before 70 CE, it would have been the earliest physical evidence of Jesus. Hershel Shanks, the editor of the *Biblical Archaeology Review* who orchestrated the discovery's initial press conference and exhibit at the museum, had previously arranged for epigraphic experts to authenticate it based on the letters' style and had two geologists confirm its antiquity based on a single and simple chemical test.[1] But several of my colleagues and I were already suspicious: the ossuary had not been found by archaeologists on excavation but had turned up via the shady world of antiquities dealers and collectors. When we noticed that the inscription cut deeper into the stone than two rosettes on the other side, we were more apprehensive. Even behind Plexiglas and at a distance, some letters appeared remarkably clear for a two-millennia-old stone box. Our hunch turned out to be right; the initial "expert" advice only ruled out a clumsy forgery, but this was a crafty forgery.

A later two-pronged investigation by the Israel Antiquities Authority convincingly showed that though the box was real, the inscription was fake. The authority's Theft Unit traced a warehouse to the ossuary's owner, Oded Golan, which served as a workshop for his other forgeries, including a more amateurish but politically explosive inscription mentioning the Jerusalem Temple. Inside his shop, they recovered dental drills and other tools, chemicals and soils from various archaeological sites, and scores of recently inscribed artifacts in various stages of production. Leads pointed to an Egyptian jeweler as the craftsman, who would later refuse extradition to testify in the owner's trial, which after three years is still ongoing.[2] Although Golan's guilt or innocence rests on Israeli legal procedures, antiquities laws, and the tug-of-war over who has the burden of proof, the ossuary's authenticity has long since been dismissed by every single archaeologist familiar with the case.[3] Shortly after the ossuary's discovery, a scientific panel was set up by the Israel Antiquities Authority to examine the James-Joseph-Jesus inscription, which concluded that the box was ancient but the inscription modern, cutting through the ancient surface and what geologists call biovermiculation, the bacterial erosion that takes place over centuries and under magnification looks like tiny coral-like pits. The patina, a thin weathering that forms on stone surfaces over time, covered most of the ossuary with a grayish-beige crystalline sheen and a cauliflowerlike appearance. It apparently also covered parts of the inscription; but microscopic examination revealed that parts around and in the inscription had been carefully coated with a fake patina, and other portions had flaked off all too easily and even before examination. The James Ossuary, it would turn out, was a hoax. Most archaeologists suspected as much when it was announced, and none today take it seriously. It does not prove anything. Of course, as a hoax it does not disprove anything, either.

THE IMPORTANCE OF *IN SITU*

The saga of the James Ossuary added the cloak-and-dagger excitement of clandestine workshops and legal machinations to the legacy of biblical archaeology. And in the process, it raised two immediate concerns for archaeologists. First, it cast a spotlight on the problem of unprovenanced artifacts. And second, it reaffirmed the absolute imperative of what archaeologists call *in situ*, a Latin phrase for "in place" that applies to all finds discovered by excavators where they had remained for centuries or even millennia. Many prominent scholars, including Eric Meyers, the former president of the American Schools of Oriental Research, used the opportunity to stress the society's position on unprovenanced artifacts, namely, that the "trade in antiquities, especially illicit trade, encourages the looting of archaeological sites and thus is a direct cause of the destruction of sites and the loss of the information they contain."[4] The reason why unprovenanced artifacts are so problematic for field archaeologists is often unknown or underappreciated by laypersons. The past and present acquisition of artifacts not found in excavation by museums or individuals has created an industry of tomb raiders and site looters. Their activities degrade the archaeological record at an alarming rate. The voracious appetite of the very rich for antiquities—whether coins, vases, statues, or mosaics—sustains an enormous illicit international trade network.[5] By placing an intrinsic value on an isolated artifact like the James Ossuary (and a high cash value—it was insured and offered for sale for $2 million!), demand is created in the black market, so that looters try to find more ossuaries for sale, with forgers adding inscriptions. Few field archaeologists are able to protect the sites they work at with surveillance and guards in the months they are not digging, and when they return to excavate, potholes from poachers with metal detectors litter those sites. The problem is so serious that many archaeologists and all professional archaeological societies refuse to publish or analyze unprovenanced artifacts from private collections, since that implies an endorsement that also enhances the object's value (and encourages more looting).

In addition to raising the ethical issue of unprovenanced artifacts, the James Ossuary raises the intellectual problem of how archaeology operates in relation to the fields of history and anthropology—that is, understanding past events and past cultures. Archaeology can only do so with integrity when it deals with artifacts found *in situ*. Archaeologists today distinguish themselves from Indiana Jones of present-day Hollywood, relic hunters of the religious past, or cultural looters of the colonial past by carefully excavating *in situ* finds and recording their context, whether sealed in a cave or cistern previously undisturbed or embedded in a layer of soil or under rubble not previously touched. This is an archaeological ideal in part because, unlike the James Ossuary, which appeared to the public through the murky world of private collectors and shady antiquities dealers, the authenticity of *in situ* finds is unequivocal. But more importantly, all *in situ* objects, however mundane or unspectacular, are tied to a specific context, an identifiable place in time and space within a web of chronological and spatial relationships made up of thousands of other artifacts. It is those chronological relationships between strata of various sites that help experts in the field of ceramics, for example, to refine their understanding of a pot's typological development and enable other archaeologists to date the layers of their excavation by the sherds in its soil.[6] Any object that lacks an *in situ* pedigree is disqualified from contributing to such typological studies, however beautiful it might look in a museum as an *objet d'arte* or however revered it might be in a church as a relic.

By treating a single unexcavated object as important, the false impression is created that there is a New Testament archaeology whose goal is to find an artifact mentioned, however obliquely, in the New Testament—the Holy Grail, the True Cross, the Holy Spear or so-called Lance of Longinus, the Shroud of Turin, or any number of items that belong to the realm of legend. In a more subtle manner, it also creates the impression that New Testament archaeologists only look for everyday items mentioned in the Gospels, like Jewish stone vessels or widows' mites, which can be used as visual aids in books and lectures as a way of suggesting the reliability of the Gospels. Yet instead of single artifacts, archaeologists care about the spatial relationship between any given artifact to many others, which is fundamental to reconstructing ancient social, cultural, or religious practices.

Thus archaeology only has ethical integrity if it is based on the collection of *in situ* artifacts, and it has academic integrity as a historical or anthropological discipline only if it considers the relationship and interpretation of *in situ* artifacts within the context of patterns derived from all other artifacts found on excavations. The James Ossuary serves as an object lesson for the importance of stratigraphic excavations. It also serves as an opportunity to reflect on the legacy of biblical archaeology and to examine how biblical scholarship and archaeology should be brought together.

THE OSSUARY IN THE CONTEXT OF BIBLICAL ARCHAEOLOGY

The publicity surrounding the James Ossuary at the beginning of the present century momentarily revived the fantasy that had sustained biblical archaeology for the better part of the previous century. By the middle of the twentieth century, biblical archaeology had become a thriving discipline at seminaries, colleges, and even universities that buoyed popular hope of finding buried in the sands of the Middle East or covered by the ruins of a lost ancient city an artifact that would confirm the Bible's truth. In the past several decades, however, archaeologists trained within and outside of biblical archaeology have alternatively abandoned or condemned this approach. Even conservative biblical scholars now recognize the limitations of such a biblical archaeology, and theologians tend to eschew relying on archaeology to affirm faith or support doctrine. But the James Ossuary not only generated great popular excitement for that possibility; it even lured some scholars back into the old-style way of relating archaeology to biblical studies, namely as an arbiter of faith.

For the better part of the twentieth century, biblical archaeologists focused on the Hebrew Bible/Old Testament and dug with a focus on the vertical and monumental. That is to say, on the one hand, they examined the sequential layers at a site and tried to link them with events mentioned in the Bible, with the goal of correlating biblical history with archaeological stratigraphy. The burning questions revolved around the biblical sites like Jericho, Ai, and Hazor and whether their destruction layers dated to the Israelites according to stories in the biblical book of Joshua. On the other hand, these archaeologists focused on large-scale public architecture at sites mentioned in the Bible with the goal of linking them to Israelite kings. Thus the sites of Gezer, Lachish, and Hazor were excavated, and the key question was whether the city gates dated to the tenth century BCE and were the Solomonic fortifications described in book of Kings. But the enterprise unraveled over the course of the second half of the twentieth century, as more doubt was cast on biblical texts than was historicity confirmed. Even the name "biblical archaeology" was dropped and is now widely out of favor, with many preferring the term "Syro-Palestinian archaeology" to describe a discipline whose main focus is not the Bible but the region whose sites are excavated and whose societies are examined. As part of this trend, the flagship journal of the American Schools of Oriental Research, *Biblical Archaeologist*, was renamed *Near Eastern Archaeology*.[7]

The older approach of biblical archaeology had never left much room for New Testament scholarship, however, since archaeological methods looked for destruction or construction—burn layers of cities destroyed or monumental architecture built by Israelite kings as mentioned in the Bible. But neither Jesus nor his early followers destroyed cities or built buildings, so no similar evidence came into question as the basis for a "New Testament archaeology." Indeed, the earliest Christian art dates to a century after Jesus, and the earliest Christian architecture to a century after that. Excavations and artifacts had for a long time no impact on historical Jesus research, even though there were a few inscriptions that mentioned some New Testament figures. These include one dug up in Israel's Caesarea Maritima that mentioned the Roman governor Pontius Pilate, who condemned Jesus to crucifixion; the bone box discovered in Jerusalem belonging to high priest Caiaphas, who participated in Jesus' trial; an inscription found in Greek Delphi that names Gallio, the procurator who stood trial over Paul in Acts 17; a pavement stone in Corinth inscribed with Erastus, perhaps the very person Paul cites in his letter to the Romans; and several inscriptions from the prominent Roman Sergii Paulli family, one of whom Paul converted according to Acts 13.[8] For many, these archaeological artifacts guaranteed the New Testament's validity. Yet one has to wonder, how can their now archaeologically proven existence verify the spiritual, moral, or religious claims of the Bible? Many might agree that it makes those claims more plausible, but it really cannot prove them true. Nevertheless, these inscriptions offer an important lesson. All of those New Testament characters whose names were written in stone had attained considerable power in the Roman world and had acquired some measure of wealth. In contrast, we have no inscriptions from the New Testament's main characters, whether Jesus or John the Baptist, Mary the mother of Jesus or Mary Magdalene, Peter or Paul—all of whom were people of no power or wealth. That does not mean they did not exist. But it does mean that they lived like the mass of people throughout history, flying under radar and leaving behind neither inscription nor building.

They vanished without a trace in the archaeological record. For that reason alone, the discovery of an inscription mentioning James and Jesus was surprising, if not suspicious.

Nevertheless, the James Ossuary was immediately hailed as the most important archaeological discovery for Christians *ever*—and discussed in a way that seemed to turn back the clock half a century in Hershel Shanks and Ben Witherington's *The Brother of Jesus: The Dramatic Story and Meaning of the First Archaeological Link to Jesus and His Family*. This book was the "official" version of the ossuary's story and its significance, but the biblical-archaeological approach was all too apparent, as it began to make the artifact an arbiter of faith; indeed, the latter author stretches to confirm a particularly Protestant kind of faith. Witherington concludes the book in an overly defensive manner by stating that the bone box provides "confirmation that the Bible often is speaking of real historical figures and real historical events, despite the skepticism about its historical truth that has emerged from many directions in our times. The historical confirmation of Gospel accounts is welcome news in a skeptical age that demands that you 'show me' the evidence before I can believe."[9] Witherington of course sets up a false dilemma for the reader: either the Bible is true or you are a doubting Thomas. His presentation asks archaeology to settle matters of faith or theological conviction without recognizing the limits of archaeological contributions, or for that matter the nature of faith, in my estimation.

Those limitations are serious even if one naively accepts the James Ossuary's inscription as authentic. How can we be sure, after all, that the inscription actually refers to the "right" James, Jesus, and Joseph? A statistical analysis of names in first-century Jerusalem by André Lemaire suggested that it is highly likely that the James-Joseph-Jesus name combination referred to the Gospel characters.[10] But "highly likely" is not proof. In this light, we should remember that those were very common male names for first-century Jews, and they have been found on other ossuaries in the past. An ossuary found early in the twentieth century had etched into its side *Yeshua bar Yehosef*, Aramaic for "Jesus son of Joseph."[11] Another ossuary discovered in 1980 at Talpiot outside of Jerusalem also bore this Aramaic inscription, although this time it was more clumsily written. A nearby ossuary was inscribed with *Yoseh*, a commonly contracted form of *Yehosef*, and another nearby was labeled in Greek with "of Mariamne, who is (also called) Mara," a form of the common name "Mary" that appears centuries later for Mary the mother of Jesus or Mary Magdalene.[12] The collection of names catapulted that tomb into the limelight recently as the Jesus family tomb in a sensationalizing book and made-for-TV special, all backed by a clever though disingenuous statistical analysis.[13] But archaeologists, historians, and biblical scholars rejected the claim, and even an array of statisticians rejected the overly optimistic identification based on mathematical calculations. Of course for the believer, any alleged statistical probability that these are the Gospels' Jesus, Joseph, and Mary is opposed since no bone box would be needed for a resurrected body. And of course for the historian, a myriad of problems make the identification implausible, improbable, or impossible.[14] These latter ossuaries show the elusive nature of "archaeological proof" for the existence of Jesus or James. No serious scholars doubt their existence anyway, and even if James's ossuary (and not Jesus' ossuary!) has been discovered, would it make the resurrection claims more plausible or the teachings of the Gospels more true? Making archaeology a means of proving or disproving the historicity of the Bible is a quixotic if not perilous enterprise for both archaeologists and people of faith.

If this approach to biblical archaeology is abandoned, that does not mean that archaeology cannot be brought to bear on our understanding of the New Testament and early Christianity. Even a scholar as theologically conservative as Craig Evans has stressed the problematic relationship between archaeology and faith and has used the James Ossuary as an opportunity not to prove the Bible, but to examine the archaeological record to help him understand aspects of the Gospels. In his book *Jesus and the Ossuaries: What Jewish Burial Practices Reveal about the Beginning of Christianity* (2003), Evans is much more judicious in bringing archaeology and the Gospels together than is Witherington. Rather than focusing on the single artifact of the James Ossuary, Evans examines all the evidence for the use of ossuaries by Jews in the first century. He notes where that evidence might be of help in assessing a Gospel text, and he wisely concludes that "as in the case of archaeology in general, little is proven, but much is learned. The value of this study lies not in apologetics, but in what light it sheds on customs, beliefs, historical events, and meaning in texts."[15] His study is, as he himself admits, limited to a series of *direct* correlations between artifact and text, ossuaries and Gospel passages. In that sense, he can be considered to practice biblical archaeology, with a biblical exegete appropriating (here in a positive sense) key findings of relevance to the New Testament. Thus Evans speculates on some very direct links with the biblical text, such as whether or not some names inscribed on ossuaries relate to those of New Testament characters—like one "Alexander called the Son of Simon from Cyrene," who is said to have carried Jesus' cross (Mark 15:21); or more probably, the Sadducee and high priest Caiaphas, whom we will look at again below. In addition, Evans shows how four ossuary inscriptions containing the word *qorban* clarify Jesus' denunciation of this potential legal loophole in Mark 7:6–8; how Jewish burial practices make sense of Jesus' comparison of his opponents to whitewashed tombs in Matthew 23–27; and how they provide the context for what he means when he says "to let the dead bury the dead" in Matthew 8:22. And finally, Evans speculates on the historical question of what happened to Jesus' body in light of the only crucified victim ever found, the anklebone pierced by a nail and redeposited in an ossuary labeled with the name *Yehochanan*. At this point, Evans cannot resist the lure of biblical archaeology as proof when he suggests that the Gospel stories of Jesus' burial after his crucifixion seem reasonable, since Yehochanan's ankle shows that, at least on one other occasion and against the common practice, the crucified victim's remains were obtained for family burial.[16]

BEYOND THE SHADOW OF BIBLICAL ARCHAEOLOGY

There is another way in which archaeology can be brought to bear on biblical scholarship, which need not be crippled by the obsession to prove (or disprove) the Bible and is not limited to direct links between archaeological artifacts and New Testament texts. Instead, this approach looks at wider patterns in the material culture, assesses aspects of the general cultural, social, or political trends at the time, and only then turns to how that evidence helps us understand the New Testament. Knowing full well that the particular (the James Ossuary) is a hoax, we turn to three aspects in which the general (ossuaries in first-century Jerusalem) helps us understand the historical Jesus and Christian origins. In bringing together archaeology as it relates to the historical Jesus, we begin with an archaeological description of ossuaries and burial practices in first-century Jerusalem and only then turn to its implications for early Christianity. In an approach that preserves the integrity of archaeology, we avoid the more usual approach by New Testament scholars, which is to begin with a New Testament text and then scan the archaeological record for any item that illustrates the text, in which case artifacts are often mere visual aids.

Jewish burial practices and socioeconomics. The first aspect of ossuary use in first-century Jerusalem to be considered has to do with shifting the focus away from religious interpretations of burial artifacts and toward socioeconomic observations concerning burial practices, a feature ignored by most New Testament scholars. Often, patterns in the material culture related to burial tell us less about religion than they do about socioeconomics. Byron McCane's excellent study, *Roll Back the Stone: Death and Burial in the World of Jesus* (2003) stresses how too often the archaeology of death is limited to interpretations of ancient theologies rather than the broader social context of death rituals.

With regard to the ossuaries, it has often been assumed that this Jewish practice emerged as a result of theological developments within Judaism, either from the emergent Hellenistic notions of individuality (hence each individual needs a box) or the Pharisaic belief in the bodily resurrection (hence the bones need to be kept together until they resurrect).[17] But by examining the relevant archaeological evidence in and around ossuaries, it is apparent that these theological explanations are less than convincing. Only a few of the ossuaries that were found contained a single individual. The vast majority held several skeletons, and the names etched on their sides make plain that family burial was still the norm in Judaism, with endearing terms like the Aramaic *Abba* ("Daddy") or *Emma* ("Mommy"), along with "son of," "wife of," or "father of." These identifications served like a tag to help the survivors at a later time add a child, spouse, or parent with the desired loved ones. Charnel pits with anonymous multiple interments of entire extended families might have been abandoned in the late Second Temple Period, but the numerous family members inside single ossuaries in no way implies individuality as the ideal. Each person, even in death, was bound to his or her family.[18]

We should also be cautious about connecting ossuaries to resurrection. Several ossuaries have been found that can be tied to Sadducees, a group of ruling priests who are known from literary texts (including the New Testament) to have disavowed belief in the bodily resurrection, or life after death for that matter (see Mark 12:23–33 and Acts 23:7–8). In addition to the Caiaphas ossuary, others from known Sadducean families have been excavated, like that inscribed with "Yehochana daughter of Yehochanan, son of Thophlos, the High Priest" (the "Thophlos" referred to is Theophilus, son of Annus, high priest from 37 to 41 CE). Other common high priestly family names have been found on ossuaries, like Boethos, Ananias, and Ananus, but it is unlikely that these Sadducean families collected and preserved the bones of their loved ones in anticipation of the resurrection. It is more likely that they simply adopted the common burial practice among the urban Jews of some means in Jerusalem, and they did so in rather elegantly decorated style.[19]

Burial practices and tombs often have more to do with contemporaneous social statements than they do with future hope in the afterlife. I stress the underlying socioeconomic factors in ossuary burial to a considerable degree with John Dominic Crossan in *Excavating Jesus: Beneath the Stones, Behind the Texts* (2002) in a chapter titled "How to Bury a King," which summarizes various hierarchies in burials and their role as status markers across the broader Mediterranean world. Similarly, Jodi Magness recently showed in some detail how ossuaries were used by the upper classes, while the lower classes either dug shaft or shallow graves and the lowest classes were simply discarded.[20] With regard to the James Ossuary, she concludes that: "the evidence that James was buried in a trench grave dug into the ground and not in a rock-cut tomb renders the controversy over the 'James Ossuary' moot. Even if the inscription is authentic, it would not refer to James the Just, the brother of Jesus."[21] In other words, Magness shows how ossuary burial in underground chambers was a practice of *Jewish elites* and stresses that most people, and certainly the poor, were interred in "individual trench graves or cist graves dug into the ground."[22] James, she reminds us, represents that characteristic combination of poverty and piety, and he would therefore not have been revered with an elite-style burial. This line of reasoning is not entirely airtight, since we know that in second-century Rome, Peter's tomb had been transformed into a relatively upscale burial in the Vatican, but for first-century Jerusalem the point is rather convincing. Be that as it may, I am absolutely sure she is right in saying it is a moot point, if only because I am convinced that the inscription is a forgery.

What is clear from the archaeology is that elite Jewish families in first-century Jerusalem used secondary burial in ossuaries placed underground on plots of land around the city. The lower classes could not afford such burial, be it plot of land or ossuary; thus it is not surprising that we have no evidence for Christian burial whatsoever until later in the second century, when some Christians—all outside Jerusalem and in Rome—had risen to higher levels of society. And the upper classes around Jerusalem made sure their burials reunited the extended family in death. Family burial was the ideal. Thus the Gospels' claim that Jesus was placed inside a "new tomb" (so Matthew 27:60) or a tomb "in which no one had yet been laid" (so Luke 23:53) may sound attractive to modern ears, but to ancient Jewish ears that must have sounded like a lonely, isolated, and tragic end to Jesus' life.[23]

The Caiaphas ossuary and its contents. A second way that ossuaries are of value for understanding the context from which early Christianity emerged has nothing to do with the boxes themselves, but what the bones inside them reveal about life in antiquity. There is no better illustration for this than the Caiaphas ossuary, an example that underscores the limitations of biblical archaeology. Its discovery illustrates how archaeologists do not work with any single item to understand the ancient world, but instead rely on the accumulation of finds anchored *in situ*, each of which has a specific and known relation in space and time to others. The Caiaphas ossuary was found in 1990 by construction workers south of Jerusalem's Old City when they broke through a Jewish burial cave sealed since the Roman War in 70 CE. Immediately, the Israel Antiquities Authority's salvage archaeologists were called, but they could not complete their work on the tomb after protests and pressure by ultraorthodox Jews led to its resealing and the human remains being handed over to the Ministry of Religious Affairs for reburial on the Mount of Olives in accordance with current policy. But the archaeologists had enough time to examine and photograph most of the tomb and its ossuaries *in situ*, which differs enormously from how the James Ossuary was thrust onto archaeologists at a press conference. The burial chamber had a five-and-a-half-foot ceiling that made it hard to stand upright, and four shafts, large enough to lay out a body, extended fingerlike from the main chamber. In one of those shafts was an ornately decorated ossuary, one of most beautiful ossuaries ever found, with the name *Yehosef bar Qafa* crudely etched on one side in Aramaic. The rarity of that name combination ("Joseph son of Caiaphas") left little doubt (though not absolute proof!) that this was the final resting place and ossuary of the high priest known as Caiaphas in the Gospels and infamous for his role in Jesus' arrest and trial.[24]

The find (probably) offers tangible evidence for Caiaphas, but no serious scholar had doubted his existence in the first place, given his mention in other ancient sources like the Jewish historian Flavius Josephus.

The decorated ossuary of Caiaphas, the high priest of Jerusalem (Courtesy of the Israel Museum)

And the ossuary's discovery could not determine if the Gospels accurately assessed his presence and role in Jesus' trial. But the discovery had an additional, often neglected, significance because of what was found alongside it. The Israel Antiquities Authority's forensic archaeologist Joe Zias was able to identify sixty-three other skeletons in the burial chamber, several of which were actually inside that one Caiaphas ossuary.[25] The demographic distribution of the dead is a grim reminder that even a wealthy high-priestly family was not immune to premature death or infant mortality. Of those buried with Caiaphas in the tomb, some 40 percent never made it past their fifth birthday. An additional 20 percent never reached puberty. Those statistics are shocking, especially when one considers that high-priestly families ate more meat than other groups since they received a share of the animal sacrifices and lived in a wealthy part of the city with ample flowing water and underground sewage. We can be sure that Jerusalem's urban poor were worse off. The distribution of ages in the Caiaphas Ossuaries matches other evidence from antiquity that shows that death at that time came less frequently than it does today from degenerative diseases such as cancer, heart attack, or stroke; most people of that era died from contagious respiratory or gastrointestinal diseases like tuberculosis, typhoid fever, or malaria, making the grim reaper's activities more unpredictable and holding little regard for age or social location.[26] The accumulation of artifacts in Caiaphas's tomb, as well as other Roman-era tombs in Judea, underscores the frailty of life in antiquity.[27] It is no wonder, then, that stories of Jesus' healings resonated with its inhabitants. Curing the sick was an urgent, not peripheral, concern. The context of Caiaphas's ossuary shows how students of the New Testament must look beyond the obvious connections between artifact and Gospel and more broadly at the world of the New Testament.

Ossuaries and outside influence. It has often been stated that the use of ossuaries is uniquely Jewish. To some extent, this particular kind of secondary burial of several individuals inside soft limestone boxes in an underground chamber is exceptional, occurring only around Jerusalem in the Early Roman period. But a few scholars, including Gideon Foster, Lee Levine, and most recently Jodi Magness, have suggested that ossuaries themselves might have been influenced by common practices in the Eastern Mediterranean during the Roman period.[28] Similar small stone boxes, carved out of both limestone and marble and about the same shape and size as ossuaries, are often on display in museums in places like Ephesus and Bodrum, though rarely are they published or well studied. They were used, along with urns, for secondary burials, albeit mostly of ashes following cremation. Of course, literary evidence in the Diaspora and archaeological evidence in Israel strongly supports the notion that Jews never cremated and interred ashes, but the similarity between these Roman ossuaries—which for some time were mistakenly thought to have been children's sarcophagi—and Jewish ossuaries is obvious. In the first century CE, they are frequently found from the northern Levant throughout modern Turkey, and they are especially numerous in Asia Minor, even though they are not well published.[29] They would appear to continue a common Aegean tradition seen in the Hellenistic period of mostly round, limestone containers, but which by the imperial period were increasingly rectangular—one would presume under the Roman influence of sarcophagi, which became dominant among the Roman elites in the second century CE.

In the late first century BCE, the ruling Herodian dynasty in Jerusalem was cultivating an intimate relationship with Rome and then especially

Small sarcophagus from Asia Minor, displayed at the Bodrum Museum in Turkey (Photograph by Jonathan Reed)

with the emperor Augustus and the imperial family. Herod the Great also increased pilgrimage to Jerusalem as he rebuilt the Temple, and he fostered closer relations between Diaspora Jews and Jews in Jerusalem. It is quite possible that this context encouraged Roman influences on the burial practices of the Jewish nobility in Jerusalem, and frequent interaction between Diaspora Judaism with Jerusalem led to the high frequency of Diaspora Jews who were interred in first-century Jerusalem.

The significance of this comparison lies not in the origins of burial practices in and of themselves but in the fact that the pattern seen in underground Jerusalem—Jewish elites adapting Roman styles—is also apparent above ground. This is, of course, apparent immediately in above-ground tomb structures such as those of Bene Hezir in the Kidron Valley, the tomb of Queen Helena, or Nicanor's tomb on Mount Scopus, whose Hellenistic-Roman influences have frequently been noted.[30] More particularly, these tombs, and that of Herod himself at Herodion (which is not unlike Augustus's in Rome), illustrate how Jewish elites in Jerusalem were adapting Roman styles as status markers at an accelerated rate beginning with the rule of Herod. The very same phenomenon can be seen in the architectural features and imported wares of the Jewish elites in Jerusalem. Whether in construction techniques with mosaics, *opus sectile* floors, frescoes, and columns or the use of imported ceramics like wine amphorae or Eastern Sigillata A and their imitations, there are many recent examples that support Nachman Avigad's observation of over twenty years ago that the Sadducean inhabitants of the upper city were living "according to the dominant fashion of the Hellenistic-Roman period."[31] Roman-inspired architecture, dining, and burial styles provided a vocabulary in the material culture for the Jewish nobility (which was heavily Sadducean and priestly) to distinguish themselves still in an aniconic manner; on the one hand, these things separated them from Jerusalem's lower classes and the Judean peasantry, and, on the other hand, it aligned them with the urban monoculture of the Roman Empire that was developing since the rule of Augustus. Jesus' message of the Kingdom of God was occurring right at the time when Rome was encroaching, and some elites in Jerusalem were embracing a lifestyle that was very different from that of their predecessors.

THE PROSPECT OF ARCHAEOLOGY AND THE NEW TESTAMENT

By dismissing the ossuary as a forgery, I hope nevertheless to have shown that ossuaries, in light of their patterns and associated artifacts found on archaeological excavations, help us understand the more general context in which Jesus and James lived and from which the early church emerged. And by dismissing the traditional approach to biblical archaeology, I certainly do not intend to undermine the contribution that archaeology can have to our understanding of the New Testament. It is just that biblical archaeology, if one chooses to call it that, must focus on how archaeology can comment on, or relate to, the context in which Christianity originated. It must spend the bulk of its energies on the big picture, on looking at the broader trends and patterns in the material culture. In the case of ossuary archaeology, this would largely consist of studying how their use shapes our understanding of the Jewish nobility in Jerusalem and analyzing the inextricable relationships between Roman influence and status markers, Sadducees and Temple, and Roman collaboration and socioeconomics. And it is in this context that Jesus' Temple action, along with his execution, need to be interpreted by equally careful exegetical and historical work. And it is in the same context that Jewish Christianity in Jerusalem—the pious poor James and his death at the hands of the high priesthood in the city—must be understood.

As a concluding aside, it is worth noting that New Testament scholarship working on Jesus and the Gospels has been transformed by archaeology over the past few decades in such a way through the influence of excavations at Galilean sites and not in Jerusalem. Rather than being obsessed with any single discovery, as was initially expected of the James Ossuary, or by any single artifact or place mentioned in the Gospels, renewed interest in how archaeology could help our understanding of the historical Jesus was the result of meticulous fieldwork in Galilee at places that were never mentioned in the New Testament. In the 1970s and 1980s, Eric Meyers, Carol Meyers, and James Strange excavated upper Galilean villages unknown in the Gospels, such as Meiron, Gush Halav, Khirbet Shema, and Nabratein, with their synagogues that postdate Jesus by at least a century. This introduced the notion of Galilean regionalism as a factor in historical reconstruction and stressed the necessity of examining the village as context for the synagogue, rather than just as an isolated architectural structure. A bit later, Israeli archaeologists excavated at the ruined towns of Gamla and Jodefat, which are likewise nowhere connected to Jesus in the Gospels or Byzantine tradition but which led to enormous strides in understanding Jewish life in the larger villages of Galilee. Beginning in the mid-1980s, excavations were conducted at what was once the largest city of Galilee, Sepphoris, a site notoriously omitted by the Gospel writers, and a decade later excavations began at Tiberias, the other Galilean city that the Gospels never associate with Jesus. These excavations made urbanization and rural-urban relations foundational for assessing Jesus' life and message. But all those excavators were less concerned with directly and immediately tying their site or finds to Jesus, though some biblical scholars often debated premises such as "Jesus and Sepphoris" or "Jesus and the Theater."[32] Instead, each excavation contributed to the underlying debate about the more general Galilean context in which Jesus must be understood. The healthy by-product of not having any direct relationship between Jesus and the site or discovery was the necessity of articulating how concepts like urbanization and socioeconomics, Hellenization and Romanization, diverse or common Judaism, and household purity and public religion apply to the world of Jesus and his first followers. The James Ossuary, albeit a forgery, serves as an effective object lesson for the importance of stratigraphic excavations and the consideration of the entire archaeological context, while revealing the limitations of artifactual prooftexting that have plagued biblical archaeology since its inception.

NOTES

1. See, initially, André Lemaire, "Burial Box of James, the Brother of Jesus: Earliest Archaeological Evidence of Jesus Found in Jerusalem," *Biblical Archaeology Review* 28, no. 6 (2002): 24–33, 70; and later, Hershel Shanks and Ben Witherington III, *The Brother of Jesus: The Dramatic Story and Meaning of the First Archaeological Link to Jesus and His Family* (San Francisco: HarperSanFrancisco, 2003), 7–22.

2. The best impartial account is by Nina Burleigh, *Unholy Business: A True Tale of Faith, Greed, and Forgery in the Holy Land* (New York: HarperCollins, 2008).

3. In spite of Shanks still holding out on its possible authenticity; see Hershel Shanks, "First Person: Help Me! I'm Desperate!," *Biblical Archaeology Review* 34 (2008): 6.

4. The 2003 ASOR Policy on Preservation and Protection of Archaeological Resources is available at: <http://www.bu.edu/asor/policy.htm>.

5. To get a sense of the scope of the problem, browse the "Archaeology Watch" portion of the Archaeological Institute of America's website (<http://www.archaeological.org/>). A concise statement is also provided in Neil Brodie and Colin Renfrew, "Looting and the World's Archaeological Heritage: The Inadequate Response," *Annual Review of Anthropology* 34 (2005): 43–61.

6. Although designed with pedagogy in mind, the essays collected in Milton Moreland, ed., *Between Text and Artifact: Integrating Archaeology in Biblical Studies Teaching* (Atlanta: Society of Biblical Literature, 2003), offer a good starting point for the problems and promise of integrating archaeology and biblical studies.

7. For a sense of the current debate, contrast Israel Finkelstein, "Bible Archaeology or Archaeology of Palestine in the Iron Age? A Rejoinder," *Levant* 30 (1998): 167–74, with Seymour Gitin, "The House That Albright Built," *Near Eastern Archaeology* 65 (2002): 5–10.

8. For more details on these discoveries, see John Dominic Crossan and Jonathan Reed, *Excavating Jesus: Beneath the Stones, Behind the Texts*, rev. and updated ed. (San Francisco: HarperSanFrancisco, 2002); and John Dominic Crossan and Jonathan Reed, *In Search of Paul: How Jesus's Apostle Opposed Rome's Empire with God's Empire* (San Francisco: HarperSanFrancisco, 2004).

9. Shanks and Witherington, *The Brother of Jesus*, 220.

10. Ibid., 54–63.

11. Levi Y. Rahmani, *A Catalogue of Jewish Ossuaries in the Collections of the State of Israel* (Jerusalem: Israel Antiquities Authority, 1994), 77 (no. 9).

12. Ibid., 223–24 (nos. 701–9); first published in Amos Kloner, "A Tomb with Inscribed Ossuaries in East Talpiot," *Atiqot*, English ser., 29 (1996): 15–22.

13. Simcha Jacobovici and Charles Pellegrino, *The Jesus Family Tomb: The Discovery, the Investigation, and the Evidence That Could Change History* (San Francisco: HarperSanFrancisco, 2007). See my criticisms in the 2007 *Review of Biblical Literature* (<http://www.bookreviews.org>).

14. The statistical analysis was eventually published by Andrey Feuerverger ("Statistical Analysis of an Archaeological Find," *Annals of Applied Statistics* 2 [2008]: 3–54), but with responses that ranged from polite reservation to scathing criticism, including the charge that accepting the assumptions of Jacobovici was a breech of professional standards. The statistics did not settle anything.

15. Craig Evans, *Jesus and the Ossuaries: What Jewish Burial Practices Reveal about the Beginning of Christianity* (Waco, Tex.: Baylor University Press, 2003), 124.

16. Ibid., 90–123.

17. Steven Fine, "A Note on Ossuary Burial and the Resurrection of the Dead in First-Century Jerusalem," *Journal of Jewish Studies* 51 (2000): 69–76.

18. Crossan and Reed, *Excavating Jesus*, 237–40.

19. Ibid., 240–44.

20. Jodi Magness, "Ossuaries and the Burials of Jesus and James," *Journal of Biblical Literature* 124 (2005): 121–54.

21. Ibid., 122.

22. Ibid., 123.

23. Byron McCane, *Roll Back the Stone: Death and Burial in the World of Jesus* (Harrisburg, Pa.: Trinity Press International, 2003), 89–106; but see Magness, "Ossuaries and Burials," 140–49.

24. Zvi Greenhut, "The 'Caiaphas' Tomb in the North of Jerusalem," *Atiqot*, English ser., 21 (1991): 63–71; and Ronni Reich, "Ossuary Inscriptions from the 'Caiaphas' Tomb," *Atiqot*, English ser., 21 (1991): 72–77.

25. Joe Zias, "Human Skeletal Remains from the 'Caiaphas' Tomb," *Atiqot*, English ser., 21 (1991): 72–80.

26. Walter Scheidel, "Problems and Progress in Roman Demography," in *Debating Roman Demography*, ed. Walter Scheidel (Leiden: Brill, 2001), 1–81.

27. Yossi Nagar and Hagit Torgeé, "Biological Characteristics of Jewish Burial in the Hellenistic and Early Roman Periods," *Israel Exploration Journal* 53 (2003): 164–71.

28. Gideon Foerster, "Sarcophagus-Production in Jerusalem from the Beginning

of the Common Era up to 70 C.E.," in *Sarkophag-Studien 1: Akten des Symposiums 125 Jahre Sarkophag Corpus*, ed. Gunthram Koch (Mainz: Philipp von Zabern, 1998), 295–309 (see especially 303–4); Lee Levine, *Jerusalem: Portrait of the City in the Second Temple Period (538 BCE–70 CE)* (Philadelphia: Jewish Publication Society, 2002), 264–65; Magness, "Ossuaries and Burials," 133–40; contra Rahmani, *Catalogue of Jewish Ossuaries*, 58–59.

29. A recent catalogue by Cengiz Içten, the retiring archaeologist of the Ephesus Museum, with a discussion by Christine Thomas, will go a long way toward rectifying the situation; see Christine Thomas and Cengiz Içten, "The *Ostothekai* of Ephesos and the Rise of Sarcophagus Inhumation: Death, Conspicuous Consumption, and the Roman Freedmen," in *Akten des Symposiums des Sarkophag-Corpus 2001*, Sarkophag-Studien 3, ed. Guntram Koch, (Mainz: Phillip von Zabern, 2007), 335–44. See also Christine Thomas, "The Ephesian Ossuaries and Roman Influence on the Production of Burial Containers," in *100 Jahre Österreichische Forschungen in Ephesos: Akten des Symposions Wien 1995*, Denkschriften 260/Archäologische Forschungen 1, ed. Herwig Friesinger and Friedrich Krinzinger (Vienna: Österreichische Akademie der Wissenschaften, 1999), 549–54.

30. Andrea Berlin, "Power and Its Afterlife: Tombs in Hellenistic Palestine," *Near Eastern Archaeology* 65 (2002): 143–47.

31. Nachman Avigad, *Discovering Jerusalem* (Nashville: Thomas Nelson, 1983), 83.

32. Jonathan Reed, *Archaeology and the Galilean Jesus: A Reexamination of the Evidence* (Harrisburg, Pa.: Trinity Press International, 2000), 100–138.

RYAN BYRNE & BERNADETTE MCNARY-ZAK

Epilogue

Objects, Faith, and Archaeoporn

Six years after its display in Toronto, the James Ossuary phenomenon remains a unique case study for scholars of religion, a cautionary tale for archaeologists, and a point of contention among some faith communities. What makes ossuaries resonant as artifacts with potential religious power or insight is not merely the fact that many bear biblical names from the biblical period. It is the possibility, however remote, that these are tangible, accessible objects with the prospects of housing the literal human remains of biblical characters. It is the *body*, or what the body once touched, that tantalizes the imagination of the faithful. And so on one hand, we see in the sensational merchandising of these artifacts a new kind of titillating exploitation of the body, which Byron McCane has dubbed "archaeoporn."[1] On the other hand, we see resistance from some religious sectors to construct a relationship between faith and physical evidence by embracing the body or its repository as a substitute or even catalyst for spiritual enrichment.

This recurring intersection with the material body perhaps reached its crescendo with the publication of Dan Brown's *The Da Vinci Code* precisely because it centered on the secreted tale of a Jesus whose body was neither crucified nor resurrected, a Jesus whose body went on to procreate a human line of descent that stripped that body of all the trappings of divinity so intertwined with Christian tradition.[2] Although a work of fiction, this novel also pushed certain buttons among communities of faith, who took umbrage at the liberties an author would take with the necessary narrative of the body through whose biblically reported fate laid the foundation for traditions of human salvation. In spite of its controversial premise, or perhaps because of it, *The Da Vinci Code* dominated the *New York Times* best-seller list for more than two years.[3] Brown had clearly tapped into popular cultural curiosities bubbling beneath the surface.

In a multimedia circus, which one might consider a sequel of sorts to the *Da Vinci* phenomenon, a carefully orchestrated commercial blitz filled the airwaves and Internet with news of the discovery of a tomb in the neighborhood of Talpiot in Jerusalem.[4] Funded by Hollywood producer James Cameron, the documentary filmmaker Simcha Jacobovici, who had created the 2003 film *James: Brother of Jesus, Holy Relic or Hoax?* for the Discovery Channel, presented a new investigative film claiming that the sensational artifacts inside the Talpiot tomb allegedly included the ossuaries of none other than Jesus of Nazareth, his wife, and children. A Jesus encased in an ossuary meant no resurrection of the body. A nuclear family interment meant a pedestrian human life ending with a conventional human burial and secondary burial. It was *The Da Vinci Code* all over again, except this time the argument did not rest upon the fictional speculations of a former high school teacher but upon the material results of an archaeological excavation conducted with scientific controls in the early 1980s. To accompany the documentary, on February 27, 2007, Jacobovici and coauthor Charles Pellegrino released a popular book, *The Jesus Family Tomb: The Discovery, the Investigation, and the Evidence That Could Change History*, detailing the results of their research.[5] This reawakened interest in another book, *The Jesus Dynasty: The Hidden History of Jesus, His Royal Family, and the Birth of Christianity*, by James Tabor, a biblical archaeologist at the University of North Carolina at Charlotte.[6] Tabor focused his interests on the ten ossuaries discovered in the Talpiot tomb. The inscriptions and placement of the ossuaries, as well as the location of the tomb, led Tabor to argue that this was the family tomb of Jesus and the original site of the James Ossuary, which had *mysteriously* disappeared only to make its way into Oded Golan's hands, presumptively via the black market.

When the Discovery Channel aired Jacobovici's sixty-minute docudrama, *The Lost Tomb of Jesus*, on March 4, 2007, viewers were treated to portions of the investigation, selective (and sometimes misleading) representations of scholarly commentary, historical reenactments, and the insinuation that although the Talpiot tomb had been excavated more than a quarter-century earlier (complicating media headlines of Cameron or Jacobovici having "discovered" much of anything) and *published* more than a decade earlier, there was still something fishy about its relative obscurity in the public realm.

The film's premiere was followed by a panel discussion led by Ted Koppel titled "The Lost Tomb of Jesus: A Critical Look," which intended to address some of the issues raised by the docudrama. A press release explained the reason for the discussion: "This documentary touches on many sensitive issues. The experts' findings reported in the documentary rely on the application of the most current forensic patina analysis, Paleo-DNA techniques, and statistical evaluation. But it is the beginning of a complex archaeological journey, not the end. Because of that, we believe that this film should be viewed in the context of a spirited dialogue and viewers should decide their own viewpoints and conclusions."[7] The questions asked and the answers provided by the discussion echoed, with almost uncanny similarity, those surrounding the James Ossuary phenomenon. On a stage that appeared set for a mock trial, Koppel facilitated discussion from his chair at the center of the room; he was flanked on his right by Jacobovici and Tabor and, for the first half of the hour, on his left by Jonathan Reed and archaeologist William G. Dever. Discussion focused first on the film's evidentiary claims. Because the proposed reconstruction of the Talpiot tomb supplied a response to one of the many challenges to the authenticity of the James Ossuary (namely, its place of origin), panelists debated whether acceptance of the docudrama's reconstruction merely extended the leap of faith employed by many with regard to the James Ossuary. Debate continued when three theologians later replaced the biblical archaeologists and scholars on the panel as Koppel's questions addressed the probative content of the film. Panelists expressed concern about the theatrical aims of the docudrama and the potential confusion caused by its claims about the relationship between ancient objects and biblical narratives.

This time around, the scholarly community did not embrace the arguments on behalf of the Jesus family tomb. The evidence against Jacobovici's claims was overwhelming and the hints that the scholarly community had somehow deemphasized sensitive, incendiary evidence did not pass muster. Responding to Koppel, Reed borrowed McCane's neologism to describe the film's stab at titillating entertainment as archaeoporn. Subsequent to Reed's citation of this neologism, the term "archaeoporn" quickly entered the realm of Associated Press coverage and ultimately the blogosphere.

The vetting of the James Ossuary, like that of the Talpiot tomb, challenges the limits of reasonable evaluation of evidence and, in this, reveals something relevant about contemporary American religiosity. It is the commodification of ancient objects and places to inform a sense of identity in the present that bears attention and defines their meaning for religious persons. Indeed, as we have seen, there is nothing self-edifying about the ossuary; rather, it is the extent to which it allows for the appropriation of a particular Christian heritage, which functions as a way of actualizing the present, that remains its value. For the scholar of religion, such an act in itself becomes *the* category for observation. It becomes *the* datum of religion.

NOTES

1. Byron McCane, personal communication. Compare his remarks on archaeological pornography in his essay in this volume.

2. Dan Brown, *The Da Vinci Code* (New York: Doubleday, 2003).

3. Edward Wyatt, "*Da Vinci Code* Losing Best-Seller Status," *New York Times*, November 4, 2005.

4. The late Yosef Gat excavated the Talpiot tomb in 1980 on behalf of Israel's Department of Antiquities and Museums. The ossuaries from the tomb were published in Levi Y. Rahmani, *A Catalogue of Jewish Ossuaries in the Collections of the State of Israel* (Jerusalem: Israel Antiquities Authority, 1994). See the final publication by Amos Kloner, "A Tomb with Inscribed Ossuaries in East Talpiyot, Jersualem," *ʿAtiqot* 29 (1996): 15–22.

5. Simcha Jacobovici and Charles Pellegrino, *The Jesus Family Tomb: The Discovery, the Investigation, and the Evidence That Could Change History* (San Francisco: HarperOne, 2007).

6. James D. Tabor, *The Jesus Dynasty: The Hidden History of Jesus, His Royal Family, and the Birth of Christianity* (New York: Simon & Schuster, 2006).

7. Jane Root of the Discovery Channel, Silver Spring, Md., PRNewswire, <http://www.bwtorrents.com/showthread.php?t=88300> (March 1, 2007).

Index